*Books by Fran Stewart*

<u>The Biscuit McKee Mystery Series</u>:

*Orange as Marmalade*
*Yellow as Legal Pads*
*Green as a Garden Hose*
*Blue as Blue Jeans*
*Indigo as an Iris*
*Violet as an Amethyst*
*Gray as Ashes*

*Red as a Rooster*
*Black as Soot*
*Pink as a Peony*
*White as Ice*

*A Slaying Song Tonight*

<u>The ScotShop Mysteries</u>:

*A Wee Murder in My Shop*
*A Wee Dose of Death*
*A Wee Homicide in the Hotel*

Poetry:

*Resolution*

For Children:

*As Orange As Marmalade/
 Tan naranja como Mermelada
 (a bilingual book)*

Non-Fiction:

*From The Tip of My Pen: a workbook for writers*
*BeesKnees #1: A Beekeeping Memoir (#1 of 6 volumes)*
*BeesKnees #2: A Beekeeping Memoir (#2 of 6 volumes)*
*BeesKnees #3: A Beekeeping Memoir (#3 of 6 volumes)*
*BeesKnees #4: A Beekeeping Memoir (#4 of 6 volumes)*
*BeesKnees #5: A Beekeeping Memoir (#5 of 6 volumes)*
*BeesKnees #6: A Beekeeping Memoir (#6 of 6 volumes)*
*Clear as Mud*
*Clearly Me*
*Crystal Clear*

# Crystal Clear

Fran Stewart

Crystal Clear

Fran Stewart

© 2021 Fran Stewart

All rights reserved. No part of this book may be used or reproduced in any manner whatsoever without written permission from the author, except by a reviewer who may quote brief passages in a review.

ISBN: (Softcover) 978-1-951368-24-1

This book was printed in the United States of America.

Published by

My Own Ship Press
PO Box 490153
Lawrenceville GA 30049
myownship@icloud.com

franstewart.com

Dedicated to:

Diana
Erica
Eli
Veronica
Darlene
Savannah
Aiden
Marcia
and Peggy

(This is the order in which I met you.)

## Author's Note

This third volume of my Facebook memoirs has been a real joy for me to compile, not only because it's given me a chance to take a deep look at 2020, this tumultuous year that we've lived through, but to review all the times I've felt so connected to those of you who have followed my posts so faithfully.

You mean a great deal to me.

I've re-read your comments—and even included a few of them in this volume—and wondered what later generations who won't have access to my FranStewartAuthor FB page might have thought to comment about.

Whether you've followed me for years, whether you were new to this page, or whether you're someone who has discovered my words long after I've joined all my cats on the other side of the rainbow bridge, I hope you'll find joy in reading (or re-reading) these words of mine.

I hope my words can bridge whatever gap may exist between us, no matter whether it's measured in physical distance or in time.

If you can, please keep in touch. If that's not possible, know that I send you all my best wishes for a life filled with purpose. And with joy.

 —Fran
 from my house beside a creek on the other side of Hog Mountain
 January 2021

# January 2020

### January Reading Challenges

**Wednesday 1/1/2020** – Let's start the year out the right way, with lots of reading. I love this calendar of themed books to read during January. You get to choose the theme you like the best. If you follow the "Librarianuary" month, you can add my Biscuit McKee series (all eleven books), since Biscuit is a librarian!

"Meow," adds Marmalade (the library cat), which means "Happy New Year."

~ ~ ~

### Your diet

**Thursday 1/2/2020** – I've decided to go on a diet this whole year. Not the kind of diet you probably have in mind, but the kind of diet where I choose to be aware of everything I put into my mind and spirit, as well as my body.

I'm going to watch the books I read even more than I have in the past.

I'm going to sing more, and praise more, and laugh more.

And as for what I put in my body – I think I'll start with some homemade fudge.

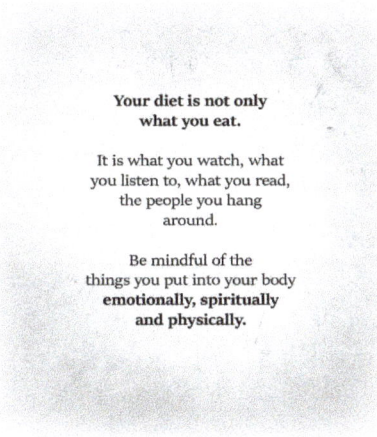

# Fran Stewart

~ ~ ~

## Veins on the Bottom

**Friday 1/3/2020** – Did you ever think much about what's underneath stuff? The part of everything that we don't see and hardly ever consider.

Lily pads, for instance. Something has to strengthen those fragile-looking green circles. After all, frogs have to sit on them. I was fascinated by the pattern of veins on this one. How I wish Internet photos were all tagged with the source. Where was this photo taken? Who is the person? What's the genus and species of that particular lily pad?

Years ago I started turning things over (carefully) and checking out what holds them together or supports them. It was meant to be an exercise in exploration. What it's uncovered recently—in my house at least—is a whole bunch of dust bunnies and cat hair.

<<sigh>>

~ ~ ~

## Stop Shrinking Yourself

**Saturday 1/4/2020** – This past year, and specifically this past month, has been one of the most momentous years (months) of my life. As I look back over my journal entries for the past year, I see so often where I envisioned some miracle and then stepped into it.

Years ago, when I sold cosmetics—I won't name the company, but if you think PINK you'll be pretty close—I first heard the phrase "Act as if, and you will become."

I secretly thought it was a bunch of hooey at the time, since I'd never set goals in my life. I couldn't see myself even one year ahead of then, much less five or ten or twenty. Except to assume that I'd be dead by that time. Needless to say, with an attitude like that, I did not move more than a rung or two up the pink ladder.

What's changed in all this time? What changed last month, last year? Maybe I've grown up. Maybe I've had the "sea change" that so many writers have referred to. Over the past year I've been priming myself (unbeknownst to me) to take an uncompromising look at my life, which I did several weeks ago. I realized that I've spent most of it "thinking poor."

I've always been a frugal person. I like frugality. I like conserving energy and not spending excess amounts on new things when there's so much used stuff going to waste. I like bringing home a doggie bag from a restaurant. I like washing clothes in cold water and not bothering with fabric softeners that are just going to clog up the septic tank anyway.

That may be, but I finally realized I was doing all that for the wrong reason. I was doing it out of terror of becoming a bag lady someday.

Get this, Frannie – you are nowhere near being a bag lady. Not even within spittin' distance.

So I decided to spend some of the money I've been saving (compulsively) for decades. I was counting on those savings to sustain me in my old age.

Get this, Frannie – old age isn't way far off in the distance. It's here. It's now. I'm 73, for criminey's sakes. So I called both my (well-grown) children and told them I was planning to spend a chunk of their inheritance. One said, "Go for it, Mom!" the other said, "It's about time!"

So, here I am at the Tesla place in Atlanta with my completed order.

I picked her up on December 21st, the Winter Solstice, so the official name of my beautiful new deep blue winged chariot is Pegasa Solsta Tesla.

What have you been envisioning? What are you ready to step into?

Fran Stewart

~ ~ ~

**Carrots, Eggs, and Coffee**

**Monday 1/6/2020** – In my beekeeping blog, I wrote the following little essay exactly ten years ago today. And it's included in *BeesKnees #5: A Beekeeping Memoir,* which will be out in print late next month. The thoughts are still pertinent, so I'd like to share it with you.

=========

**Day #451**

Here's another blog post that has nothing to do with bees.

A friend of mine in Australia shared an interesting story with me recently about a wise old woman who helped a younger woman deal with adversity. "Dig up some carrots," she said, "and gather some eggs, then bring me some ground coffee beans."

The young woman did as directed, and then was instructed to put them all in boiling water. So she took three pots, brought water to a boil, and put the carrots in one, the eggs in another, and the coffee in the third.

"Look at them," the older woman said after a while. "What do you see?"

The young woman replied, "They've all cooked."

"Yes," said the wise woman, "but look at the differences. The **carrots** were hard and resistant when they were put in the water, but they softened up and gave in to the heat. The **eggs**, with their soft vulnerability, became hard in the boiling water. As for the **coffee**? Well, it changed the water!"

We all have adversity. But how each one of us reacts to that adversity is up to us. Will we be carrots, eggs, or coffee?

**BeeAttitude for Day #451:** Blessed are those who cook with joy no matter what they cook, for they shall spread happiness.

=========

p.s. All six volumes of my BeesKnees memoirs are available as e-books. And so far, the first three are in print, with the final three still to come. Here's the cover of #3, that was released just a week ago.

~ ~ ~

**Twelfth Night**

**Tuesday 1/7/2020** – Are you planning to see *Twelfth Night* at the Atlanta Shakespeare Tavern sometime this month?

You're not?

Why not?

I was there celebrating my 73rd birthday along with a LARGE number of friends last Saturday evening who took me up on my invitation to 1) eat a meal from the great pub menu at the Tavern; 2) see a timeless, funny, heart-warming play; and 3) enjoy my birthday with me.

They're not quite sold out for the rest of the month-long run, so it's not too late to call for tickets 404-874-5299. You won't want to miss Rachel Frawley playing Viola and Marlon Burnley as Orsino.

Thanks to everyone who showed up for the play, it was one of the best birthday parties I've ever had!

*Photo Credit: Atlanta Shakespeare Tavern*

# Fran Stewart

~ ~ ~

### Waist of Time

**Wednesday 1/8/2020** – I have a friend who must have fifteen wristwatches, more than enough to make a "waist of time." They come in all sorts of styles and colors, and she's always changing her watch to match her outfit.

Whatever floats her boat is fine with me.

I've been using the same watch since March of 2002. Twenty minutes after my father died, I took it off his wrist, put it on mine, and I've worn it ever since. Why twenty minutes?

I'm glad you asked.

I'd read somewhere or other that it takes up to twenty minutes after death for all the cells of a body to shut down. So my sister and I sat beside our father and held his hands and stroked his hair back off his forehead and talked gently to him, thanking him for all he had taught us over the years. We rubbed his gradually cooling arms and patted his shoulders.

Then I began wearing his watch. Every time I look at it, I remember the timeless love of that good man. That's more important than fashion, as far as I'm concerned.

~ ~ ~

### Barkalounger

**Thursday 1/9/2020** – While we're talking about relaxing—well, we weren't talking about it, but we should have been—I've been considering the way my cats can drape themselves over almost any obstacle and look perfectly at ease. Although I didn't have this picture in mind when I wrote *Violet as an Amethyst*, my 6th Biscuit McKee Mystery, this sort of relaxation is precisely what I had in mind when Marmalade began to nap atop Gracie, the lost dog who adopts Biscuit's sister, Glaze.

"She is very warm," Marmalade says, but her people think she's simply purring in contentment.

I don't have a warm dog to curl up beside when I take a luxurious nap, but slipping into the corner of my bed where the afternoon sun streams through an upstairs window is almost as good.

Wooly Bear agrees with me.

~ ~ ~

**Wooly Bear on comforter**

**Friday 1/10/2020** – "Where'd that sunshine go?" Wooly Bear asked me the other day. One moment she was lying in a puddle of warmth, the next the skies clouded over and she was left wide-eyed in disbelief, as you can see.

I know just how she feels. One day I'm all sure of myself, basking in the sunshine of my accomplishments. The next I'm wondering how I'm ever going to do everything I'd like to do before I croak.

But then, when I feel that way, someone comes along with a smile or a song, with a friendly word or an encouraging note – or I buck myself up by reminding myself to go one step at a time. After all, that's how every journey is accomplished.

~ ~ ~

**Fit your Future**

**Saturday 1/11/2020** – At my Shakespeare Tavern birthday party last week, I realized that this saying reflected precisely where I am now in my 73 years. All the people who came to share the evening with me are people I want in my future, and although I've known some of them all their lives (daughter and grandchildren), and others a great deal of my own life, I want that sweep of history to continue growing for a long time to come.

I'm gonna keep hanging out with these folks. Their energy, their vision, their humor, their various areas of expertise, are all factors I want in my life as it unfolds. I am rich indeed in the love of good friends and family.

And—I'm open to finding new friends. That's certainly happening as I teach the memoirs classes. Life is good indeed.

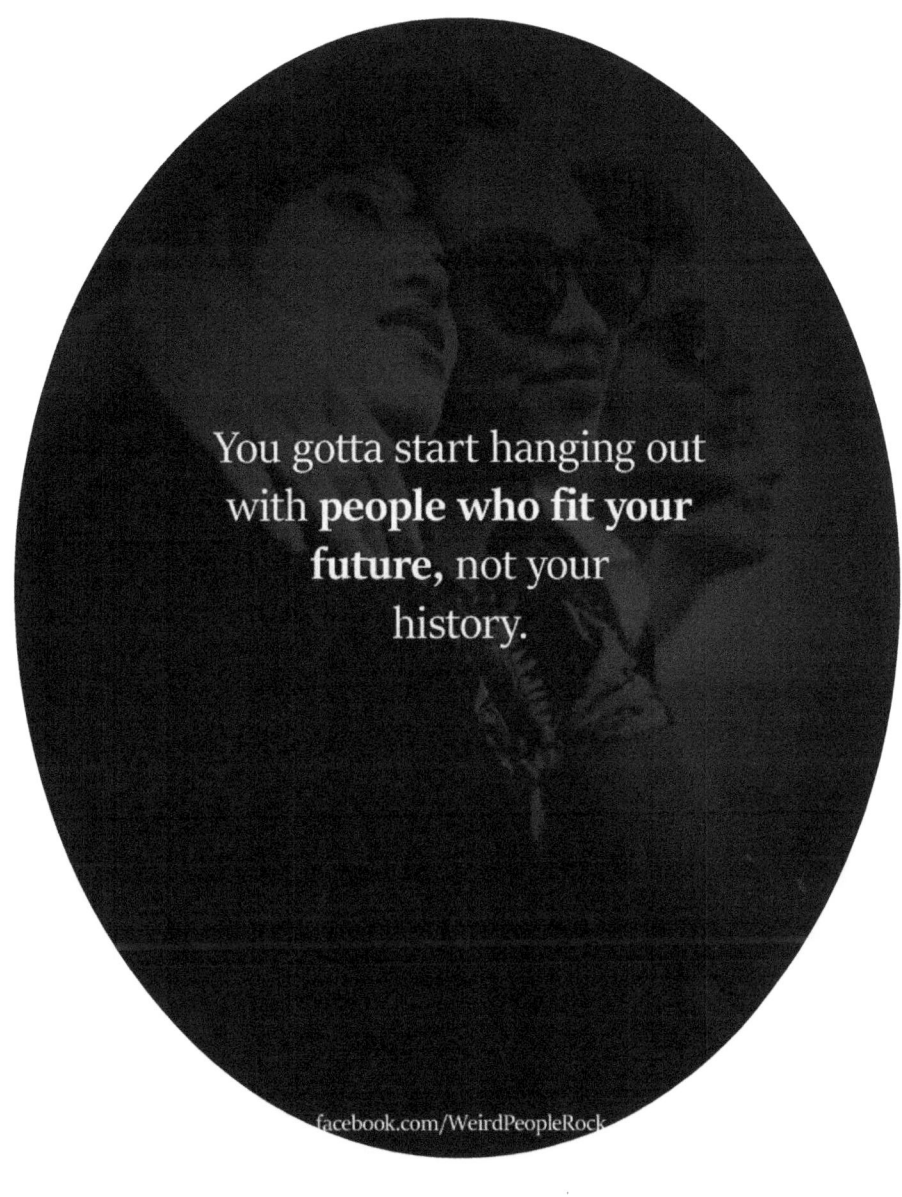

~ ~ ~

**Who? Me?**

**Monday 1/13/2020** – Saturday I drove to Tyrone GA to visit Marcia Dunscomb, a dear friend. On Sunday morning, she and I attended a discussion group she's been a member of for several years. Sometimes they talk about the environment, particularly since one of the members is an active volunteer with the Citizens' Climate Lobby. Sometimes they discuss the driving political issues of the day, since all of the members are active in their political parties. Yesterday they were talking about philosophy – in particular the philosophy that governs communication.

I read once that most people's idea of communication is listening in order to reply instead of listening in order to understand.

Wouldn't it be lovely if we could all talk with "the other side" (no matter who or what we consider that to be) with the goal of understanding, rather than simply slapping on a label and discounting everything they say?

Marcia had told me ahead of time that her usual question at each of these discussions is "What can we do?"

What a good question.

What can we do? We can take a first step.

When we ask, "Who? Me?" the answer is YES.

~ ~ ~

**You're Your Yore**

**Tuesday 1/14/2020** – Today I begin a new six-week Memoirs class at my local library branch. I am passionate about helping people write the stories of their lives, in large part because my aunt gave me copies of my grandparents' and great-grandmother's daily diaries that she transcribed years ago. Although these documents give tantalizing glimpses into what went on in the early years of the 20th century, they don't TELL THE STORIES as fully as I wished they did. Every entry is a basic list of what jobs they accomplished (washed, visited, sold this many chickens or that many dozens of eggs, had a baby, named it, the cow had a calf, snake in the outhouse, helped lay out body of neighbor's child who died last night, funeral at 3pm).

Any one of those events could have been rich in detail, but they knew what they were writing about, and didn't think it would be important to give last names, talk about the relationships between people, relate the importance of those sales, let me know how the pregnancy went, tell me the cow's age or whether she had trouble delivering her calf. What about the snake? What about the child? My grandmother had 12 pregnancies, but only 8 live births. Nowhere in her diary or in my grandfather's, is there any mention of a) her pregnancies, or b) her miscarriages. The births are recorded—but it took my grandfather nine months before he even mentioned the name they'd given my father.

You ARE your yore. And if you're willing to write those stories, you'll leave a priceless legacy to those who come after you.

Don't know how to start? Maybe you need to take one of my classes.

## Our heritage makes us who we are.

## You're your yore.

~ ~ ~

### Cardinal Mohawk

**Wednesday 1/15/2020** – Somebody asked me the other day what book I was reading. Book? Singular? I never read just one book. I read multiple books, and lately I've been reading nothing but non-fiction (except for re-reading "Still Life" by Louise Penny, which was my book club's selection for this month. Of all fiction writers, Penny is my favorite).

*Seven Skeletons* by Lydia Payne – the seven iconic skeletons that helped change the way we think about human life on earth umpty-kazillion years ago.

*Of Orcas and Men* by the journalist David Neiwert – I never knew there was so much to learn about orcas. Well, I did know I was ignorant about them, but I didn't realize how much until I read this moving tribute to the Orca. Orcas were originally called the *whale killer* because Orcas hunt other whales (and dolphins and seals and such). They never ever kill humans in the wild. The only instances of orcas killing humans has been when the whales are in captivity. Not a wonder; orcas who are separated from their families and forbidden to roam the oceans must be quietly going crazy in their restricted pools.

*Planet of the Bugs* by Scott R. Shaw – a fabulous follow-up to the Bugs 101 course I took a few months ago from the University of Alberta.

*What Happened* by Hillary Rodham Clinton – there is hope for the women of America (and the men as well), but seeing from the inside all the ways in which the first woman to run for the Presidency was blocked on so many fronts was sad indeed.

*Without a Doubt* by Marcia Clark – about her prosecution case for the Orenthal James Simpson trial.

# Fran Stewart

And *The Other Side of the Coin* by Angela Kelly – the behind the scenes story of Queen Elizabeth's clothes. The book includes so much more information, though, about the ways the royal household works. After reading it, I realized I know a number of women like the queen: women who are older than I, but who glow with a love of life, who have a hearty laugh and love to use it, who face life's challenges head on, who are unafraid to voice their opinions, but who are consistently thoughtful of the people around them. I'm honored to know those women.

How do I keep all these books straight at one time? It's very simple. When I'm in the mood to read about Orcas, I pick up that book. When I need something a bit lighter, I choose Kelly's book. When I'm upstairs I work on Clark's book; in the family room, it's Clinton's.

I've talked with people who think I'm crazy, but I won't think less of them for reading only one book at a time. Of course, I returned Payne, Neiwert, Shaw, and Kelly to the library yesterday. The others I didn't have to return because I own them.

Now I have a whole raft of new books to start. I'm going to start with *Shade* by Pete Souza, which was a gift from one of those special women I mentioned earlier.

Life is rich indeed.

Oh, and the cardinal's Mohawk? I just thought you'd enjoy it.

~ ~ ~

### More Libraries than McDonald's

**Thursday 1/16/2020** – Yesterday I stopped by the library for a quick look at their new shelving system. Quick—or so I thought. I'd gone there to find the book my book club is reading for next month, *Hillbilly Elegy* by J.D. Vance. I couldn't find it where I thought it ought to be. It's a memoir of growing up in Appalachia, but I couldn't find a memoir section. So I looked under biography. Nope. Turns out it was shelved under Social Science.

You see, like many libraries across the country, our Gwinnett County libraries have switched away from the Dewey Decimal System. Now, before you howl in dismay, let me tell you that I spent quite a long time roaming through the non-fiction section, trying to get my head around this new system that classifies non-fiction books based on their genre.

"It's just like the Dewey system," one of the librarians told me, "except it uses words instead of numbers."

Easy for him to say.

Still, I know I'll eventually get used to it. In the meantime, I'm either going to have to look up the books I want online before I leave home or ask a librarian for help while I'm roaming the shelves. The system doesn't quite make sense to me yet. I looked for *Becoming* yesterday. It's an autobiography, right? So I looked under the O's in the Bio section. Nope.

Gave up. Asked the same librarian. I'm listening to the book on CD (loaned to me by a wonderful friend), but I'd like to read along with it as I listen to Michelle Obama telling her fascinating story.

The librarian led me to the politics shelf.

I remember so well the days of the old card catalogs, which I dearly loved. But I've gotten used to looking up books in the online catalog. Now I suppose I'll adapt to this new system. Wonder how long it will take me ? ? ?

Bye-bye Dewey, hello Words.

Fran Stewart

~ ~ ~

**Coati – San Diego Zoo**

**Friday 1/17/2020** – About a month ago I posted a picture of "baby brontosauruses." I've had people email me to ask what they actually were. Although at first glance, they looked like cats with their tails up in the air, if you looked carefully, you'd see that their noses were long and pointy. So, to clear up that mystery, here's an announcement. The baby bronts in that December photo are coati, a South American omnivore.

One of the coolest things about them is that their ankles can rotate 180 degrees, which makes it easy for them to climb down a tree headfirst.

I found out about them at the San Diego Zoo site when I was looking for a good link to pass on to a friend about reindeer. Check it out – it's fascinating.

https://animals.sandiegozoo.org/animals/coati

~ ~ ~

**playroom outside**

**Saturday 1/18/2020** – Usually the rule was "Come in before the streetlights come on." Or "Come in before the sun sets." But I remember one snowy winter day on an Air Force base in Germany when my sister and I went out sledding on a nearby hill. She had a watch. I didn't. "Be back by five o'clock," was the order.

I was six years old and had no concept of what time was, but I knew quite well that we'd be punished if we came in late. I spent the first half of our sledding time asking my big sister, "Is it five o'clock yet?"

She finally told me to quit bothering her. So I quit asking.

I still remember the look on my sister's face when she finally got around to looking at her watch. We ran, even though there was no hope of mitigating the results of our inattention.

Sure enough, the flat-bottomed wooden spoon came out as soon as we walked in the door.

I remember thinking it would have much safer if I'd just stayed inside with a book.

Still, when I walk around my neighborhood now on a Saturday, I seldom see any of the children outside playing, even though the sun is still bright.

What a shame.

Maybe we need some snow to entice them outside.

~ ~ ~

**Happiness is a choice**

**Monday 1/20/2020** – I've been thinking about this a lot recently. There are quite a few things that don't come to us—things we have to generate, things that have to bubble up within us.

Things like courage and compassion, kindness and determination, serenity and joy.

It helps if we have circumstances around us that serve to nourish the goodness inside. Still, the choices are always ours, always yours, always mine. Many years ago I heard someone described as the kind of person who'd complain when he got to heaven. The one speaking paused a beat and added, "If he ever even gets there."

The judgment implicit in that comment was something my seven-year-old mind registered, and I found myself looking at the speaker differently than I had before. "She's not very happy," I remember thinking.

If only we could see ourselves with that kind of clarity. If only we could lighten up a bit and realize that others carry a heavy load not visible to us.

Today, I plan to let nothing but joy bubble up through my thoughts. Will you join me?

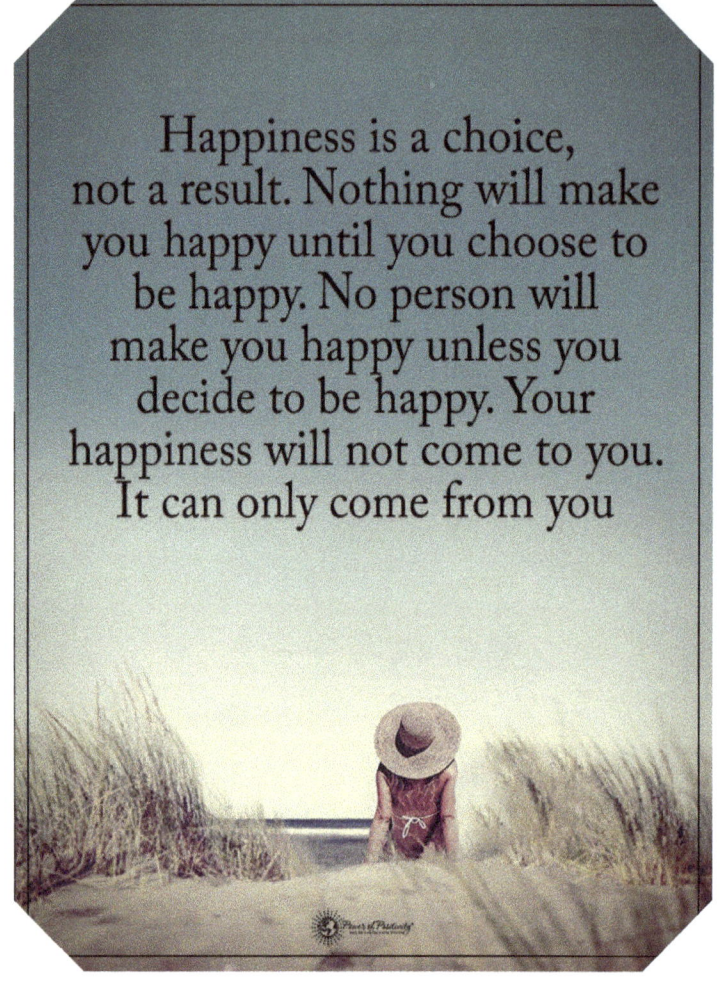

~ ~ ~

**Someone Else's Candle**

**Tuesday 1/21/2020** – Over the past week, I've had the distinct feeling that someone I knew was, in three different conversations, trying to blow out my candle. My first reaction was pique, my second was resentment. It took until the third try that I realized she was feeling completely overwhelmed and had barely enough energy to keep her own candle lit, much less contribute to my light.

Now, why couldn't I have figured that out the first time around instead of holding onto my negativity?

Ah, well. I got it eventually.

If there is a next time, I hope I'll get smarter a lot faster.

~ ~ ~

**Redundancy**

**Wednesday 1/22/2020** – Redundant. Superfluous. Inessential. Unnecessary. Uncalled for. Something I never want to be thought of as.

There have been many times when I've felt that way. I remember many years ago when I took my daughter and some of her friends roller-skating and tried to get them involved in a game on skates. I can still feel the shock of having my daughter roll her eyes at me—the first time I ever saw her do that. I tucked my tail between my legs and retreated to the side of the rink.

Talk about feeling outdated and unnecessary.

In my life, such feelings will no longer ever be tolerated in my life any longer.

So there!

Hee-hee-hee…

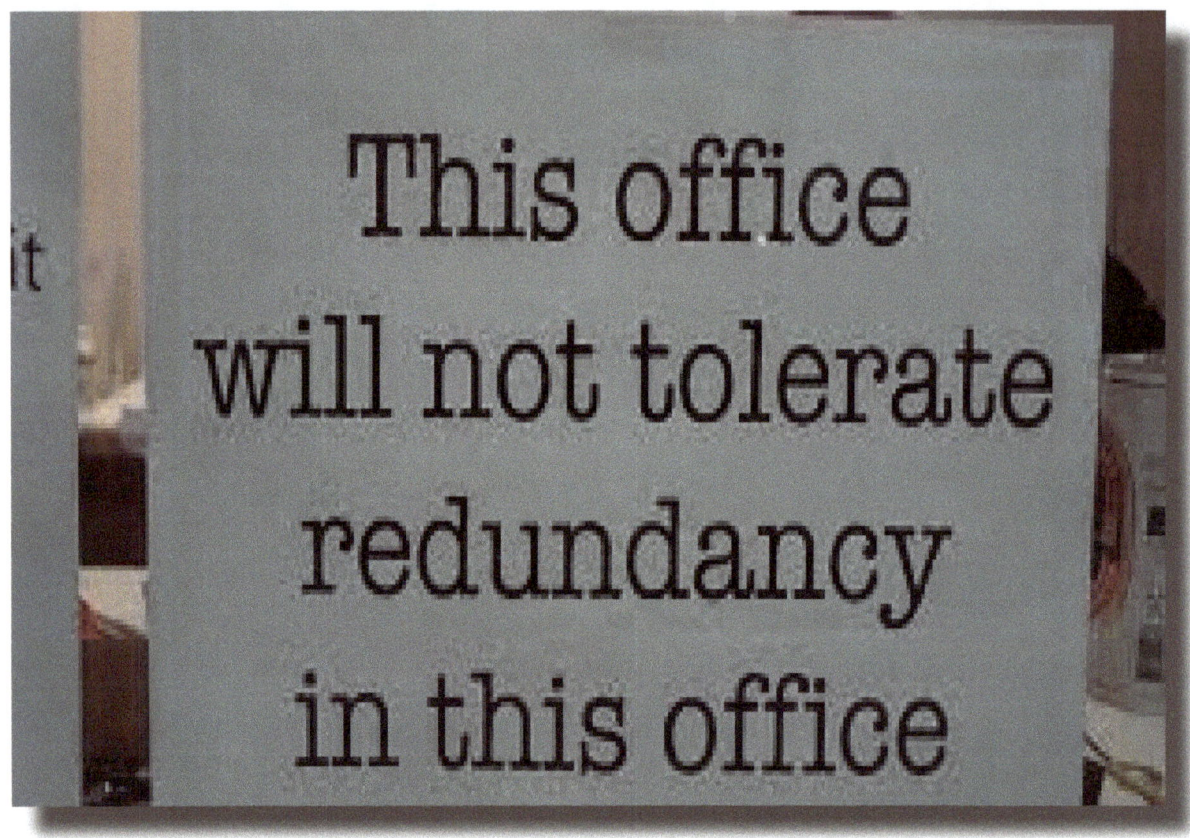

~ ~ ~

**Wish Them Healing**

**Thursday 1/23/2020** – This quote for today kind of ties into what I wrote about two days ago. Thank you for all the private messages of support, but I hope I was able to reassure each of you that my only problem was waiting two or three days to get the lesson.

I truly do wish healing for those who strike out in anger or because of deep hurts.

> Never wish them pain.
> That's not who you are. If they
> caused you pain, they must
> have pain inside. Wish them
> healing.

~ ~ ~

**Yelling**

**Friday 1/24/2020** – Did you ever yell at a pinecone by grumping about something that you then found out had no basis whatsoever in fact?

I did one less-than-memorable time [translation: I wish everyone around me had never seen it happen], and I've done my best to forget the details. But I got to wondering how many other times I've walked right into negativity without seeing the full picture before I took that first step.

Probably more often than I realize.

Doggone it.

Starting here, starting now – no more pinecone moments for me. How about you?

# Fran Stewart

~ ~ ~

### The Second O

**Saturday 1/25/2020** – This remonstrance was posted on April 1st last year somewhere or other. I don't want to wait for another April Fool's Day before I enjoy it again.

I hope that the rest of your Saturday is filled with joy . . .

and that you come back here on Monday. I'll be waiting for you!

~ ~ ~

**Hidden Brain – Melting Permafrost**

**Monday 1/27/2020** – Last Friday I listened to NPR's *Hidden Brain* program as they explored the ways in which the Alaskan permafrost is melting. One of the questions they asked is why, for almost the entire history of humankind, so many people have refused to believe the prophets who warn us of impending danger.

That's a good question. When the permafrost is melting, how can we possibly deny the results of global warming?

Just as the way in which the Trojans brought the big horse inside their gates despite Cassandra's warning, so too do several otherwise intelligent people I know refuse to see the Greeks inside the horse, the climate catastrophe within what we're experiencing now.

Why don't we listen? Why don't we wake up? Why don't we pay attention to Andrew Natsios (who is interviewed on this show)?

The answer to these questions was complex, but it pretty much boiled down to this: we don't listen because we don't want to face the uncomfortable truths that prophetic people have pointed out.

It's time to face up to what we've done to this earth.

To find the original podcast from 5/16/2019, search for "How to See the Future No Crystal Ball Needed"

Fran Stewart

~ ~ ~

**Can Do Anything**

**Tuesday 1/28/2020** – It's time for us to stop trying to take on every unfilled job.

I speak from experience.

Nobody wants to serve on the board of a particular organization, which shall remain unnamed on this FB page. I'm already on the board and said I was willing to continue to serve in that position – but then there's the president and 1st VP. There are no volunteers.

Do I volunteer to be president as well as the position I already hold?

Or do I go to bat to have the whole organization dissolved? We never accomplish anything anyway (mostly because not only is there nobody in leadership positions, but nobody volunteers for committees).

That settles it. I can do anything, but I'm not going to try to do everything. I'm gonna try to dismantle the whole thing.

Wish me luck.

# Remember, you can do anything. But you cannot do everything.

## (And that's okay)

SOUTHERN PLATE

## My First Tunic

**Wednesday 1/29/2020** – I've always liked uniforms. Such a mindset is probably the result of my having grown up in an Air Force family. In fact, I read a book called *Military Brats* many years ago in which the author said that the majority of military brats end up in jobs that require uniforms once they're grown.

So it made a lot of sense for me to decide that as long as I like a "uniform" look, I ought to dress that way. Now, that doesn't necessarily mean all the same color all the time. But it could mean the same relative shape most of the time.

If you've read these daily postings for any time, you also know that I live frugally—and don't like wasting ANYTHING. I read an article about how one of the big problems in landfills is the tremendous number of clothes that Americans throw away. Fabric does not decompose easily in the airless environment of landfills. It just takes up space.

I decided to do something about both of these problems (my lack of a uniform and my wish to use old fabric rather than throw it out).

Aha! I've had some old flannel bed sheets that were too ratty to use, but that I wasn't willing to toss.

Ta-da! My first tunic top! It's incredibly comfortable. It fits me exactly the way I want it to fit (unlike the store-bought things that always have too-short arms or too-wide shoulders). Before I made it, a friend said, "If it doesn't work out, you can always use it as a pajama top." Whenever I wear it, though, I always get lots of compliments and requests to know where I bought it.

Since then, I've sewn three more tunics without having to buy any new fabric. The landfills are happier. So am I!

## Blue Planet

**Thursday 1/30/2020** – Today seems like a good day to recognize miracles.

I woke up this morning and opened my eyes.

And saw my cat gazing at me with her golden eyes. I stroked her luscious black fur and relished the feel of it.

When I brewed my morning Teeccino, I sniffed that vibrant smell and felt so fortunate.

I brushed Fuzzy Britches and listened to her deep resonant purr.

I'll sing the special birthday song to a friend of mine later today, and even though my voice has gotten croakier as I've gotten older, I still can bring joy to someone by calling them on their special day.

And these are only the five senses we concentrate on the most. There are multiple other "senses" that are miracles in and of themselves. The sense of love, the sense of compassion, our sense of integrity, and the wonder of the intellect. Friendship, family, humor, empathy. All of these are miracles.

Which miracle will you focus on today?

~ ~ ~

### One for the Chipper

**Friday 1/31/2020** – Last Saturday I was one of 180 volunteers with a county cleanup program called Bring One for the Chipper. I was the only grandma there. The others were young people from local schools getting credit for community service, their teachers, middle-aged folks who believe in environmental activism, and the employees of several companies that turn old Christmas trees into mulch to be used throughout the county's park system.

Good for us!

When I reached Bethesda Park at 7:45, there were three long piles of trees that stood well more than head-high and that stretched from the far end of the big parking lot down to where we volunteers gathered. The workers had already started the chipping at 7:30. A few minutes later, we early birds joined them.

I started the morning all gung-ho, hauling trees to one of the five chippers where the yellow-garbed employees shoved them into the enormous maw of the grinder. We had to examine each tree and set aside the ones that had metal spikes in the trunk (so as not to damage the chippers), the ones with tinsel, the ones with that disgusting sprayed fake snow, the ones that still had strings of lights on them (yes, really!), the ones wrapped in plastic netting. We had to discard the wreaths and evergreen ropes because all of them have metal frameworks. We also had to rip off the various plastic tags and markers, and the reams of plastic string used to tie the trees up.

Within about an hour I had to take a break to catch my breath and rest on the curb for a while. Then I had to ask one of the young folks for help getting up—the old knee joints just didn't want to cooperate.

Finally I found my niche. Instead of hauling those heavy trees, I became the self-appointed garbage picker-upper. Not only did I amass my own personal pile of all those items mentioned above, but I collected reams of plastic people used to contain the pine needles. There were also dozens of broken plastic tree stands and several handfuls of ornaments – some broken, some still intact. One of these pictures shows my waist-high pile of gatherings about halfway through the morning.

When we all finally left, after the last chippable tree was chipped, the workers were facing more hours of work dealing with the mulch. And there was an enormous blue dumpster that had to be hauled off, as well as the piles of garbage near each of the chippers.

I plan to go back next year. All said, it was great fun.

So was the nap I took when I got home!


**(December 2020 Note:** I didn't do it this year because of COVID.)

*before we started*

*halfway through*

Crystal Clear

*my personal pile of garbage by 9AM. It's almost waist-high.*

*getting closer to the end*

## February 2020

### Groundhog Day

**Saturday 2/1/2020** – Just a little reminder. Tomorrow is Groundhog Day. I always feel sorry for the poor groundhogs who are forced to leave their cozy winter nests just so a bunch of people can cheer or groan. Does that make me a Groundhog Grinch?

~ ~ ~

### ASC

**Monday 2/3/2020** – Yesterday afternoon Ingrid and I had great fun attending *Romeo & Juliet* at the Shakespeare Tavern in Atlanta. Those actors have such tremendous energy – and every time I see a show there (even if I've seen that particular play a dozen times before) the performance I'm watching is always new and vital and vibrant.

Because I sponsor the Tavern's Playbill, they often introduce me during the house speech before the play. So, during intermission, a delightful woman named Rebecca bought all three of my ScotShop mysteries from the Tavern's gift shop and asked if I'd sign them for her.

Well, of course I would – and was delighted to do so.

Anyway, it was a great way to spend an afternoon. Ingrid and I talked about the play all the way home afterwards. That's half the fun of seeing a good play – being able to discuss the nuances.

Have you seen any great plays recently?

Crystal Clear

### Hedgehog

**Tuesday 2/4/2020** – When I had a wall taken out several years ago, they had to leave a column sort of in the middle of the room.

Why?

Because it held up the roof.

But they left a funny little shelf off to one side of the column.

Every morning, when I come down the stairs, there's a friendly hedgehog to greet me and wish me a lovely day. Today I've asked her to greet you as well.

Great way to start the morning!

**The Four Agreements**

**Wednesday 2/5/2020** – These four things I can do.

Will you join me in striving to meet these standards?

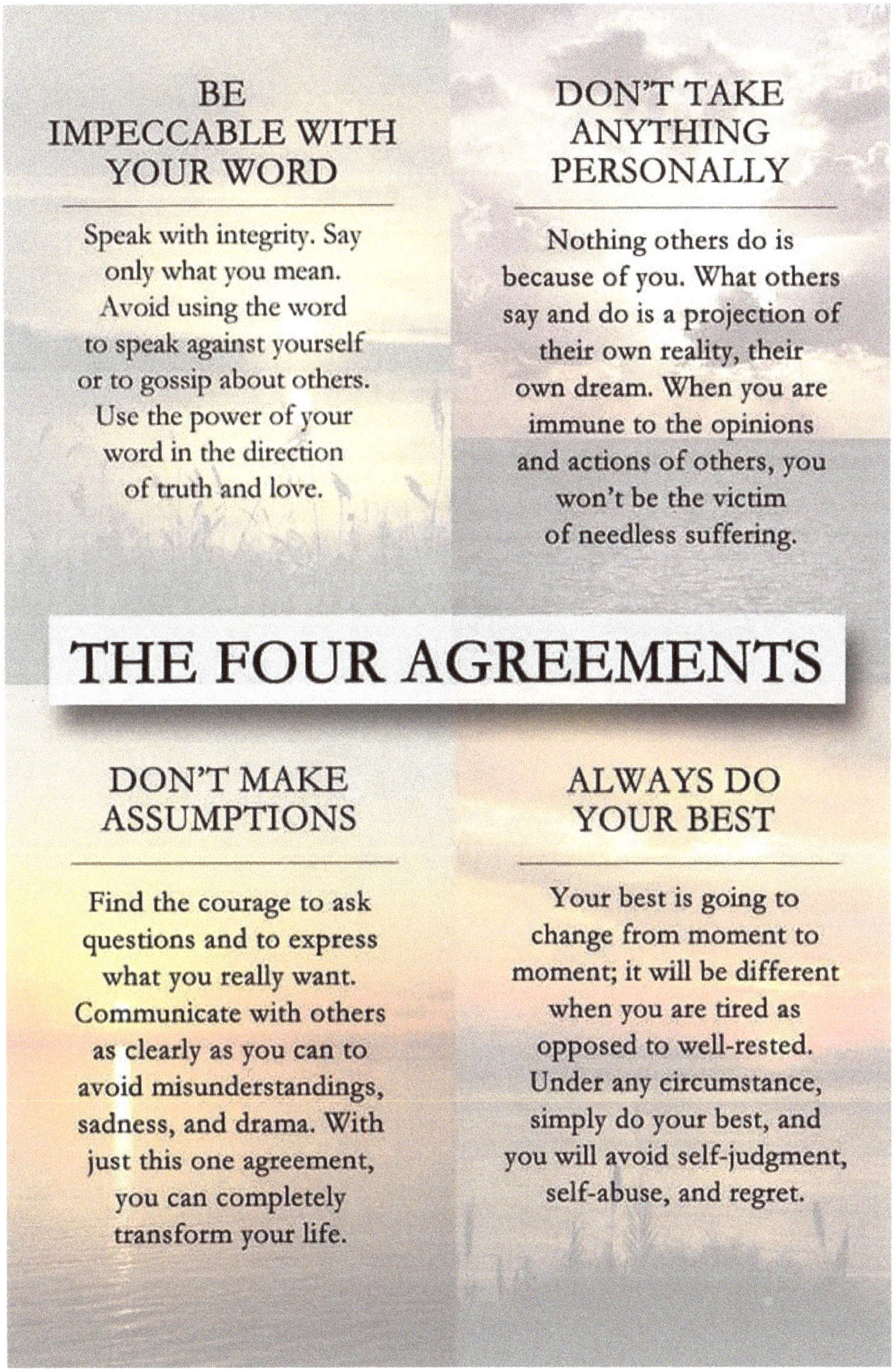

## THE FOUR AGREEMENTS

**BE IMPECCABLE WITH YOUR WORD**

Speak with integrity. Say only what you mean. Avoid using the word to speak against yourself or to gossip about others. Use the power of your word in the direction of truth and love.

**DON'T TAKE ANYTHING PERSONALLY**

Nothing others do is because of you. What others say and do is a projection of their own reality, their own dream. When you are immune to the opinions and actions of others, you won't be the victim of needless suffering.

**DON'T MAKE ASSUMPTIONS**

Find the courage to ask questions and to express what you really want. Communicate with others as clearly as you can to avoid misunderstandings, sadness, and drama. With just this one agreement, you can completely transform your life.

**ALWAYS DO YOUR BEST**

Your best is going to change from moment to moment; it will be different when you are tired as opposed to well-rested. Under any circumstance, simply do your best, and you will avoid self-judgment, self-abuse, and regret.

Fran Stewart

~ ~ ~

### Flower in Concrete

**Thursday 2/6/2020** – We're faced with a senate that has abrogated its constitutional mandate to provide checks and balances. They've caved in to the bullying of a vindictive POTUS, but I still have to believe that somewhere there is a flower popping up through the concrete.

Maybe more people will vote in the next election. Maybe more people will pay attention and try to heal the deep divisions within this country.

COMMENT: **Marcia Foster Dunscomb** Well said, Fran. I believe in "us." "We the people" are smarter, wiser, kinder and better than what recent actions suggest. My driveway has many cracks - they give me hope.

~ ~ ~

### The Price of Libraries

**Friday 2/7/2020** – Yesterday I spoke to a group of people at the Bethesda Senior Center, giving them an intro to writing their memoirs. The class was sponsored by the county library system—which sponsors a large number of highly informative programs.

So, yes, I agree with Walter Cronkite.

Here is something to think about, though. It was an ignorant, cowardly nation that allowed Joe McCarthy to take over the senate 60+ years ago, despite the number of libraries at that time.

Now that we're headed up by another Joe McCarthy, it is past time to stand up and speak our conscience. And vote our conscience. And say no to tyranny. I hereby stand. And I will vote (of course). And I say no.

> **WHATEVER THE COST OF OUR LIBRARIES, THE PRICE IS CHEAP COMPARED TO THAT OF AN IGNORANT NATION.**
> —WALTER CRONKITE

~ ~ ~

**First Mistake**

**Saturday 2/8/2020** – Doggone it, I'm still making that year/date mistake.

How about you?

Ironically, the first time I wrote it, well more than a month ago, I got it right—maybe because I was concentrating so much on the change. But the next time or two (okay—three or four), I wrote 2019 without even thinking about it.

Are we creatures of habit?

I just finished reading *Garbology* by Edward Humes. It's a report on the garbage industry in this country, and he points out that people are more willing to go out weekly to clean garbage off the beaches rather than reduce the number of things they buy. Why? Because one practice gives a feel-good result while the other one makes people think they are somehow having to sacrifice something. "WHAT????" they say. "Stop buying brand new [made-cheaply-in-China] whatevers, even though I know I'll have to throw them out within a year [or a month]?????"

Living simply is truly much easier. And it will save your children or grandchildren the bother of throwing out all your accumulated "stuff" when you croak. But people don't want to consider life "without" all the disposable stuff.

# Fran Stewart

That's why each person in America will produce 102 TONS of garbage (per person!) in their lifetime.

Not I. Not if I can help it.

Except for those checks I had to void out and rewrite because I messed up the date.

~ ~ ~

**Morning Coffee**

**Monday 2/10/2020** – Oh dear. I grossly overestimated the time I had available to do a job for which I have a looming deadline – and I grossly underestimated the total amount of work involved.

What's the solution?

I'm glad you asked.

1. No extraneous activities this week.

2. No time-consuming cooking. Of course, I almost always consider that an extraneous activity anyway, so I suppose this lumps into #1.

3. No winding-down time before lights out.

4. No brewing of early-morning tea. WAIT A MINUTE! Delete this one. There are certain lines I will not cross.

~ ~ ~

**Landed This Way**

**Tuesday 2/11/2020** – I could hardly believe my eyes when I went out into my yard after a particularly windy day and found this hollowed-out broken twig into which a tuft of pine needles had blown.

What are the odds that that particular clump of pine needles would get itself blown into that precise opening on that exactly proportioned hollow broken-off branch?

What are the odds that you, exactly proportioned as you are for filling the roll you came to this earth to fill, would find precisely the niche you were meant to be in? Or that I would find my niche?

And then, when we each grow out of that role, what are the odds that we will find exactly what we are meant to do or where we are meant to be in the next phase of our lives?

I'd say the odds are pretty good. After all, it happened with the pine needles!

~ ~ ~

**Three Simple Rules**

**Wednesday 2/12/2020** – I love these three simple rules, but I'd like to add another one:

If you don't say no (at least occasionally), you will easily get overwhelmed with all those volunteer things other people ask you to do.

If it doesn't bring you joy—if it doesn't fulfill some yearning in you—if it feels icky or boring—don't do it.

"Three simple rules in life. 1. If you do not go after what you want, you'll never have it. 2. If you do not ask, the answer will always be no. 3. If you do not step forward, you will always be in the same place."

### The Dog is Happier

**Thursday 2/13/2020** – My granddog, Limerick, is unabashedly enthusiastic about everything. That should be Everything with a capital letter—or maybe EVERYTHING with all caps.

Each time I dogwatch, we play tug-o-war with the same battered toys, but she never tires of it. If I take a nap while I'm at my daughter's house, Limmie is content to curl on the floor next to the couch, with her head resting on my slippers.

That kind of contentment is so very relaxing—for me as well as for her.

In a way, I have my own favorite play-toys—treasured books that I read again and again for the simple pleasure of the words. And my favorite head-resting place, a battered pillow that cradles my cheek in exactly the right way.

Maybe I'm more like a dog than I thought I was.

Not a bad way to be at all, wouldn't you say?

Fran Stewart

~ ~ ~

**Crazy Hats at Eri's House**

**Friday 2/14/2020** – Okay. It's time for a silly photo. A whole bunch of years ago, I traveled west to visit my sister, and we stopped in at her daughter's house. Erica (my niece) loves crazy hats, so Diana and I had to try on a few, and Eri took this picture of the two of us.

Why was I holding a broom? Don't ask. Or rather, you're welcome to ask, but I don't have a clue what the answer is. Maybe it was just a fun prop to evince a gothic American look—except that we were grinning too much to look truly gothic.

We all have a picture like this somewhere or other, right?

So, why don't you haul out yours and have a good laugh over it (them)?

This one certainly brought a chuckle to my heart. I rather enjoyed being a sunflower for a few hours.

[from the comment section]: **Erica Jensen** I do not remember this. It's my house. And my hat/scarf and I remember that broom. Wow.

**[My Reply]:** I can't laugh, Eri. Yesterday as I was proofing the sixth volume of my BeesKnees memoir, I came across an entry about a "Gathering for Gardner" I attended in Atlanta back in 2012. I was fascinated to read about all the marvelous events, the great entertainment, and the delicious dinner–and I don't have a clue about who I went with or how we got there. In short–my mind's a complete blank around that entire evening. And the sad thing is that it sounds like it was so much fun!

So don't worry about not remembering the hat goofiness. You're in good company. (And it was a LOT of fun.)

~ ~ ~

### Read to Your Children

**Saturday 2/15/2020** – I was looking through one of my bookshelves the other day and came across Tolkien's Ring trilogy. Couldn't help recalling the joy my son and I had one summer when he was just out of kindergarten. He saw me reading *Fellowship of the Ring* one afternoon while his little sister was napping. He asked what it was. So I pulled out *The Hobbit*—you have to start with the first book—and read him the first page.

And the second. And the third.

We ended up barreling through all the books that summer. He was already pretty good at reading (I'd started him early), so sometimes he'd read half a page to me and then I'd read fifteen pages to him. He liked the listening most of all.

The funny thing was that he "got" the story and could make the connections between the dark rider glimpsed in one chapter and the awful happenings three chapters later. Sometimes he was on my lap. Sometimes we lay stretched out on the floor beside each other.

No matter where or how we sat, though, it was an app built in heaven.

# Fran Stewart

~ ~ ~

### Wooly's TP Toy

**Monday 2/17/2020** – This is what I get for sleeping late.

My alarm sounds at 4:30 every morning, so 8:13 is really late for me. There's a reason for my lie-abed today, though. I wrenched my back late Thursday afternoon. My chiropractor's office is closed on Fridays and over the weekend. The only position where my back doesn't hurt is when I'm lying face-up.

So I'd say I had a fairly good excuse to turn off the alarm this morning.

Wooly Bear didn't agree.

How she managed to get the cabinet door open, I'll never know, but she obviously had a great deal of fun while I was deaf to the world. Yes. I hide my TP in the cabinet. No way am I going to leave an enticing roll out in plain view on one of those roll-y holders.

Sure hope my chiropractor's in her office today.

If not, there's no telling what Wooly Bear will open next …

~ ~ ~

**No More Car Turds**

**Tuesday 2/18/2020** – Why did I buy a Tesla?

I'm glad you asked.

Take a look at this clever video from PBS's Nova. Wish I had a photo to show you.

No more car turds for me!

        https://www.pbs.org/wgbh/nova/video/carbon-car-tailpipe-solid-chunks/~ ~ ~


**Fran, Heifer, and Pepper Can**

**Wednesday 2/19/2020** – From the ridiculous to the sublime: car turds yesterday to pepper cans today.

Why did I carry around an old empty pepper can when I was a kid? I have no idea.

Why was I so fascinated by cows? That's easy to answer. I've always liked cows. Watching my grandfather milking their cow, watching my grandmother churn the milk to make butter – everything about the process intrigued me.

By the way, rather than using a butter churn, Grandma put the milk in 1-gallon glass jugs. Then she and my aunts and my mother would hold the jugs on their laps while they rocked on the side porch, shelling peas, talking, laughing, knitting, doing whatever sittin'-down jobs needed doing. Eventually, the milk would clabber, they'd all migrate to the kitchen to complete the process of turning white milk into sheer gold.

There's something special about fresh butter from a cow you know personally!

# Fran Stewart

~ ~ ~

### London Statue

**Thursday 2/20/2020** – Have I shared this picture with you before this? Somehow I think I might have, but then again, maybe not. I just seem to be in an old photo mood, probably because I'm trying to complete the "Mom Tell Me Your Story" book my son gave me a couple of years ago. He's going to be here in two weeks (so he and I can take the Landmark Forum together), and I'd really like to have the book finished before he arrives.

Here I am teaching memoirs classes, in which I encourage my students to write their stories, and I'm woefully behind the schedule in writing my own. <<sigh>>

Anyway, one of the pages in the book says, "Tell me about the best vacation you ever took." Naturally, I wrote about a childhood trip, since these pages were talking about those long-gone days. But as an adult, one of the loveliest trips I took was to London for five glorious days, all by myself.

While I was there, I took one of the only three good pictures I've ever taken. The sidewalks were busy, the day was partially cloudy, the traffic kept zipping from right to left across the camera view. I wanted to show those iconic London chimneys, and the marvelous outline of the statue, which just happened to be in the middle of the street. I also wanted to avoid any electric lines and telephone poles – not easy to do unless I crouched down right on the curb and leaned out into the traffic lane.

So I waited and waited and waited . . . until there was a sudden break in traffic. I took one more quick glance to my right to be sure there were no lorries bearing down on me, crouched down for just the right angle, and snapped the photo. When I lowered my camera, there stood a lorry with a dear, patient, good-humored driver who had come upon me suddenly from around the slight bend, slowed—well, actually he stopped—his truck so as not to behead me. He leaned out the window as he drove past, once I was out of the way, and called, "You should have taken a snap of me, lovie!"

How I wish I'd had the presence of mind to raise my camera and capture him the same way I captured this quintessential ancient London scene. As you can tell, this picture is a photo of a photo. Sorry about the reflections off the plastic picture-protector.

Funny how one picture can make an entire vacation come flooding back. I don't need hundreds (or even dozens) of pictures to recall those five magical days. This one does it perfectly.

(**Later Note**: Doggone it! As I was going through these posts to get them ready for publication in *Crystal Clear*, I found that I'd written this same story in somewhat different words on June 6th. That's the trouble with memoirs—it's easy to forget which stories you've told and which ones you've only *thought about* telling. At any rate, you won't have to worry about remembering this story, since you'll get to read it again when you get to page 133.)

~ ~ ~

**Honeybee Socks**

**Friday 2/21/2020** – Are these not the cutest socks you ever saw?

A couple of weeks ago, just before Valentine's Day, I went to a regular monthly meeting in Atlanta. One of the members greeted me. "I just had to thank you, Fran," she said, "for writing those BeesKnees books. I just finished the first one last night, and I felt so warm and comfy while I was reading it. I could hear your voice talking to me the whole time."

She handed me a little red-heart bag with a red ribbon tying it shut. I assumed it was chocolate, told her I'd open it when I got home, and went on with getting ready for the meeting.

When it came time to introduce guests, Anne stood and said, "I didn't bring a guest this month, but I wanted to tell everybody about Fran's bee books." She went on to give one of the nicest 'book reports' I've ever heard.

After the meeting, after I'd unloaded the car, I opened her gift, thinking that a little afternoon snack of Valentine chocolate would hit the spot.

It wasn't chocolate. It was this pair of long, warm, comfy honeybee socks. A perfect gift. A delightful surprise. A frequent reminder that when we write the stories of our lives (and that's what my BeesKnees memoirs are) we touch the lives of other people in ways we can't even begin to imagine.

By the time she gets to *BeesKnees #3: A Beekeeping Memoir* she'll see that the book matches these socks. Sort of. Thank you, Anne.

### Two Different Concepts

**Saturday 2/22/2020** – Several days I spoke to a genealogy study group about the importance of writing their own memoirs. "Wouldn't you," I asked them, "love to find old journals that give you a picture of what your great-great-great grandparents thought of the events of their lives?"

Everybody nodded, of course.

"Now, think about what it will mean to your descendants to find your life stories written down. Don't leave them in the dark. Shine a light on the last of the 20th century and the beginning of the 21st."

Then we proceeded to talk about the ways our viewpoint of life events change over time. Like this "Boat! Land!" dichotomy. Something that seemed devastating to us when we were five can, many years later, be seen as the impetus that helped us craft our life in a unique way. This new way of viewing that event, from the perspective of years down the line may bring us to a more empathetic outlook; it may show us that we have the courage to begin a new career; it may spur us to fight injustices.

A sense of perspective is a good sense to cultivate, wouldn't you agree?

**TWO DIFFERENT CONTEXTS, TWO DIFFERENT VIEWS**

**THIS IS LIFE.**

## Change the Ending

**Monday 2/24/2020** – My grandson drove over to help me with some yard work this weekend. Well, to tell the truth, he did most of the work and I just puttered around the edges. I can't change what I did to my back two weeks ago, but I can change the ending. I'm following my chiropractor's instructions (ALL of them) and am feeling considerably better.

Do you remember four or five years ago when I grew potatoes in an old plastic trashcan on my deck? I shared with you a picture of my harvest. This year I've started FOUR trashcans of potatoes. Now, why, you may ask, do I have all those old trashcans on hand?

I wish I knew. Hard to believe how much we accumulate over the years, isn't it? But I believe in the 4 R's [refuse, reduce, reuse, recycle]—another thing you'll know about me if you've read these posts for any length of time—so I wanted to avoid throwing the trashcans away. After all, I can't change the fact that I collected all that stuff, but I sure as heck CAN change what I do with it.

Now I've run out of old trashcans, and I still want to plant peas and tomatoes and pole beans. But where? The only sunny place in my yard is on the side where all those porcupine eggs [that would be the spiny seed cases of Sweetgum trees] sprouted up after the dying pines were removed four years ago. The last thing I want to do is spend my time combatting more sprouts while trying to avoid digging up veggies.

Ergo (!) more back-deck plantings. But what to put them in?

I saw a great little video on the Mary's Heirloom Seeds site about using old rain barrels. And I just happened to have two on hand. Their spouts had been damaged, and they weren't usable for their original purposes, so on Saturday Aiden (the aforementioned grandson) hauled them onto the deck and sawed them in half. Now all I have to do is drill a few more holes for plant drainage, fill them with good soil, and be ready to plant as soon as Mary sends me the seeds I ordered.

I'll be sure to let you know how it turns out.

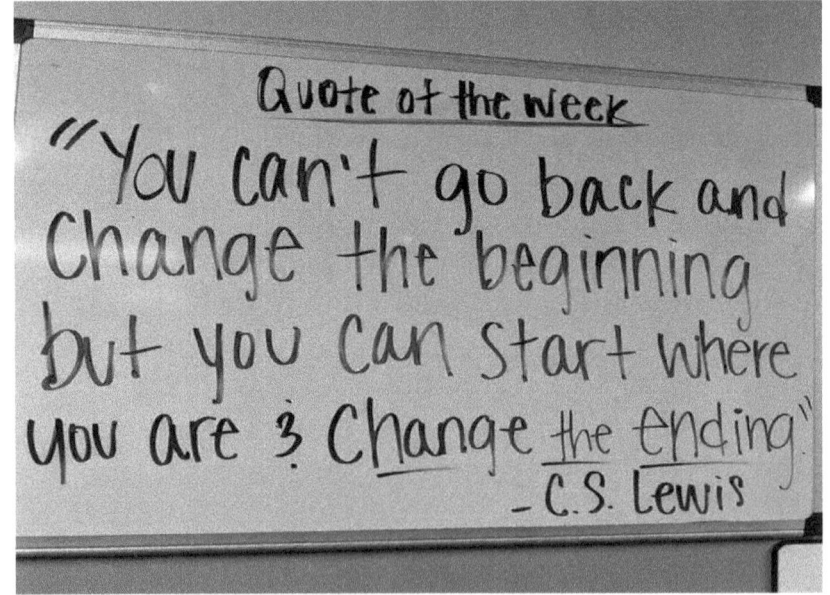

~ ~ ~

**A Few Rotten Years**

**Tuesday 2/25/2020** – I found this picture somewhere or other. It had a caption that said, **"You can have a few rotten years and still survive."** How true that is.

Long ago, I wallowed for a long time (it's embarrassing to think just how long) bemoaning the circumstances I'd gotten myself into and trying to blame everybody else (but never poor little misunderstood Frannie).

I'm so glad I dug my way out of that hole. Now I can look back on those times and see that they were simply growth rings that looked and felt rotten. I wouldn't, however, be the person I am today without having had those experiences.

The point of it all is that the tree (and I) (and you) kept growing.

## Sigh – Living Bathroom

**Wednesday 2/26/2020** – Whenever I see a gorgeous house-beautiful picture like this one, I always wonder where they put the litterboxes? Wooly Bear has hers in the bathroom. Of course she does. I poop in that room, so why shouldn't she as well?

And where are the cat toys or the dog bones?

*House Beautiful* would throw up their hands in despair over me.

~ ~ ~

### great stairs

**Thursday 2/27/2020** – This stairway is the very embodiment of inclusiveness. Years ago, my then-husband took on the job of fostering a service-dog in training. She failed practically every test, so he ended up keeping her. But before she flunked out, we rented a wheelchair for her to practice with around our house. Naturally, the kids loved popping wheelies and zipping around.

But we found out quickly just how almost insurmountable some barriers were. The little ridges that separate carpeted from non-carpeted areas, for instance. It's amazing how hard it can be to get a wheelchair over those unless you have room to build up a bit of speed ahead of the bump. And getting from the den out onto the back deck? Forget it. Completely insurmountable. I needed a push every single time.

The rest of the house? Stairs up to the top floor and down to the basement. Steps up to the front door. Steps into and out of the sunken living room. Whatever were the builders thinking?

Even now, I live in a split-level. Three steps up to the front door. Nine steps up to the top level (where my bathroom is). Five steps down to the lower level (where another bathroom is).

So, if I ever end up unable to manage stairs I'll have to choose between living on the main level where the kitchen is (so I can eat), or staying upstairs (or downstairs) where I'll be able to poop, but I won't have access to food.

Hmmm . . . sounds like Hamlet's dilemma—to pee or not to pee.

 define-space

i really admire the design for these stairs and how they incorporate a wheelchair access ramp. in a world were barrier free design is essential to living a full and happy life, its amazing to see landscape architect Cornelia Oberlander has taken literal steps to design stairs AROUND a ramp, instead of the other way around.

~ ~ ~

**Bottled Water**

**Friday 2/28/2020** – Who on earth was the marketing genius who decided to convince Americans that water from the tap isn't acceptable? I know, I know, there are areas where the water quality may be less than optimal, but when we have perfectly good, perfectly safe water available just by opening a tap—water we already pay for—why would we choose to spend more money buying plastic bottles?

I made a decision some time ago not EVER to accept bottled water. I have a couple of sturdy bottles I recycled from somewhere or other, and I make a point of filling them and taking them along with me. Whether

# Fran Stewart

I'm teaching a memoirs class or speaking at a public event or just driving a long way in my car. Especially during hot weather, but (really) year-round.

After all, water's good. Notice I didn't say, "it's good for you." I shudder when someone tells me what's good for me. I'll make my own decision about that, thank you. But when someone says, "It's good," that leaves the choice up to me.

And I choose not to support bottled-water companies.

I'd love it if you'd join me – but it's entirely up to you.

> **bottled water companies don't produce water, they produce plastic bottles.**

~ ~ ~

**Live Every Day**

**Saturday 2/29/2020** – I thought this would be a great thought to end the week with.

I plan to live every single day. Every. Single. Day.

# March 2020

## Yellowstone Early Touring Bus

**Sunday 3/1/2020** – I know I post only six days a week. Not on Sundays. But I couldn't resist this happy birthday message.

Happy 148th Birthday, Yellowstone National Park!

I remember going to Yellowstone with my mother and my sister when I was a kid. We had a little tow-along-behind-the-car pop-up Coleman camper, which was basically a fold-up tent on wheels.

The first night we were there, we heard somebody or something scraping a cooler out from underneath the camper. Contrary to common sense, Mama grabbed a flashlight, jumped outside, grabbed the other end of the cooler the bear was dragging away, shone the light in the bear's eyes, and yelled, "Scoot!"

Then she lifted the cooler into the camper (where it should have been in the first place) and shook with the what-ifs for the rest of the night.

It never occurred to me at the time to think that a bear might not be as scared of my mother's anger as I was.

I think people should be banned from the park—sent outside every night into fenced enclosures—leaving the park to the animals who have every right to be there, and who should never have been acclimated to handouts (voluntary or otherwise) from humans.

Then private cars should be banned from the park—the way they do at Denali. Let people take touring buses, like this one I found on the National Park Service's Yellowstone website.

## Septic Tank Pumping

**Monday 3/2/2020** – Last Friday was septic tank clean-out day. Today will be landscapers-coming-to-repair day. They won't have to repair Davis Septic Tank Service's work, It's the rest of the yard that needs help, particularly the area I've mentioned before that grew up with junk trees after I had to have six huge dying pines removed four (five?) years ago.

Davis is a family business. Sheila takes care of the office side of it. Cecil and his son do the onsite work. When they arrived, Cecil took a look at the leach-field area while Nick probed to find the two ends of the tank and began digging to access the holes on either end of it.

Once the concrete access lids were revealed and opened, they stuck in a long wide hose to suck out the contents of the five-foot deep tank. I asked if there was any problem. Could I change anything I was doing in order to create—how can I say this?—a better quality of sewage?

"Nope," Nick said. "This looks incredibly good. Whatever you're doing, just keep right on doing it."

That was a relief!

"You know," he said, "even though it's been twelve years since we were here last time, I remember you."

I remembered him as well—a dozen years ago he was only 13 years old, but he'd worked like a real trooper.

While I was recalling that, he went on. "I've been telling this story to customers ever since, whenever they ask me, *'what's the strangest thing that ever happened to you in this job?'* I tell 'em we did some work for a writer once, and when we got here and started digging, she asked us if we'd ever found a dead body in there, and how hard would it be to hide a murdered person in a tank."

Although I didn't remember having asked them about that, I do know it was a perfectly logical question. I always researched my mysteries carefully, and although I never used the septic tank idea for hiding a body, I did work in septic tanks a couple of times in the Biscuit McKee series. What had been an all-in-a-day's work question for me was a we're-gonna-remember-this-forever moment for them.

After the pumping was complete, I asked Nick to place a big paving stone over one end and a gorgeous rock over the other. That way, next time they come over for preventive maintenance, he won't have to spend extra time probing for the location of the tank.

The birds have forgiven me, now that I put their feeders back in place – and I've put them farther from the trees so the squirrels (hopefully) will not find it quite so easy to get onto them.

Crystal Clear

# Fran Stewart

~ ~ ~

### Library Card

**Tuesday 3/3/2020** – Lately I've had to charge my phone every day. The battery must be wearing out (planned obsolescence?) but I can't see buying a new phone with 40-kazillion bells and whistles on it, when all I use my phone for is phone calls, text messages, and photographs.

I don't want to get my emails on my phone. I check my messages two (sometimes three) times a day on my laptop. I don't want to surf the web on my phone. I limit those times severely so as not to wander into time-wasting byroads.

I've memorized my 14-digit library card number, so I don't even need to rummage around in my purse when it's time to check out books. Some of the books I read are timeless; some are timely. Some are both!

Yes, my card is wireless—and unlike my telephone, I never have to worry that its battery might give out.

~ ~ ~

### Coal Dragon

**Wednesday 3/4/2020** – Instead of my usual blurb about marching forth on March Fourth, I decided to share some information about a new fossil. *Carbonodraco lundi* is a recently discovered parareptile, from the Permian Age (before the age of dinosaurs). It had discernible (big) fangs. The fossil was found in an Ohio coal dump, hence the name—which means Coal Dragon. I love that name.

You can tell I'm still enraptured by the online Dinosaur course I took from the University of Alberta. Are you as enthralled by newly discovered fossils as I am?

No? That's okay. But I hope you at least like the name!

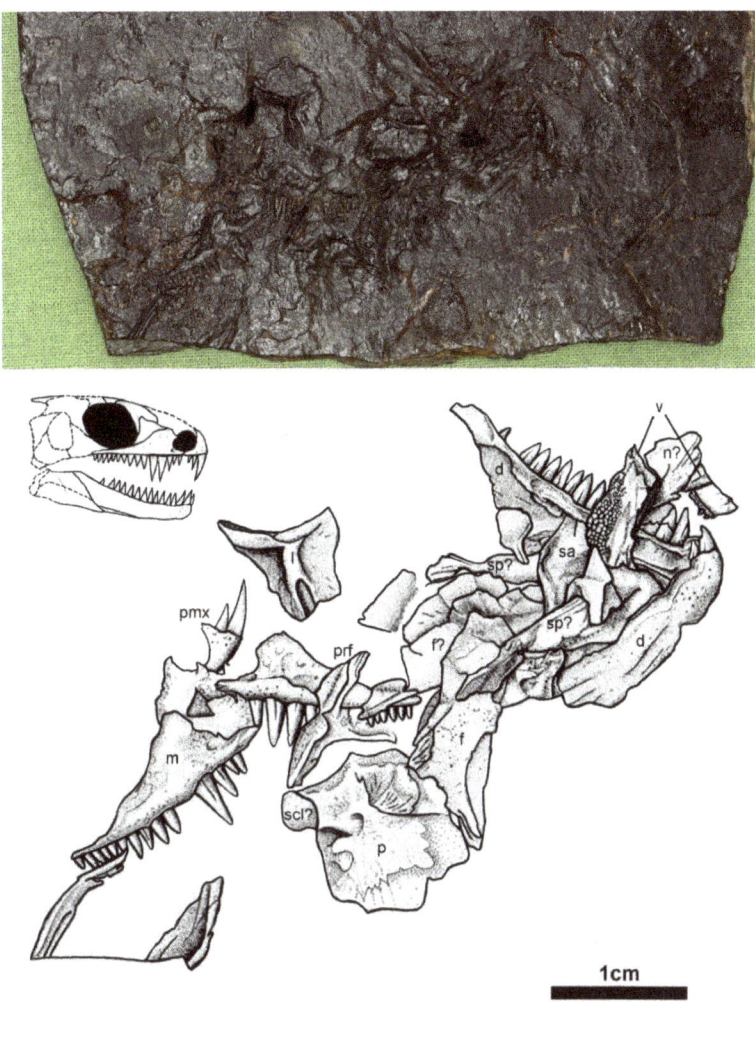

~ ~ ~

**Eli's Moon**

**Thursday 3/5/2020** – I love my son's photography. This ethereal moon captures so well the feeling I had when I first read "The Highwayman" by Alfred Noyes. It's a soap opera of a poem, but I loved the language, the rhythms, the repetitions—and particularly the line "The moon was a ghostly galleon, tossed upon cloudy seas."

It was first published in 1906, but the story can still speak to us today.

Whether or not you read the poem in its entirety, I'm sure you can appreciate the "ghostly galleon" quality of Eli's photo.

He's here in the Atlanta area for a visit – and I feel blessed indeed.

~ ~ ~

**Jain 108 Mathematics**

**Friday 3/6/2020** – I love stuff like this! Periodically I check out the Jain108 FB page and find math treasures (like this one) to enjoy.

Or I marvel at a Kakuro puzzle. I gave up on Sudoku long ago, since it became so unutterably, predictably easy. Sure, sometimes I goofed, but as long as I was careful I could always get the Sudoku square completed. Kakuro, though? A well-crafted Kakuro grid gives my brain a real workout.

Earlier this month, this "times 8" lineup had me stopping in my tracks. There are plenty of math games built around the number nine – and I've probably seen most of them – but I'd never come across an 8 one as intriguing as this in all my seven-plus decades.

What brand new thing have you learned recently?

Crystal Clear

$$1 \times 8 + 1 = 9$$
$$12 \times 8 + 2 = 98$$
$$123 \times 8 + 3 = 987$$
$$1234 \times 8 + 4 = 9876$$
$$12345 \times 8 + 5 = 98765$$
$$123456 \times 8 + 6 = 987654$$
$$1234567 \times 8 + 7 = 9876543$$
$$12345678 \times 8 + 8 = 98765432$$
$$123456789 \times 8 + 9 = 987654321$$

~ ~ ~

**Books on Llamas**

**Saturday 3/7/2020** – Did you hear about the woman who walked into a library and asked, "Do you have any books on llamas?"

"No," the librarian said. "As you can see, all our books are on shelves."

Bye for now. See you Monday.

~ ~ ~

**Perfect Cabbage**

**Monday 3/9/2020** – Just look at these three perfect spirals coming off the center of this red cabbage. There is so much beauty around us every moment of every day.

Remember high school English lit? I'm sure you had to read Wordsworth's poem that begins "My heart leaps up when I behold / A rainbow in the sky." Then again, maybe that was only my English class.

Well, my heart leaps up when I behold the nebula in the center of a cabbage, or the star in the center of an apple. Or a ghostly galleon moon (the kind I wrote about last Thursday). Or any one of a thousand other daily miracles.

We're alive. There is hope.

~ ~ ~

**Spring Forward at Stonehenge**

**Tuesday 3/10/2020** – I always feel sorry for the people who have to take on this chore each year, moving all those monolithic stones in all the henges throughout the world. I hope they're taking a couple of days to recuperate. I try to make it a point not to drive anywhere on the day after the Spring time change, just because sleep deprivation does crazy things to people—and then they go out and get in a vehicle that weighs a ton or so.

This year I finally got smart about the spring-forward thing. Three months ago I set my morning alarm to 4:30, rather than 5:30. I got S-L-O-W-L-Y used to waking at that time (slowly, because I used the snooze button a lot for a couple of weeks).

So, this past Sunday I woke at what my body told me was the usual time, although the clock now said it was 5:30. Yes, I have an hour less to get ready if I have to go somewhere early in the day, but for all those months when I got up at 4:30, I had an hour EXTRA that I just spent reading or knitting. Now I need to be a little more efficient with my time in the morning, and I'm a LOT safer when I get on the road.

It's a good system. Want to try it next year?

~ ~ ~

**Wednesday 3/11/2020** – Last night my son and I completed taking the Landmark Forum in Atlanta—I for the second time, he for the first. If you've never heard of the Forum, rest assured that it's a life-changing weekend seminar (plus a Tuesday evening session).

Whew! I felt like I was on a roller-coaster with so many insights into how I've been living my life, how I've been making decisions, how I've been relating to the people around me.

It's been a very good ride. And now I'm ready to move mountains.

~ ~ ~

**Moon over Landmark**

**Thursday 3/12/2020** – Here's your chuckle for the day. If you've read my posts for any length of time, you will have figured out that I have a lousy phone camera. I'm always slightly surprised by the clarity of the pictures other people take.

# Fran Stewart

Sometimes, though, a photo from a crummy camera can surprise one all on its own. Take this one, for instance. When Eli and I left the final session of the Landmark Forum earlier this week, the moon was just peeking over the building. Naturally, I had to take a picture. Imagine my astonishment when I saw the next day that the moon was square.

Really! The corners are slightly rounded, but the moon itself is a perfect (almost) square.

I think this is funny.

Am I nuts?

Possibly. But I'm happy.

~ ~ ~

**Gorgonzola & Pepper Jack**

**Friday 3/13/2020** – I love the cheese section at Sprouts, a fresh foods grocery store I discovered only recently. They have these little bitty packages of weird kinds of cheeses. Okay, so maybe Gorgonzola isn't truly weird, but it's one I'd never tried before simply because I hate the idea of buying a big chunk of something I might not like. And the look of it reminds me of bleu cheese, which has a taste I truly do not enjoy.

Guess what? Gorgonzola has its very own unique yumminess. And I never would have known that if it hadn't been for being able to buy a teeny package for less than $3.00.

The price per half-ounce was probably something like four kazillion dollars, but was this worth the cost? Absolutely!

Here's a portion of the cheese plate I made for myself the other day. It looked tidier when I started, but I took this pic after I'd already rummaged around a bit.

Crystal Clear

~ ~ ~

**Mona Lisa's Cat**

**Saturday 3/14/2020** – Keep me straight, please. Let me know if I've already used this picture in one of my earlier posts.

I kinda think I did.

I kinda think I didn't.

Anyway, it'll serve as the laugh for the end of this week, right?

p.s. Yesterday I sent out an email to my fan list reminding them about the Sisters in Crime event this Saturday: Crime Fest Atlanta. As one of the featured authors, I'd been looking forward to it, but doggone it (or as my grand-dog would say, humangone it) the Smyrna Library closed its doors and cancelled the event. Please, stay safe. Wash hands. Either curtsey or do the "jazz hands." Remain calm. If I haven't told you lately that I love and appreciate you, please know that I do.

**When We Run Out of TP**

**Sunday 3/15/2020** – The last time I went to the grocery store, the cart bay just inside the front door was empty. That's right. Empty. Needless to say, there were numerous shelves just as bare as the day they were first installed. So, if you find yourself running out of toilet paper, step outdoors and find a soft leaf or two or three.

Helpful Hint: Be sure the leaves you pick are not *toxicodendron radicans*.**

**otherwise known as poison ivy.

~ ~ ~

**Power of Chickens**

**Monday 3/16/2020** – If I'd had a way to fence in my backyard years ago, I think I would have gotten a flock of chickens.

Just look at the wonderful things they do for the world!

Of course, I would have had to get over my fear of chickens before I could have followed this path. I know you know about it. Well, you do if you've been reading these daily posts for a couple of years. I wrote all about how Julie Porath introduced me to her sweet chickens and taught me that they're not the "peck-me-in-the-eye-monsters" I thought they were.

I like the "eat the weeds" part of this illustration.

Can you guess that I spent a fair amount of time this past week pulling invasive weeds?

I wonder if you can talk a chicken into leaving the dandelions for the bees?

# Fran Stewart

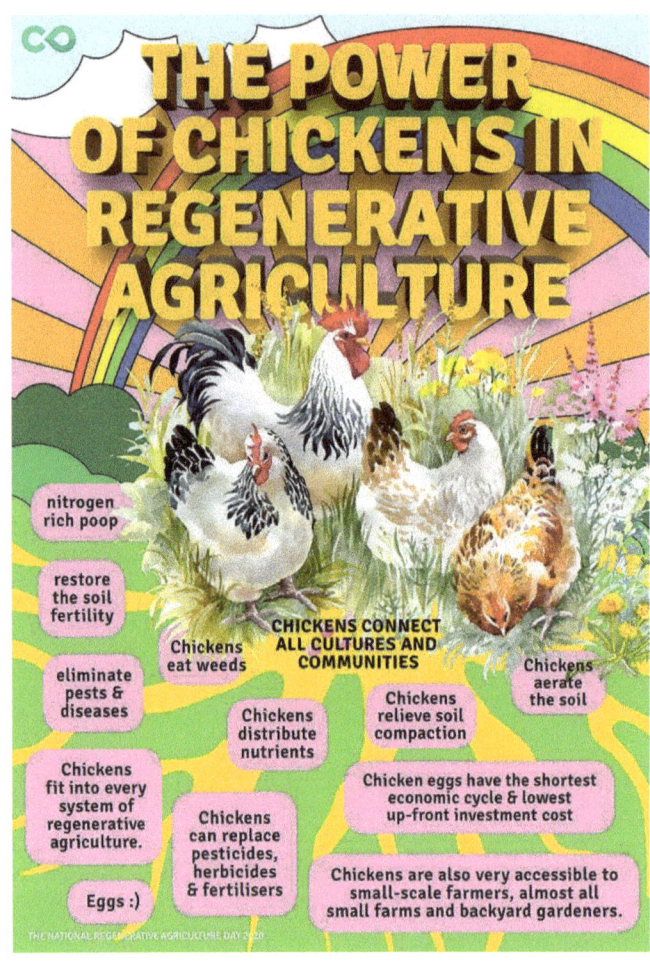

~ ~ ~

**Snowdrift**

**Tuesday 3/17/2020** – I used to live in Vermont. I see nothing strange about this photo. After all, I still recall the day I opened my front door to find it completely blocked by a six-foot high drift of solid snow that extended about 12 feet out along my front walkway.

Luckily, I had a snow shovel inside. Unluckily, there wasn't anywhere to put the snow if I shoveled it.

Luckily, I had a neighbor who tackled the other end of the drift and made a tunnel for me.

You know what the funny thing is?

I completely forgot *I had a back door* that wasn't blocked at all. I could have carried my snow shovel out that door, walked around to the front, and shoveled myself out.

I also could have let the dog out the back so she wouldn't have had to cross her legs. She finally just couldn't hold it any longer. So while my neighbor shoveled and shouted encouraging words, I cleaned up dog pee.

Serves me right for being back-door-blind.

~ ~ ~

**Connected the World**

**Wednesday 3/18/2020** – It would be easy to get all gloom-and-doomish about the number of people who are so tied to their phones that they never look into the eyes of the people around them, but earlier this month (before the pandemic lockdown) I spent three days and one evening in a room with 131 other participants, one Landmark Forum Leader, and 25 very helpful volunteers, all of whom got it that connection between people is our raison d'être. Without other people, where would we be?

When I was a child, one of my most horrific nightmares was the fear that someday I might have to be trapped inside an iron lung to prevent death by polio. That kind of isolation (to say nothing of the claustrophobia aspect of it) terrified me.

Then again, there was the 10-day period I volunteered to maintain complete silence. I experienced this at the Vipassana Center in south Georgia some years ago. Even though we had all vowed not to speak (or sing or write or raise our eyes to look directly at anyone else), and even though we had no access to any sort of technology, we ended those ten days feeling a thorough connection to everyone else in that program. In fact, you might think that at the end of the ten days we would have been so anxious to TALK that we'd all go at it nonstop. Chatter, chatter, chatter – all this information to impart.

That's not what happened. Most of us waited and waited and waited until we found the perfect moment to speak what was most important. My first words after those ten days of complete silence were, "Thank you," which I said very slowly to one of the dedicated volunteers who had cooked and served our meals. I looked her in the eyes—the EYES—when I said it. And I truly saw her. And she saw me as she paused and said, "You're welcome.

I plan to try every single day to connect—truly connect—with the people I meet.

Let's start a movement, shall we?

The only trouble with this plan of mine is that I've self-isolated for the next two or so weeks, so I won't be meeting any people. Hmmm. Guess I'll postpone the plan till later. Meanwhile, I can walk outside, listen to the birds, do a bit of weeding, laugh at the antics of the squirrels. Inside I can knit, work Kakuro puzzles, play the piano, read, and of course, write. What more could I ask?

p.s. Don't you love the texture of the paper this note was written on?

[**Later Note:** I can hardly believe how optimistic that "two weeks" of self-isolation was when I posted this. As I write now, I've maintained physical-distancing for seven months—with a lot of months still to go. But I'm still alive, alert, and enthusiastic. Life is good.]

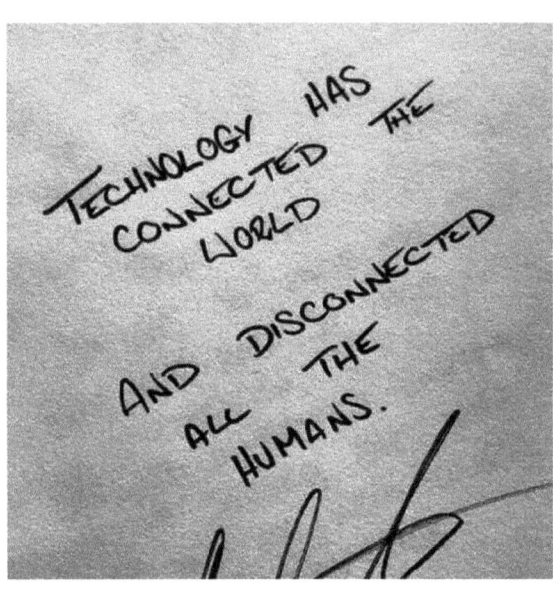

~ ~ ~

**Because of You**

**Thursday 3/19/2020** – I agree with the statement in this picture, but I'd like to point out something I thought was quite revealing.

Did you notice that the photo could have been cropped right up to the bottom of this person's shoe, but instead, the photographer chose to include the reflection in the rainwater?

It's not just the actions we take (or don't take) that impact the world. It's also the reflection we leave (or don't leave) with each step we take.

Is that entirely too esoteric?

Sorry. Had to get it off my chest.

At any rate, I plan to leave kind (virtual) reflections today. Let's do it together, shall we? At a safe distance of six feet, of course.

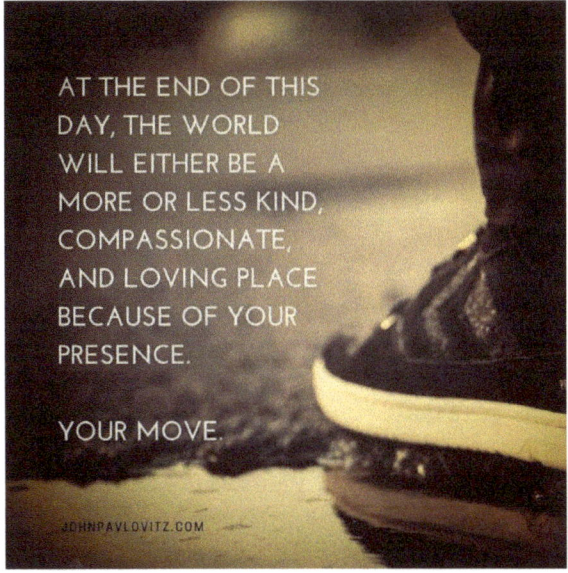

~ ~ ~

**Uncomfortable with Honesty**

**Friday 3/20/2020** – I asked someone recently if the church they attended was open to admitting people in the LGBTQIA community. "Of course," he replied. "We accept anyone who wants to worship with us."

There was a bit of a pause, and then he added, "Of course, someone like that could never be admitted to the ministry."

Someone like that?

"Ah," I said.

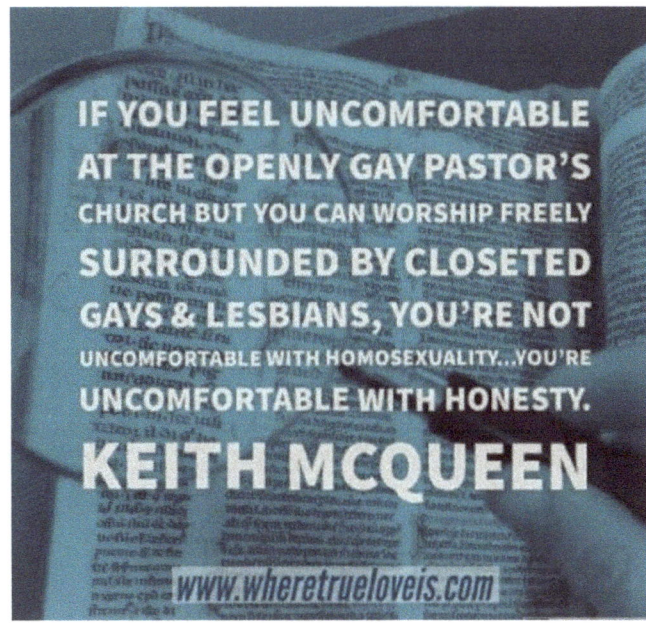

# Fran Stewart

~ ~ ~

## Perkatory

**Saturday 3/21/2020** – We need a laugh to end this week.

So here it is.

In my case, it's a fresh pot of herbal tea called Teeccino, which is advertised as "herbal coffee." I don't care what they call it. I just want to enjoy a cup of it while I sit on my deck if the weather cooperates or on my roofed porch if it's rainy.

Do you go through perkatory each morning?

Or do you have one of those robotic pots that brews everything before you open your eyes?

Obviously, I don't have one. Instead I watch the pot while it gets around to boiling.

I take that back. While I wait for the water to boil, I feed the cats and clean the litter boxes and make sure the bird feeders are full and . . .

And then I relax with my morning cup. And then I post this morning communication to you.

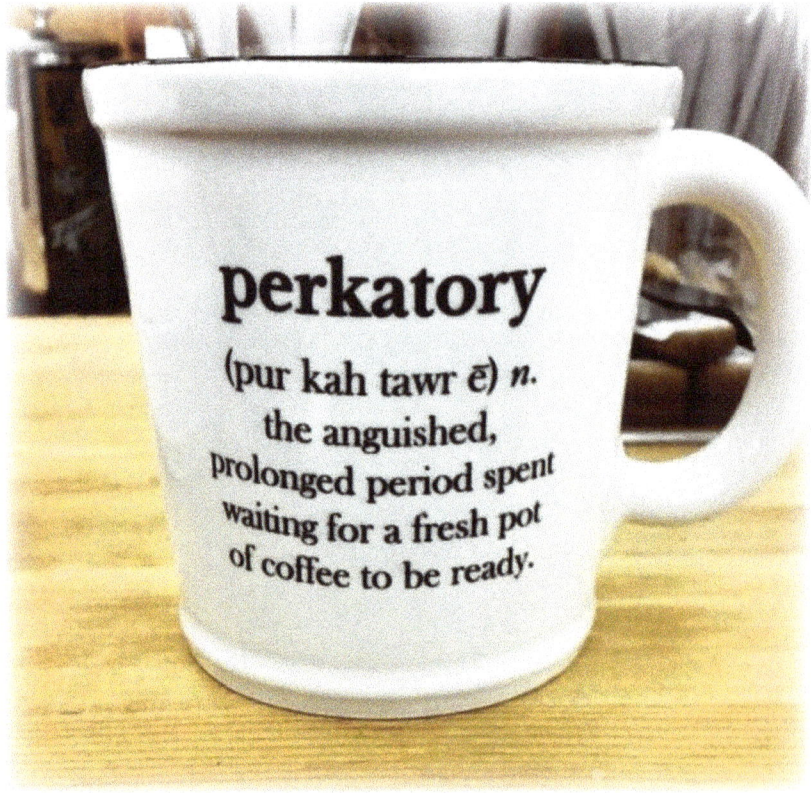

**The One Who Stayed Away**

**Sunday 3/22/2020** – This is why I've chosen to self-isolate.

~~~

### One of You

**Monday 3/23/2020** – I just love this thought. Figured it was a great way to start this week.

I hope you agree.

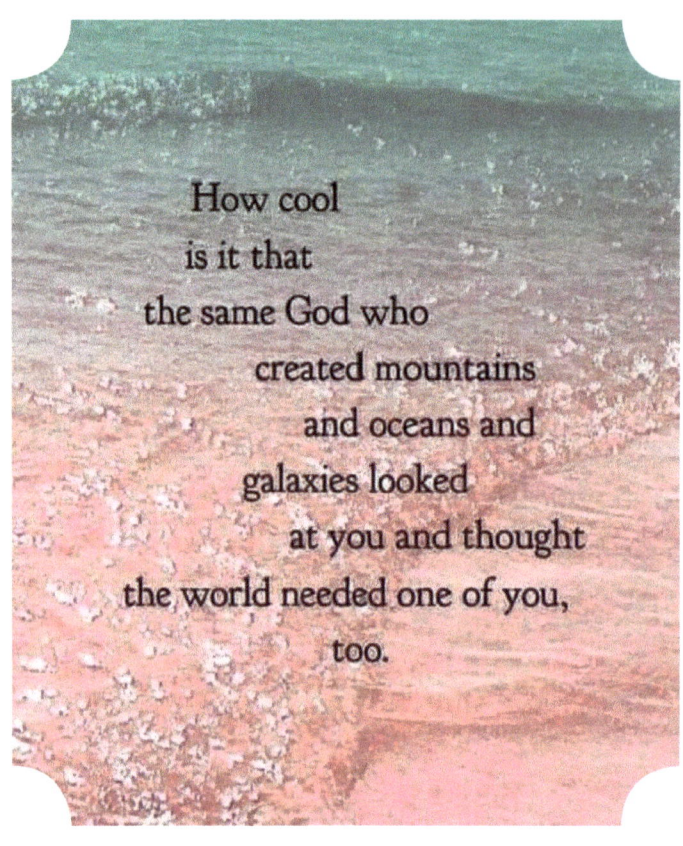

~~~

### Where You Are Celebrated

**Tuesday 3/24/2020** – I know you know this. If your circle doesn't support you 100%, you need a new circle.

In the memoirs classes I teach, I've had a number of people ask me where to find like-minded people. I prefer to think of it as like-hearted people. It's not a good mind that celebrates a friend. It's a good heart.

Where do my friends pop up? My family, my book club, the classes I teach, the chorus I used to sing with, the library programs I've attended.

There are folks out there just waiting to join your circle—and wanting someone like you to be in *their* circle. All we have to do is open our eyes. And our hearts.

~ ~ ~

**Don't Regret What I've Done**

**Wednesday 3/25/2020** – I'm fairly sure I've received more phone calls during these weeks of self-isolation than I had for the first two months of this year.

Why?

I'm glad you asked, although you've probably already figured out the answer. The calls have been from people "just checking to see how you're doing." How lovely. I've talked with folks I've had little phone contact with for ages. Emails—yes, text messages—yes. But phone calls? Actual hear-the-other-person's-voice phone calls? In the past there weren't very many.

Something about isolating our bodies has seemed to free up our voices to connect. In many ways, it's lovely.

I finished an editing job last night (my self-imposed deadline had been today), so now I feel I have extra time today just to call around and say, "Just checking to see how you're doing." If I don't call you, it's probably because I don't have your phone number. Of course, you could always message it to me, so we can connect voice-to-voice.

I don't intend to get to the eventual end of this COVID-19 mess and wish I'd called more people, made more contact, spread more cheer where I could. I'm not lonely—but I have no idea who else might be.

So—I mean it—if you'd like a call, message me through my FranStewartAuthor FB page. Let's connect.

# Fran Stewart

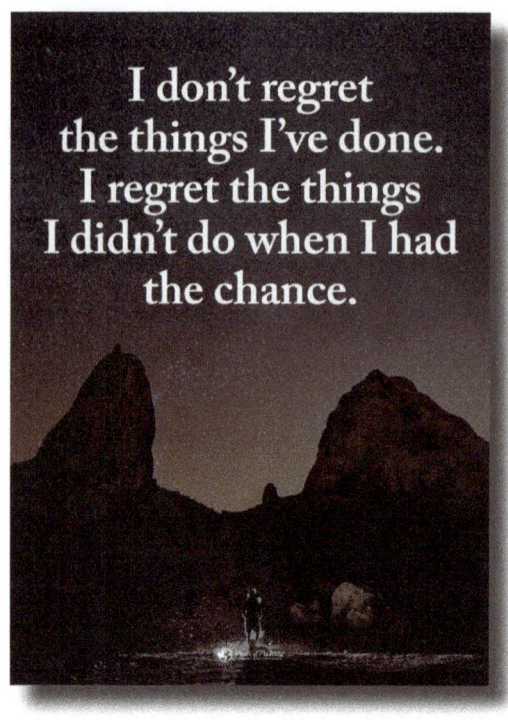

~ ~ ~

**You're Your Yore**

~~Friday~~ **Thursday 3/~~27~~26/2020** – I know I've posted this picture before – but I have something else to say about it. I wish I'd remembered it when I spoke to the Genealogy Study Group last month. But then I would have had to put together a power point so they could see it—or create another hand-out (one more wasted piece of paper per person).

When I teach, I'd rather just have it be me and the people in the room. After all, what if the power goes off or the computer cuts out or I forget and leave the handouts behind?

I've been unbelievably forgetful lately. Not Alzheimer's-type forgetful. Just blame-it-on-the-sunspots kind of forgetful.

Earlier this month—just before I started self-isolating—I went to my regular monthly meeting of the Atlanta Pen Women. I forgot to take the name tags; I'd forgotten to write the treasurer's report; someone who couldn't be at the meeting had asked me to announce one of her upcoming concerts. I did announce it, but I told everybody it was free when in fact, there was a ticket price clearly shown on the flyer she'd emailed me. I forgot to bring a copy of the Pen Women Anthology that we normally give our guest speakers; and I forgot to bring volumes 3 and 4 of my BeesKnees Beekeeping memoir series for the member who had requested them. I did remember to bring #5 and #6, but these books really should be read in order.

I do hope that the memories of me that get passed on to my descendants are not the ones of these forgetful moments. Instead, I hope they remember that I always call with a special birthday song on their birthday, that I listen to *hear* what they're saying (not simply to manufacture a reply), and that I laugh *with* them rather than *at* them. I also like to laugh at myself—it keeps me endlessly amused.

That's the kind of yore I want.

# Crystal Clear

**Our heritage makes
us who we are.**

**You're your yore.**

~ ~ ~

### Ant Acid

~~Saturday~~ Friday 3/~~28~~27/2020 – Am I getting in a rut here? There's something about ending the week with a laugh that seems to have become a habit.

Guess that's okay, though. There's no such thing as too much happy laughter.

p.s. - I just tried to delete this post, since my friend Darline pointed out that I was a day off kilter. Yesterday was Thursday. Today is Friday. <<sigh>> but FB won't let me delete it for some reason. I guess that means I need to give you yet another reason to laugh at me. I'm certainly laughing at myself right now. Wonder what I'll come up with tomorrow?

~ ~ ~

### No Rational Person

~~Thursday~~ Saturday 3/~~26~~28/2020 – I know it's Saturday the 28th, not Thursday the 26th. After two days of confusion I'm finally back on track. [Thanks to Darline Handley for setting me straight.] At least I remembered to go donate blood at the Red Cross yesterday when I had an appointment. Now on to what I was planning to talk about.

# Fran Stewart

Golly day! I love puns!

Of course, with this one, you have to remember back to math classes. We all know what pi is. Some of us know more about it than others. For instance, I once knew somebody who'd memorized the first thirty or so numbers that came after the decimal point. All I ever chose to remember was 3.1415926

But until I saw this numbered door and the caption above it, I'd flat forgotten the definition of a rational number.

Rational person – rational number. Get it? I hate it when people try to explain puns.

So I'll shut up now.

~ ~ ~

### Anne Sampson – Rare Shot of Nearly Extinct Species

**Sunday 3/29/2020** – I know I made a decision some time ago not to post on Sundays, but for the last couple of weeks, I've wanted to connect with you every day of the week. Here's a breaking news story: I'm now starting my third week of voluntary self-isolation, and I'm happy to report that I have a thriving colony of this rare species (thought to have been exterminated three weeks ago). They live in my garage.

Thanks to LetsGoGreen.biz, every two or three years I order a big supply of environmentally safe TP. The box lives in my garage, and I draw from it as necessary. Credit for this photo goes to Anne Sampson, who spotted one of them scurrying across a log near her home.

p.s. Please don't tell anyone. I'd hate for poachers to come after this vanishing species.

~ ~ ~

### Golden Ratio in Nature

**Monday 3/30/2020** – I know I've spoken—uh, written—about the Golden Mean before. Sometimes it's called the Golden Ratio. Whatever you call it, though, I think it's absolutely beautiful.

I came across this picture somewhere or other a while back and wanted to share it with you. That ratio shows up in the swirls of the Chambered Nautilus shell, but it's also in your ear and in your curled-up hand (and in bees and sunflowers and rams' horns and peacock tails and . . .)

Get the idea?

Mama Nature ain't no slouch.

~ ~ ~

**Me At 16 – No Lines**

**Tuesday 3/31/2020** – This picture was taken (by Frank Albanese, a professional photographer) on a happy day when I was sixteen years old.

As I'm sure you know, I still had so much to learn – about life, about my place in it, about my capabilities, about perspective, about death—not only about the death of a body, but about the death of hope.

I wouldn't ever want to return to that unlined face of mine, unless it would be to tell her that time does heal, that hope is ever-present, that every path we take is the right path, that joy doesn't wait around the corner—it waits within us.

Tomorrow I'll show you what joy looks like now.

Crystal Clear

~~~

83

# April 2020

### Sculptured Face

**Wednesday 4/1/2020** – April greetings. This picture was taken about three years ago, long after I'd chosen to stop wearing makeup and to stop worrying about wrinkles. Now I prefer to think of them as sculpture lines.

A fine sculpture is a good thing, right? And joy is ever-present, even within all the COVID-19 turmoil that surrounds us now. I'm staying safe at home, smiling as much as I want to—which is a whole lot!—being thankful for life itself.

And sending [virtual] hugs to you.

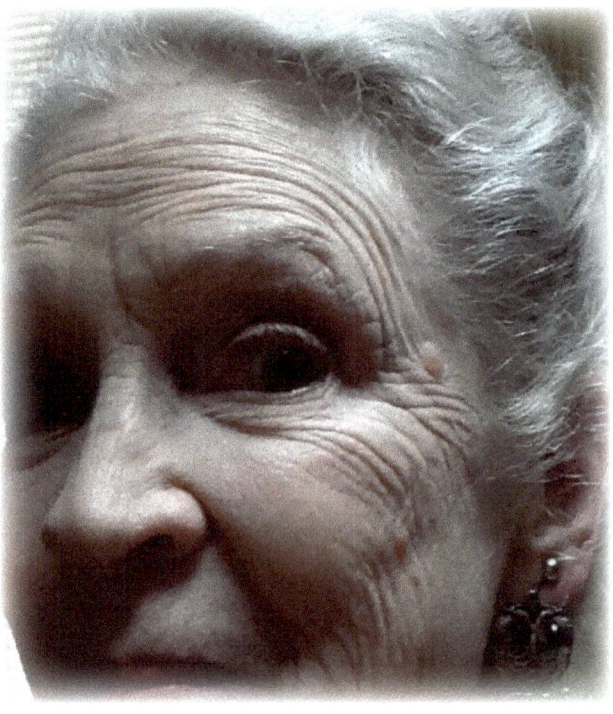

~~~

### Spring 2020

**Thursday 4/2/2020** – Spring IS just around the corner. Certainly it's already started here in Georgia, but the more northern parts of the country can rest assured that it will show up soon.

I remember living in Vermont and anticipating that first flush of spring green as trees began to leaf out. It always seemed as if one day it was winter, and the next it was not.

Except for that April 27th long ago, when we were stranded in the Burlington airport waiting for the runway to be cleared of snow … but I'm not going to think much about that  L O N G  day.

Spring is just around the corner...

~ ~ ~

**A Quiet Visitor**

**Friday 4/3/2020** – Look who came to visit me! She's been completely quiet, going about her business on my keyboard, periodically stopping to wash her hands (uh, feet). I do wonder what she could possibly find so interesting here on my laptop. I'm taking care to type around her. Later, if she'll cooperate, I'll scoop her up and take her outside.

I do wonder, too, if her navigation system is being messed up by the electronic emanations from my computer. I wonder if anyone has done any studies about such things. I'd hate to think about countless flies being stuck in computer labs just so these questions of mine could be answered, though.

So, instead, I will assume she came simply to say hello and to wish me a calm, peaceful day.

I hope your day is just as peaceful as hers and mine.

### Sunshine into Your Heart

**Saturday 4/4/2020** – Not only your Sunday tomorrow, but your Saturday today. And I've decided to take tomorrow off, so I'll see you on Monday.

### Fight Like Mike

**Sunday 4/5/2020** – I know I said I wasn't going to post anything today, but there's a good reason I changed my mind.

Last week, a man named Mike Thames died after a four-year fight with leukemia. From almost the moment of his diagnosis, he and his wife visited other people undergoing chemo, taking them tee shirts and goodie-bags, spreading love in the best way they knew how. The two of them founded an organization called "share love, that's all." You can read about it at fightlikemike.org. Every shirt you buy on their website funds another shirt that they'll give to another person who is fighting like Mike. I'm proud of the shirt I have.

His wife Lindsey wrote a moving tribute in her blog on April 3rd. These three lines in particular stayed with me:

> He lived.
>
> Every day.
>
> Every day to the fullest.

None of us could ask for more than that as a statement of life's purpose.

And so, like Mike, let's live every day we have. To the fullest.

~ ~ ~

**Terry Cloth Bathrobe**

**Monday 4/6/2020** – Years ago I had a plush, comfortable, white bathrobe. It lasted for years and years and years. My cat loved to knead doughballs on my bathrobed lap, but the robe never showed any particular signs of wear.

Until my daughter got a pet rabbit. She (the bunny, not my daughter) used to nuzzle around my legs while I was cooking breakfast – and then one day the bottom of the robe fell off. Boofus had quite literally nibbled the lower edge all the way around.

So I put up with a shorter-than usual robe. After all, the rest of it was just fine.

Eventually, though, I got around to replacing it with a brand-new terry cloth robe, thinking I would have a lot of years of usage. It took about three months of laundry cycles before it started looking like this – scroungy.

They just don't make fabric nowadays the way they used to. But I'll keep this one. After all, I still have cats, but I don't have a bunny rabbit.

~ ~ ~

**Trees Breathe**

**Tuesday 4/7/2020** – I love the way these two images show the way the lovely branching of veins and tree branches mirror each other. I rather like the idea that I have a tree inside me.

I'm doing my best to keep that tree safe. Ditto the trees outside in my yard.

You stay safe, too.

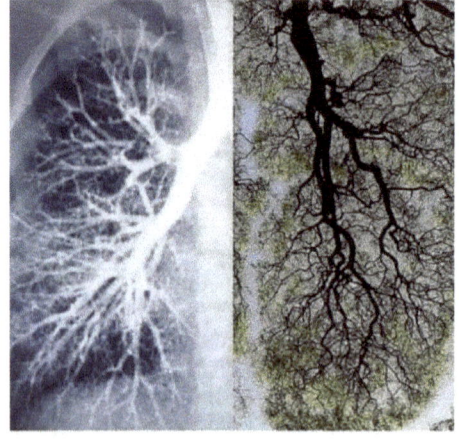

### Passover

**Wednesday 4/8/2020** – Is it possible to have a Seder via Facetime or Zoom? And next Sunday will be Easter, right? I don't celebrate either of these events, but I can't help wondering about the people who've always gotten the whole family together—sometimes travelling long distance to accomplish this. And now they're going to have to rethink that tradition.

At least, I hope they've rethought it all. Is it worth the risk? Will Grandma be dead in three weeks just because you felt the need to get together? Or what about the new baby you're looking forward to showing off? A tiny coffin is not a happy sight.

Okay – I know this is a bummer of a post, but all of us are in this together. The person you infect today may be the person my daughter passes by in the grocery store five days from now.

So, make a new tradition. Find a new and safe way to celebrate, no matter what traditions you honor. The "loving families" mentioned here don't travel.

Now I'll get off my soapbox and wish you well.

# Fran Stewart

~ ~ ~

## Duct Tape and a Sock

**Thursday 4/9/2020** – Amazing what you can do with duct tape and a sock. Are you old enough to know what I'm talking about?

Yesterday marked the 50$^{th}$ year since the Apollo 13 mission to the moon had to be scrubbed because of an onboard explosion two days after takeoff. I still recall how everyone hugged their radios and TVs to find out what was happening as the three astronauts struggled to return to Earth.

One of the most amazing accomplishments was the jury-rigging of a mishmash of supplies to allow a carbon-dioxide scrubber from the command module (designed to remove CO2 from the air) to cleanse the air inside the lunar module where the men were trapped and where the scrubber wasn't designed to work in the first place. The fix, devised quickly (since the astronauts were in danger of being poisoned as their exhalations increased the CO2 level), involved duct tape and a sock among other things. I took this picture from a Smithsonian Magazine article – Smithsonian got it from NASA.

Duct tape, cardboard, a sock, a piece of hose. Three lives saved in 1970. I love stories like this.

Now, in 2020, all we have to do to save lives is to stay home, wear a mask if we have to go out, and wash our hands.

~ ~ ~

## Footprint in the Pollen

**Friday 4/10/2020** – Does anyone know what kind of footprint this is? Somebody visited the black tea table I have on my front porch a few nights ago. Yes—the table really is black. That yellow dusting is one day's worth of Atlanta-area pollen.

At first I thought it was the possum that comes around every evening. But that's not a possum print. The toes are too close together and there aren't any nail prints showing.

Then I thought maybe it was the tail feathers of a bird that might have alighted, but there were no other marks – just these five "finger pads." You can ignore the white splat of bird poop. That's from the mealworm feeder overhead. (I move the table when I put my tea down on it.)

Anyway, I went online to try to figure out what sort of critter might have left the print. The closest I could come was a polar bear. The shape is right, although there's a certain size differential. Maybe a pygmy polar bear? One who wandered far to the south of home?

Do let me know if you figure it out.

~ ~ ~

**So Hollow Inside**

**Saturday 4/11/2020** – Ever feel like this? Kinda hollow?

The best way to cure such a problem is to have a virtual meeting with lots of friends. I've had a number of wonderful [virtual] face-to-face conversations recently. It's one of the long-term benefits of all this isolation. People are discovering how marvelous it is actually to see another human face.

Sure beats texting!

I'll be back on Monday.

p.s. I still remember the first time I was every given a chocolate Easter bunny. I was thoroughly incensed to find out it was just a hollow shell. Shoulda been solid!

~ ~ ~

### What'll She Plant

**Monday 4/13/2020** – Then there's the other side to all this self-isolation. If you're considering taking up this kind of gardening, you might want to reconsider – just in case.

~ ~ ~

### April Distance

**Tuesday 4/14/2020** – Seems like all we talk about any more is how to stay safe. I've been as guilty of it as anyone else. There truly are other topics. It's just that the one about survival seems a bit overwhelming at the moment.

Still, I promise that tomorrow I'll have a gentle reminder for you that the world keeps turning regardless of what we people are angst-ing about. I'll give you a hint. It has something to do with the miracles that happen in my front yard every April, without my even having to think about it.

~ ~ ~

**Swan Lake - The Kirov Ballet**

~~Monday~~ Wednesday 4/~~20~~15/2020 (date corrected after my dear friend Marcia Dunscomb mentioned that she was glad she wasn't the only one who couldn't keep up with the date) – Last Monday I spent almost two hours watching the entirety of *Swan Lake,* performed by the Kirov Ballet. I'm sorry to say I've never seen the whole thing before this. I know that over the years I've watched bits and pieces of it, but never had a chance to be caught up in the truly lovely story.

And would you believe it? As we got closer and closer to the end, I was on the edge of my seat, for I had no idea what the outcome would be.

Turned out to be heart wrenching and thoroughly satisfying.

I recommend it highly.

### Yellow Iris #1

**Thursday 4/16/2020** – Here it is – A couple of days ago (I think) I promised you a treat. Check out the raindrops on this iris that hasn't completely unfolded yet. On the stem in back of this one are two other buds that haven't even begun to unfurl.

I'm always so amazed by irises. They pop up without my realizing it's time. They surprise me every single year. I really do need to separate the corms after they all finish blooming. But then I'll have to find people to give them to. I've already populated a large portion of my neighborhood with extra irises.

Maybe book club once we're back to meeting in person.

Maybe I could toss them from the window of the car as I drive past unlovely sections of road. Irises are incredibly hardy, even though they look so fragile. I tossed a corm in the compost pile one autumn, and it bloomed the following spring.

~ ~ ~

### Prestonia – Swan Lake Ballet

**Friday 4/17/2020** – And while we're talking about ballet—we were a couple of days ago, remember?—a dancer named Charles Riley AKA Lil' Buck created a moving presentation of "The Swan" by Camille Saint-Saens, and he did it in tennis shoes. As I mentioned in a comment when my niece Erica shared this, "I've never seen this done without toe shoes – sheer liquid and absolutely riveting." If you want to see it, try Googling "Yo Yo Ma and Lil' Buck."

I think you'll agree it's well worth watching.

~~~

**Purple Iris**

**Saturday 4/18/2020** – My grandma's irises are all in shades of purple and lavender. They seem to last longer than the golden ones, which is just fine with me.

I can remember watching my grandmother on her knees weeding her iris garden. I wished like everything that I could help her, but I was too shy to ask. I guess even then I had the feeling she wouldn't welcome my intrusion. Years later my aunt told me, "Mother never really liked small children." So maybe my self-preservation antennae were working perfectly—and kept me from trying to help. It wouldn't have been much fun at five years old to be told to go away.

Still, I wish I'd tried. Maybe … maybe … maybe.

I think that garden was her get-away place. Her self-isolation, even if only for a little while. There's something about digging in the dirt that's so thoroughly satisfying. Yesterday I spent a good deal of the morning outside putting together my rain barrel gardens, getting ready to transplant the tomatoes I'm starting indoors. I came in with my fingernails crudded up with dark rich soil – and I felt wonderful. It helped that Grandma's purple irises stood by and watched me as I puttered.

You see, I have the descendants of her iris garden. My aunt dug up a gazillion of the corms when Grandma died. She transplanted them in her yard where they spread the way irises inevitably do. Each time she moved, she'd dig up a bunch of them and take them to a new house in a new state. Eventually she divided some to give to me when I moved to Georgia. And when I moved to this current house, I did the same.

Just think about it. My grandma's irises are populating the planet!

Ain't life grand?

~~~

**Toilet Creature**

**Sunday 4/19/2020** – Here I am again, deciding to post something on Sunday. But I couldn't resist it.

If it weren't for Wooly Bear—I already showed you a couple of weeks ago what she does with toilet paper when she gets hold of it—I'd love to create a creature like this to greet me each time I approach the throne.

Wouldn't it be fun?

~ ~ ~

**Shadow Pictures**

**Monday 4/20/2020** – I haven't thought about shadow pictures for years. I used to make them all the time when I was a kid. Then I sort of got out of the habit.

Until I had grandkids. When they were young and spent each Tuesday with Grannie, I taught them how to create these wonderfully entertaining creatures. We had all sorts of conversations—quacks and cheeps and neighs and screeches and meows. I wonder if they even remember …

~ ~ ~

**Sonnet A Day with Patrick Stewart**

**Tuesday 4/21/2020** – I've been listening to Patrick Stewart read a Shakespearean sonnet each day, most every day. Usually he gets through them without stumbling, but occasionally he messes up a line. Instead of doing a retake, he corrects himself (often with wry look at the camera). When I listened to Sonnet #29, I was struck again by how composed that man is – even when he goofs. After all, this is real life. We're all trying to help each other get through this day and the next and the next.

Just as I published my BeesKnees Beekeeping blog in book format, I plan someday to publish these Facebook posts, even though there are mistakes here and there. Then, a kazillion years from now, I hope people will look back on what I've written and find some joy in it. Or at least a lot of good information about what life was like in the beginning of the 21st century.

# Fran Stewart

But, am I writing with future historians in mind? No. I'm writing with <u>you</u> in mind.

Be well. Stay safe. Find joy around and within you.

~~~

### 3D Printing of food – article from the BBC

**Wednesday 4/22/2020** – I never ever would have thought about 3D printing of food. Never.

But look what's happening. It started with taste tests five years ago. Chicken drumsticks made from cauliflower, designed for people who have trouble swallowing. This type of meal also helps if you struggle with cutting your food. It adds nutritional value to institutional food that is so often tasteless and unattractive.

I love this sort of news from the BBC!

~~~

### Architect

**Thursday 4/23/2020** – Yesterday I read an online article from a guy named Nolan Dalla. He posted it on March 8th. His photo heading has a tag line that says "Faber est quisque fortunae suae." That's not a Latin phrase I'm familiar with, so I looked it up. It means "The architect of one's own fortune."

I love that. It reminds me of the poem "*Invictus*," in which the poet wrote, "I am the master of my fate / I am the captain of my soul."

Although I memorized that poem back when I was in high school, I'm not sure I truly understood all its implications until years later.

In case you're not familiar with it, here it is:

**Invictus by William Ernest Henley**

>Out of the night that covers me,
>>Black as the pit from pole to pole,
>
>I thank whatever gods may be
>>For my unconquerable soul.
>
>In the fell clutch of circumstance
>>I have not winced nor cried aloud.
>
>Under the bludgeonings of chance
>>My head is bloody, but unbowed.
>
>Beyond this place of wrath and tears
>>Looms but the Horror of the shade,
>
>And yet the menace of the years
>>Finds and shall find me unafraid.
>
>It matters not how strait the gate,
>>How charged with punishments the scroll,
>
>I am the master of my fate,
>>I am the captain of my soul.

p.s. Happy Birth/Death Day, William Shakespeare! Thank you for all the words and phrases you contributed to our language

~ ~ ~

**Missing Dog**

**Friday 4/24/2020** – I spent a good deal of yesterday trying to put out fires. Not literal ones. The figurative kind, where emails ran back and forth as people got their wires crossed. (I'm mixing my metaphors. Sorry.)

I have to admit, I probably contributed to some of the blaze. I'm the sort of person who, when I see something not working well, looks at it carefully, figures out how it could be better, and then tends to proclaim (sometimes way too loudly) the way to repair the problem. Nor do I find it easy to understand why not everyone can see how things would be improved if they were changed.

Not everybody likes that system.

Okay—you're right—very few people like that system except for other folks who think the way I do. Hence the fires.

This way of thinking is why I started writing my Biscuit McKee Mysteries years ago. There was a particular kind of mystery I wanted to read, only nobody was writing any like that. So I wrote one. And then another, and another, and another . . .

It didn't work so well yesterday, however. I think at least one person is still thoroughly ticked off with me, while a couple of others are probably standing on the sidelines wondering what the heck was going on.

What does this have to do with the missing dog in the photo? Well, nothing I guess. But I thought she was awfully cute, and she brought a smile to my heart. Today will be better.

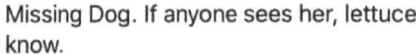

~ ~ ~

**Prickles the unshorn sheep – Smithsonian**

**Saturday 4/25/2020** – Someone who shall remain unidentified told me that quite often what I proclaim in these posts as new information is old hat because it's already been aired to the brink of boredom on TV.

<<sigh>> I can't apologize (or rather I won't), simply because I haven't had a TV set for almost three decades, so I don't see all those items that the rest of you have already been subjected to numerous times. So if this Smithsonian Magazine photo of Prickles (so-named because of the burrs stuck in her wool) is one you're used to, you can feel free to skip this post.

I think it's fascinating. A lamb escaped a wildfire in Tasmania seven years ago and returned to her home farm with all those years' worth of fleece growth still intact. Smithsonian called her coat "gloriously rotund" – love that! The article also described her as a "puffball" and a "cotton-ball." The breed doesn't grow hair on its face, which was one major factor in her ability to survive isolated for all those years.

Isolation? Hmmm…

If a sheep can do it – so can we!

I have to include some of the comments folks left for this one:

**Kay**: To let you know, Fran...I had not seen this on TV, so this post should be okay! Keep truckin', Kiddo...I love your insights and I can hear your "voice" as I read them!

**Petie**: Dear sheep looks like I feel ! ! ! Hugs, dear friend.

**Lea**: Gloriously rotund! I love that.

**Susan**: So all those TV stations have been coming to you for advice all these years???

**Linda**: Magnificent coat! Makes me smile!

**Janice**: Hey I have the same hair style!

~ ~ ~

**Pathetic seed starts (4/23/2020)**

**Monday 4/27/2020** – This is embarrassing, but since I've committed to being up front with you in these daily posts, I might as well admit it.

I'm pretty close to a failure as a gardener.

I can do the trashcan potatoes pretty well, as I've shared with you before (and I'll be showing you my harvest this fall), but seed-starting? Not so good.

As you know, if you've read my previous posts, I ordered a bunch of seed packets from Mary's Heirloom Seeds. They came. I pussy-footed around and took my sweet time about getting them started. So here we are a week from the end of April, and two (only two) of the tomato plants I started are an inch and a half tall.

I can barely see the one zinnia that's come up. Am I watering them too much or not enough?

# Fran Stewart

I have larger pots ready to put these seed-starting coconut thingies into so they can spring up in full glory. Now if only they'd start to spring …

The chives are too minuscule to show up on camera, and the gaillardia seem to be struggling. Heck! EVERYTHING seems to be struggling.

Meanwhile, I have the outside rain barrel gardens ready for the planting and positioned so they'll get the right sun exposure. I have 54" tall tomato cages ready to support my overflowing vines. I've figured out the companion plantings to deter bugs (Always plant chives with your tomatoes, for instance).

For now, though, I wait. Feels just like what we should be doing with the COVID stuff.

~ ~ ~

**They think we're cute**

**Tuesday 4/28/2020** – Revised.

Why am I revising this post? Because Facebook says the photo I used (with the note about elephants thinking we humans are cute) was incorrect. I'd rather see them checking about "facts" that are more relevant to the time, but it's no big deal. Anyway, as you can see from the "revised" photo, I cropped it to delete the captions above and below it. Here's the post as I originally wrote it:

================

Well, this just makes my day. I always wanted to be thought of as cute.

Now, to maintain that image, all I have to do is make good friends with an elephant.

There's a problem with that, though. A number of years ago, I took a course in animal communication, and for a long time I made a weekly jaunt to Zoo Atlanta to practice my skills. I was amazed at how each species of animal responded so differently. And I was truly honored that they let me even a little way into their thought processes.

The only animals I could make NO connection to whatsoever were the elephants. At one point the whole group of them turned their backs on me. So much for being thought to be cute. It looked like they heard me and decided I wasn't worth their effort. Talk about humbling.

One of the pythons more than made up for it, though. I'd stand in front of his glass-enclosed habitat for more than 45 minutes at a time. We had actual conversations. Talk about equally humbling, but for an entirely different reason. He was so generous in his responses to me. I'm sorry I eventually had to give up my regular visits there.

I didn't think he was cute at all. I thought he was magnificent.

And here's the photo I included with the revised post:

~ ~ ~

**Reading it Once**

**Wednesday 4/29/2020** – As I've mentioned before, I belong to a marvelous book club. Periodically we've talked about our reading habits:

>One book at a time or many?
>
>Multiple readings of the same book or only once through?
>
>Morning reading, afternoon reading, evenings, or bedtime?
>
>Does reading wake us up or put us to sleep?
>
>One favorite genre or many?

Naturally, we all had varying answers. I tend to read a lot of books at once (loveseat, wingback chair, red chair, dining room table, and so on). I read many of my favorite books multiple times. I read any time I have a chance, no matter what the time of day. Does it wake me up—yes if it's a good one. If it's not a good book, I scan through it and then put it aside without wasting my time. And finally, my favorite genre is the one I'm reading at the moment, whatever that moment is. Mysteries, historical fiction, memoirs, biography—I love them all (if they're well-written).

Despite all of this, though, are there pieces of music (and books) that don't open up after a second listening or reading? I'm not sure about that. I know there are plenty that I won't give a second chance. But AHHHH! The ones that need and deserve a second or third or fourth chance? Those make life worthwhile indeed.

> We'd never expect to understand a piece of music on one listen, but we tend to believe we've read a book after reading it **just once.**
>
> Ali Smith, Scottish novelist

~~~

**Dark Era of Agriculture**

**Thursday 4/30/2020** – Goodall makes a great point here. I try to be so careful about what I put in my mouth (and into my brain as well). I don't know what I'm going to do about the farmer's markets this summer. Usually I love shopping the markets, getting corn fresh off the stalk, peas bursting their pods, celery and spinach and lettuces fresh and delicious. Squashes green or gold or yellow or orange. Berries that beg to be tasted.

I'm not sure, though, what's going to happen over the next few months. Will I feel comfortable (i.e. safe) approaching market stalls?

I don't know. Nobody can predict.

I've signed up for absentee ballots for voting. I do the curbside pickup for any products I absolutely must buy. I stay within the boundaries of my yard – and if I go walking, I do it when nobody else is traveling the same route on the same side of my street.

But I still haven't solved the problem of fresh produce come summer.

I'll let you know when I do.

~ ~ ~

**May 2020**

**My Head Scarf**

**Friday 5/1/2020** – I found out that a regular mask isn't enough for me. I have one on under this enveloping scarf. Why the double-whammy? I'm glad you asked.

My hair tends to blow about, and it tickles my cheeks and my chin and my nose. I couldn't stop touching my face with just a regular mask on. Now, with this scarf, my hair is (sort of) tamed, and I keep my hands away from my face. Great idea, eh?

The rest of this post was copied from a friend's page. Feel free to copy and paste to yours if this applies to you.

> I wear a mask in public, not for me, but for YOU. I want you to know that I am educated enough to know that, although I have been very careful, I could be asymptomatic and still give you the virus. I don't "live in fear" of the virus—I just want to be a part of the solution, not the problem. I don't feel the "government is controlling me;" I feel like I'm being a contributing adult to society, and I want to teach children the same. I want them to grow up as I did knowing that the world doesn't revolve around

me ... that it's not all about me and my personal comfort ... that if we all could live with the consideration of others in mind, this whole world would be a much better place.

Wearing a mask doesn't make me weak, scared, stupid or even "controlled"; it makes me considerate.

~ ~ ~

**Strong Women**

**Saturday 5/2/2020** – Happy Birthday Veronica. You're one of the strongest women I know. I'm so blessed to have you in my life.

~ ~ ~

**Complex Carbohydrates**

**Monday 5/4/2020** – I've been eating a whole lot of carbs recently. Comfort food. It hadn't occurred to me, though, that my food might be pondering the complexities of the universe as it courses through my digestive system.

Why are we here?

That's a very good question.

When I spoke on Saturday (via Zoom) to a group from the Post-Polio Association, about the importance of writing their memoirs—the stories of their lives—some of them hadn't yet considered that what they write today could very well become a survival guide for people 100 years from now.

We're certainly learning a lot about the importance of social distancing by reading the on-the-spot stories people wrote during the Spanish Flu pandemic a century ago. We're even able to read and learn from people who faced the Bubonic Plague in the 14th century—the few who knew how to write. Although those people didn't understand the concept of germ theory (because it hadn't been discovered yet), they did know that if people with the plague came into a community, others came down with it.

What stopped the plague eventually? People with it died. The few who didn't die had developed immunity. So the plague itself died out.

That's pretty complex, wouldn't you say? And yet, at the same time such a simple concept. Keep apart. Regardless of what "government" may say, the responsibility is ours. Yours and mine. I'm not sitting around and waiting for someone out there to develop a vaccine. I'm using my common sense, knowing that I have to protect myself and others. Am I preaching? Yeah, but I hope I'm preaching to the choir. If you're not singing this song, I won't be able to attend the funeral for you or the ones you've infected.

**How do you know?**

**Tuesday 5/5/2020** – Yesterday, while I was listening to Patrick Stewart reading Sonnet 45, I thought to get out my old Shakespeare anthology and read along. Now that tome is parked next to my computer so I can read each day as Patrick voices the poetry.

But after he was finished, I began leafing through the text and I found this sticky note in one of the plays.

I recognize the printing. I wrote it. I have no idea, though, why I jotted down these questions. They're good ones, of course, but what on earth was I thinking about that spewed them forth?

It's a mystery. If you can figure it out, please let me know.

# Fran Stewart

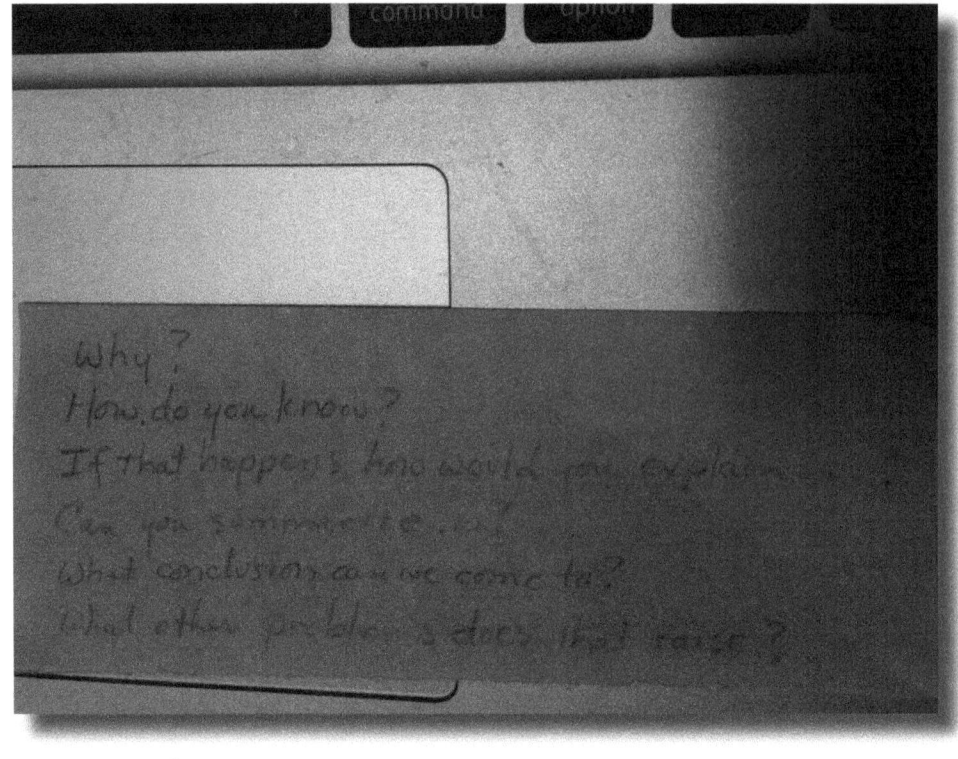

~ ~ ~

**Eaten Leaves**

**Wednesday 5/6/2020** – This container gardening I'm doing is turning out to be a lot of fun – but there are also some pitfalls.

I moved a big pot two days ago from the shady front of my porch to a sunnier more open area. The pot had a number of tall leafy violets growing around the edge of it, but I planted a cherry tomato in the middle and figured it would eventually shade the violets so they'd be happier.

Yesterday morning I walked outside and found that the tip ends of more than half the violets had been nipped off, as you can see here.

Why? I think it's because the growing tips of some plants are used by birds to line their nests. The growing generates heat, and the nipped-off leaves help to keep the eggs warm while mama bird is away feeding.

My question is, why have the birds left those plants alone for the past four or five years until now, when I moved them only 20 feet from the shade to the sun?

When the birds run out of sunny violets, will they go after my shady ones?

But then – after all this thinking about birds, I realized that the leaves they'd taken were way too big for a bird to carry off. At least not the birds that frequent my yard. I walked farther down the path and saw that the same marauder(s) had eaten the leaves off the potato plants in two of my trashcan planters. Grrr!

So I changed from blaming the birds to blaming the deer.

On the other hand, deer have to eat as well.

But not my potatoes. So I moved the plastic trash/potato buckets onto my fenced-in back deck. They won't get quite as much sun there, but at least I'll have a chance for a crop come the autumn.

~ ~ ~

**Amazing educators**

**Thursday 5/7/2020** – Let's hear it for teachers. I am constantly in awe of the people who devote their lives to teaching our children. They deserve much more respect, infinitely higher pay, and all the perks imaginable.

Years ago I did some volunteer teaching of enrichment classes (math and classical poetry) at an elementary school in Vermont. It sure helped me to appreciate what teachers go through. Just two hours of class time each week, but that doesn't include the hours of preparation that led into those two hours. I loved watching the eyes of those 4$^{th}$ and 5$^{th}$-graders as new vistas opened up for them. And when I attended the high school graduation ceremony of one of those groups, that valedictorian spent part of her speech quoting one of the poems I'd introduced them to all those years before.

Could I have managed teaching a class day in and day out, though? Nope. Don't think I could have handled it (so it's just as well I didn't go into teaching).

I'm where I am today in large part because I had some amazing teachers as I went through school. If you had a great teacher (or two or three), give a cheer!

**[Later Note:** I should mention that after that graduation ceremony, I thanked Polly for quoting from the poem I'd taught her. "Oh," she said, "is that where it came from? I had no idea."

# Fran Stewart

I hope you remember the people who taught you things, but even if you've forgotten them, their legacy lives on.]

p.s. And if you're wondering about Ken's comment on the 4th line about how they "Apollo 13'd" the problem, go back a month and look at my post for April 9th.

**Ken Buck**
3 hrs ·

We gave educators almost no notice. We asked them to completely redesign what school looks like and in about 24 hours local administrators and teachers "Apollo 13'ed" the problem and fixed it. Kids learning, children being fed, needs being met in the midst of a global crisis.
No state agency did this, no so-called national experts on curriculum. The local educators fixed it in hours. HOURS.
In fact, existing state and federal policies actually created multiple roadblocks. Local schools figured out how to do it around those too. No complaining and no handwringing - just solutions and amazingly clever plans.
Remember that the next time someone tries to convince you that schools are better run by mandates from non-educators. Remember that the next time someone tells you that teachers have it easy or try to persuade you that educators are not among the smartest, most ingenious people in society. And please never say to me again, "Those who can't do anything else just go into teaching."
Get out of the way of a teacher and watch with amazement at what really happens.

~ ~ ~

**Two hearts**

**Friday 5/8/2020** – This two-heart picture is one of those "awwwwww" photos I couldn't resist.

Hope you enjoy it. So many of the perfect little moments in life depend on our willingness to open our eyes, still our scurrying, and SEE what's around us. Did you step outside last night to look at the Super Moon? When you woke this morning, did you pay attention to the way the light filtered through your curtains? If you walked past this calf, would you see the two hearts?

I plan to enjoy my day and appreciate every heart I have access to.

Won't you join me?

~ ~ ~

**Ground-nesting bees**

**Saturday 5/9/2020** – Here's yet another reason to avoid pesticides. Were you even aware there were so many varieties of bees? If you've read any of my BeesKnees beekeeping memoir volumes, you'll be aware of some of them, but even I was surprised to find that there are so many.

I hope they all have a chance to pollinate to their little hearts' content.

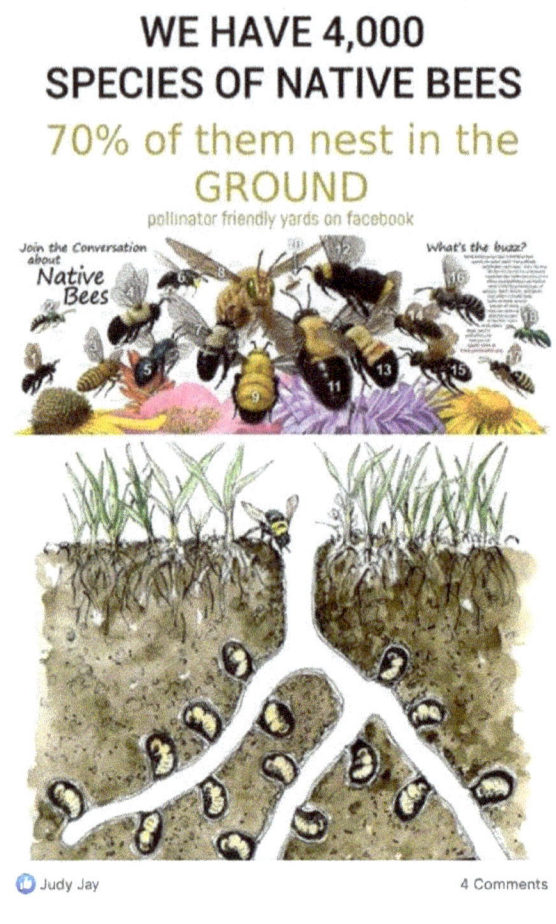

### The Perfect Mother – for Mother's Day

**Sunday 5/10/2020** – A few months ago, my son sent me a link, and I have to say, I resonated with every moment in there.

To all of you perfect mothers – and to those who had perfect mothers – and to anyone else who fits into whatever category imaginable: have a day filled with the wonder of the small perfect miracles in life.

Try it. Google "Emma Thompson Perfect Mother"

~ ~ ~

### Black Canyon of the Gunnison

**Monday 5/11/2020** – There are so many wonderful virtual tours available out there now. I hope you're taking advantage of them. Museums, parks, waterfalls, trees … there's a virtual tour for just about every taste.

On a site showing one lovely photo from each of our national parks, I found this picture of the Black Canyon of the Gunnison in Colorado. I remember visiting it when I was ten or twelve, and then going again to see it with my own children. It was just as striking both times. [Veronica and Eli – do you remember seeing this?]

Go ahead now. Take off on an adventure of your own. You won't even have to leave your room!

~ ~ ~

Spam

**Tuesday 5/12/2020** – Did you grow up, as I did, thinking that Spam was a viable Saturday evening meal?

I've cropped this picture. The original one had a caption that said:

> Hormel made their first batch of Spam in 1937.
> The company just announced that due to hoarding by consumers
> during the CV-19 crisis, they are preparing to make a second batch."

Why did I remove the caption? Because Facebook has some sort of "fact-checker" now that delights in removing pictures like this that have "untrue captions." I think it's pretty obvious that this was put together to be funny. But it brought some interesting thoughts to mind.

If I put up a picture labeled "hot dog," would they delete it because that photo is obviously not a dog?

If I post a photo labeled "a hamburger," would they come back and say, there's no ham in there?

So, I'm doing a preemptive change. No matter what you say about it, it's still Spam.

It's no wonder I never bothered to learn how to cook, when what I was raised on was so thoroughly unappetizing. I know other people coming from the same background may have made a diametrically different decision—to learn to cook so well that every meal would be a dream come true. Good for them, but that's not the path I took.

I eat two meals a day—breakfast and lunch—and then I spend half an hour or so each evening just grazing.

# Fran Stewart

I think I've shared this with you before. Sometimes it's a cheese plate, sometimes it's popcorn, sometimes a big glass of buttermilk and a handful of celery.

Beats Spam any day.

I sure did get a lot of comments on this post. Here are some of the best. (Especially Kathy's!)

**Susan:** We loved Spam! I never understand why it is put down so much. Yet everyone has eaten it, and it is still sold on the shelves. (If no one likes it, how come enough people are still buying it?)

Of course, we had to rinse it off quite a bit before cooking with it.

Dice it up, and mix it with scrambled eggs. Yum!!! (Just don't forget to rinse off the gelatin & sodium.)

> **Fran:** My mother just sliced it and fried it. It wasn't that it tasted bad -- it was just that there was no imagination involved. Never thought about mixing it with scrambled eggs. (And she never rinsed off the gelatin.)

**Barb:** My grandpa had a spam sandwich in his lunchbox everyday!

**Kathy:** Watch, someone will report this post as spam... ; )

**Cyndi:** Spam and Vienna sausage were not allowed in our house per my father's order. He was in Okinawa during WWII, a supply ship was sunk and all they had for weeks was Spam and Vienna sausage. I finally tasted Spam in college, I was not impressed.

> **Fran:** My Dad was like that with liver. He'd almost died after a car wreck. The days before transfusion. Had to eat nothing but almost-raw liver for six months. Never touched it again.

**Linda**: FYI - FB let me post the original. Growing up, we had fried Spam instead bacon or sausage with eggs at breakfast. And fried with melted cheese on toast for lunches. Usually towards the end of the month - week before payday. Spam is actually in my Hurricane Emergency kit.

~ ~ ~

**corn silk tea**

**Wednesday 5/13/2020** – Guess what I've discovered!

Corn silk tea.

Last week I went to Sprouts (wearing my mask and scarf and gloves, of course). I went early in the morning, well before any crowding. Among other things, I bought corn ("Fresh Produce from Florida," said the label).

Now, I've been eating fresh corn whenever possible for decades. I grew up on canned corn, so one of my favorite memories as an adult is stopping by a farmhouse across the lake from us in Vermont to buy corn that was way more than grocery store fresh. Or even farmer's market fresh. The man who owned the farm would walk us out to the cornfield and let us pick a dozen or so ears. Then we'd take them home, shuck them, clean off all the silk, boil them, and eat them.

They were a variety he called butter and sugar corn, I guess because of the yellow and white kernels on each ear. Back then, I never thought to do anything with the corn silk except throw it onto the compost pile.

But now, with my own butter and sugar corn in hand, I made tea. Yes, there are YouTube videos that show how to do it. You cut off the brown dried ends of the silk from the top of two corn cobs, remove the husks carefully, peel off the remaining silk—it'll be whitish yellow—and put it in a pan with about a cup and a half of water. Boil it. Let it steep for long enough to turn the water kind of golden.

Voilá! Corn silk tea.

It was used as a folk remedy way back when. It's apparently good for the digestion and for—how can I put this delicately?—for getting things moving.

It works. So don't drink too much of it at a time!

### butter and sugar corn

**Thursday 5/14/2020** – Here's the corn I was talking about yesterday. Doesn't it just make you drool?

I know, I know—no need to preach at me. Corn is largely indigestible unless we chew it lots and lots. Got it. It's full of starch. Got it.

I don't care. For me it's a special treat. Plus, it's beautiful.

Who could ask for anything more?

### newly washed hair

**Friday 5/15/2020** – When I wash my hair, I towel it off and then let it hang. Over the course of the next few hours, it crinkles up more and more until, by the time it's dried, it's turned into this.

Trouble is, when I go outside, the wind blows it around and it tickles.

Do I agonize over my crinkly hair? Not anymore. Years ago, I used to spend (waste) hours trying to get it to look sleek. I went through gels and conditioners and rollers and (once they were invented) blow dryers. Special brushes. Special everything imaginable.

HA!

All I had to do was walk outside into a humid afternoon, and all the sleekness disappeared.

Now, I brush it back, twist it around on the back of my head, and hold it in place with a big clip. Much easier. Much faster. Uses no goo and no electricity.

Before the isolating, my wonderful daughter would visit me every once in a while (like right before I had a book-signing to go to) to work her magic, and my hair would be sleek and beautiful for a day or two.

Now, I've simply revised my definition of hair-beauty. And this is it.

With so many other people concerned about things of much greater import, why on earth should I worry about hair?

~ ~ ~

**Two kinds of prickles**

**Saturday 5/16/2020** – At the northeast corner of my house, there live some prickly holly bushes that were there when I bought the house umpty years ago. All of them are prickly. None of them has ever produced a single beautiful bright-red holly berry. That probably means they're all male holly plants.

Growing up through one of the hollies is a prickly wild blackberry. Sprouting all sorts of berries.

Two kinds of pricklies. Two different lessons.

The male hollies just sit there ready to prick the fingers or legs of passing people. But they're a gorgeous vibrant glossy green.

The blackberries are equally ready to trap fingers, clothes, whatever comes within their range. But—AHA!—they're busy producing luscious, edible berries. Edible, that is, if I can beat the birds to them.

Years ago, when I first began writing my Biscuit McKee mysteries, a wise mentor of mine told me that the worst people have some good points to them, and the best people have some not-so-desirable traits. "Give your bad guys some humanity, and give your good guys some obnoxious blind spots."

Good advice.

Now I have to decide which of these plants of mine is the villain.

Oh! No I don't! They can both be the good guys.

~ ~ ~

**I'm on Patrick Stewart's FB page!**

**Monday 5/18/2020** – Imagine my surprise yesterday when I went to Patrick Stewart's FB page to listen to Sonnet 56. I scrolled down a bit, looking for Sonnet 55, which I'd missed listening to on Saturday, and saw that whatever angel handles his FB page had picked up my post from April 21st and put it where his fan base of several million people can see it.

Then I scrolled around a bit more and found that they'd also put up my post from May 5th – the one about that sticky note I found and couldn't remember having written. Facebook's automatic counter said that 425 of his fans had "liked" it. What fun!

As my dad used to say, "That and a quarter will buy you a cup of coffee."

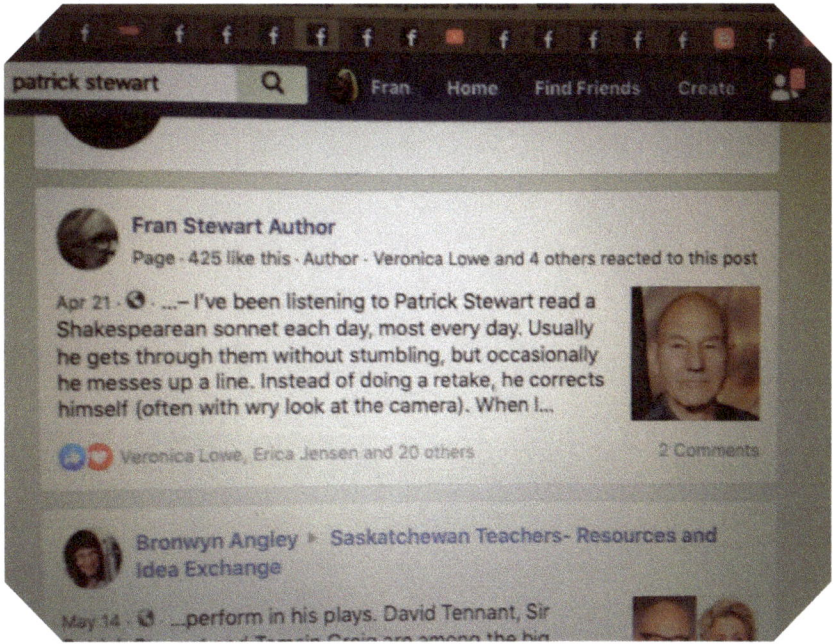

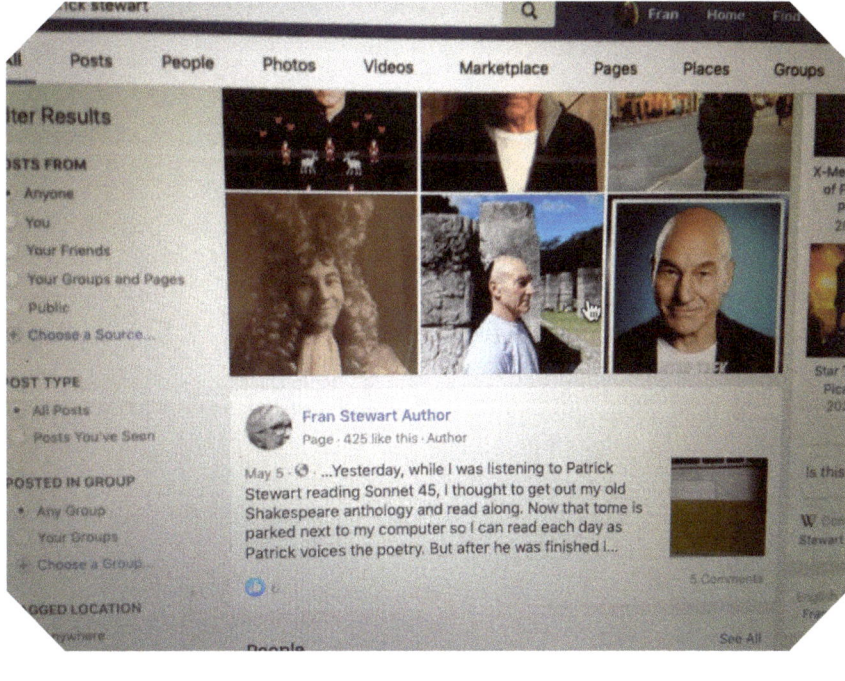

~ ~ ~

**she also needs dragons**

**Tuesday 5/19/2020** – I'll write more tomorrow. For now, I'm off chasing rainbows and soaring through the clouds on my dragon, and feeding starlight to my unicorn.

# Fran Stewart

~ ~ ~

**Who Holds Up the World?**

**Wednesday 5/20/2020** – I saw this image on the CBC Morning Brief news digest last week, and got to thinking about all the people who are holding up the world right now.

Nurses, most definitely. All the medical staff, certainly. But what about the people who clean the hospital floors and cook the hospital food and remove the hospital garbage? Of course.

And what about the people who come around each week and remove MY garbage (and yours)?

The electric linemen who keep our power on? Those who service our cell phone towers? Who staff the call centers?

What about the news reporters who gather the information we need and the ones who put it all together into pertinent stories? [Thank you NPR and CBC.]

Now, we need to do our part, whatever that may be, no matter how small our steps are.

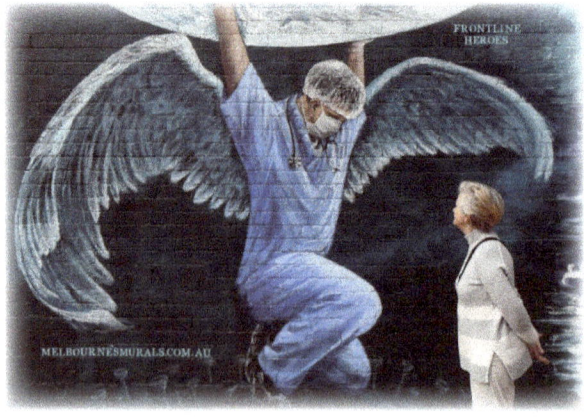

~ ~ ~

**Wolves and alpha males**

**Thursday 5/21/2020** – I know I've quoted Beau of the Fifth Column before in these posts. He's an incredibly thoughtful, well-spoken journalist, whose platform is YouTube, whose stage is his garage, and whose uniform is a plethora of tee shirts and a ball cap.

None of those last few items predisposed me to pay attention to what he has to say, until I actually started listening, thanks in large part to my niece, Erica, who reposted him so many times I began to think maybe I should give him a chance. Thank you, Eri!

In one particular video, he explains the difference between the generally accepted view of alpha wolves—as vicious creatures out only for their own good—and the truth about alphas, their generally nonaggressive stance, and their dedication to preserving their families.

The point he's making is that original studies of wolves (that developed the premise that alpha males are aggressive), were based on captive wolves who had been taken from their wild families and were put together with wolves they didn't know. Of course they were aggressive toward each other.

But when wolves are studied in their natural habitat, in the wild, scientists have found that the alpha doesn't need to act that way.

Naturally, Beau links this lesson to the political arena. He is, after all, a political journalist. But the points he makes apply not only to politics, but to our view of alpha males in general.

Do listen, please.

## Start Over

**Friday 5/22/2020** – I watched the Class of 2020's virtual graduation the other day. Since I don't have a TV set, I'm usually a few days behind on events like this, but this one was definitely worth waiting for.

I have great hopes for this upcoming generation. So many ideas, so much enthusiasm, so much willingness to help each other.

Yes, there is despair. Yes, there is sadness. Yes, there are hard times ahead.

But what a legacy of hopefulness and determination as evidenced in the messages from these young people.

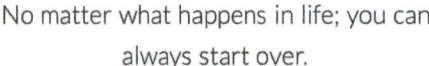

## Lazy leopard

**Saturday 5/23/2020** – Do you ever feel like this? That's how I feel today.

Seems like a good way to end the week.

I'll see you Monday.

~~~

**Rainy Monday**

**Monday 5/25/2020** – I don't complain about rainy days. When the ground is parched, as it so often is here in Georgia, why on earth would anyone grump about free moisture falling from the skies?

Of course, my house doesn't sit down beside the creek in my back yard. There's quite a hill to climb down to get from here to the waterside. Which is a good thing, because every time we get the tail end of a hurricane, that little creek (about two feet wide at the most) expands into a raging torrent twenty or thirty feet across.

But gentle rain like what's forecast for this afternoon? Perfect. I hope it soaks in to keep the trees happy.

~~~

**The woman who inspired the N95 mask**

**Tuesday 5/26/2020** – Do a search for Sarah Little Turner. She failed 90% of the time. She's the one who invented the non-woven molded bra cup, which led her directly to working to develop an effective surgical mask.

I'd never heard of her, until I listened to an NPR podcast.

She said that **if she didn't stretch, she'd never know where the edges were**.

Isn't that a marvelous thought? Like Thomas Edison's numerous mistakes, and like Babe Ruth's almost countless strikeouts, Sarah Little Turner's example can teach us to keep trying. And keep trying. And keep trying yet again.

# Fran Stewart

Without her early efforts in the 1950s and 60s, we might not have the N95 today.

Makes you think, doesn't it?

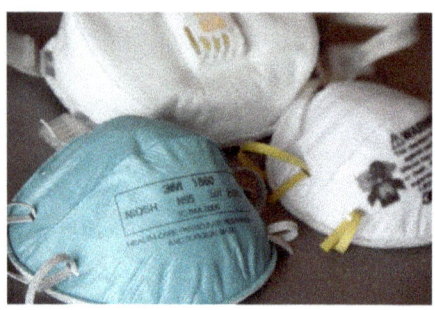

~ ~ ~

### Roman mouse

**Wednesday 5/27/2020** – This little leather mouse was found in the ruins of a leather shop in Pompeii. See the "fur" indicated with those incised lines on the back and the tail? It's only about four inches long, and I think it's cuter than a bug's ear.

Can you imagine the leather-crafter taking a few minutes out of a busy day to create such a tiny toy from a scrap? I love the way we can feel a connection to people who died almost 2,000 years ago simply by looking at what they left behind.

Thank an archeologist.

~ ~ ~

### how deep is the mud?

**Thursday 5/28/2020** – It's funny how the depth of the mud affects people differently. I'd say, though, that the tiny one who is almost up to her ears could either be intimidated by the depth of the mud, or could be delighted that she managed to trudge her way through it.

What about you? When you're in deep mud, do you give up or do you keep slogging? I'd like to think I'm in the second group. No sense in giving up. Half-empty vs. half-full. Despair vs. gratitude.

It's nice to know we have a choice.

I watched the NASA live stream of the (aborted) launch yesterday, and it reminded me so much of the feelings I had back in 1969 when I watched the moon launch and then the first steps taken on the moon. I like the fact that my life has spanned so many decades from the time when there were no computers to the time when a computer that filled a good-sized room had less than half the capacity of the phone I carry in my pocket now.

Just think how different technology will be in another four or five or six decades.

And yet, people haven't changed much in the past many thousands of years. We still have the capacity for unbelievable goodness and inexplicable cruelty. We still have the choice of how to view the mud in our lives. I choose to feed the kinder, more optimistic wolf.

~ ~ ~

**open carry / concealed carry**

**Friday 5/29/2020** – Years ago, we had one of those big have-a-heart traps. Something—we had no idea what—had been rooting around in our garage. We caught a skunk. A BIG skunk.

Now, I'm not sure we did the skunk a favor, but we didn't particularly want it in our garage, and we didn't want to kill it, so we loaded the trap into our (brand new) station wagon and drove to a wooded area some miles away. I carried the skunk-filled trap into the woods, opened it, scooted out of range, and waited for my new striped friend to meander out of the trap and into the underbrush.

Luckily, El Skunko kept the concealed weapon hidden.

I retrieved the trap and returned it to the back of the car. End of story. Almost a letdown. Hardly exciting. But much less stinky than it would have been otherwise.

Whew!

# Fran Stewart

~ ~ ~

**whether or not to say it**

**Saturday 5/30/2020** – How often have you managed to hold your tongue when the temptation to voice a subtle dig was almost too great to resist?

It takes a lot of discipline to keep my mouth shut, but I had a good teacher way back when. One of my grandfathers was what they used to call a "practical joker."

Family members (mostly my uncles) used to howl with laughter telling about the tricks their dad pulled on other people. The funny thing, though, was that Grandpa got madder than a wet hen when someone pulled a joke on him.

He could dish it out—a "joke" or a snide word—but he wasn't willing to take it.

Now, whenever I'm tempted to make that wisecrack at the expense of another person, I think about the lesson I learned way back when. It hurts to be on the receiving end of an unkind action, whether it's a mean trick or a mean word. Tearing someone else down never adds to our own stature.

That grandfather of mine may have been tall, but he was a small, small man.

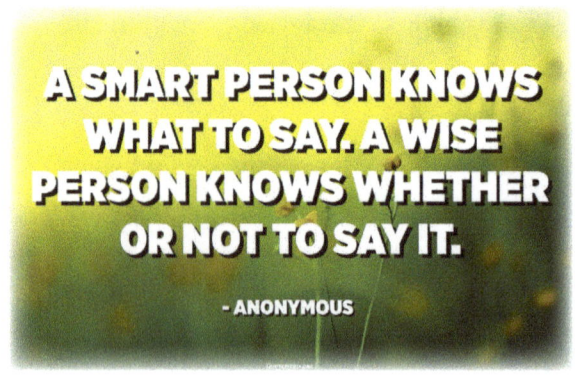

# June 2020

## Losing a library

**Monday 6/1/2020** – Why do I encourage people to write their memoirs—the stories of their lives? Alex Haley said it very well: "Every time an old person dies, it's like a library burning down."

Think about all the stories you heard your parents tell you years ago. But now you've completely forgotten some of the ones they told you. Or you've forgotten the details of the stories you do recall.

Now imagine that they'd written down their stories. What a legacy for them to leave.

Now imagine your descendants finding those stories *you've* written. As they read the funny tales, the sad ones, the uplifting stories, the depressing ones, the notes about lessons you've learned—sometimes ones you wanted to learn, other times the ones you've been forced by circumstances to learn.

How do you get started, though? Well, that's why I teach those memoirs classes—to help you jumpstart the process.

Will you write your stories? Will you share what you've learned? Or will your internal library burn down when you pass on?

As far as I can see, it's a clear choice. That's why I'm writing my stories.

~ ~ ~

## The Sounds of Nature—and how isolation has helped

**Tuesday 6/2/2020** – Frogs croaking in unison?

What happens when there is a 90% drop in the sounds people make?

An 8-minute NPR podcast addressed that question. A day or two ago. The sounds of airplanes used to be ubiquitous. Now, with fewer planes zooming overhead, birds and frogs have a chance to hear each other.

Consequently, they don't have to call or sing so loudly.

For that matter, maybe we people don't have to holler at each other in order to be heard. I love the sounds of silence.

And now, thanks to the coronavirus, those sounds are more hearable.

~ ~ ~

**silence is complicity**

**Wednesday 6/3/2020** – Speaking of silence (but a different kind this time), when I received this thoughtful and thought-provoking email from Jeff Watkins at the Shakespeare Tavern yesterday, I immediately wrote and asked for his permission to use it in today's post. He very graciously said yes. Here it is:

## To remain silent is to be complicit.

It is for this reason the Atlanta Shakespeare Company stands with our black brothers and sisters to say, "Enough is enough." We are way past the time when law enforcement or any self-entitled citizen can take the life of another human being, in any but the gravest of circumstances.

America's original sin was genocide, followed by generations of human slavery. Yet at the same time, our founding fathers created a form of self-government based on the radical proposition that each of us was endowed by our creator with certain unalienable rights, among which are "life, liberty and the pursuit of happiness". Many of the white men who articulated these ideals "owned" human slaves and it is their failure to reconcile their actions and their aspirations that continue to feed the worst aspects of America's ID, allowing any number of people to delude themselves into thinking that they are somehow "better than" or "more entitled" because of the accident of their birth or skin tone.

But to dwell on the faults of those men who endeavored to create a better world is to miss the point of the American experiment. What was articulated in our founding documents was an ideal that was not true at the time. Rather, the Declaration of Independence and the Constitution that followed, articulated the aspirations of a whole people wishing to create a better world. Give those guys some credit, they made a good start and created what we know as "America."

At our best, "America" is an idea that belongs to the world. In times past, it has inspired whole generations of immigrants from across the globe to come here and seek a better life. That diversity has made us strong and created unprecedented opportunity for millions of people to pursue a happy life.

But our "best" America has never existed for a large percentage of black Americans. With the legacy of Jim Crow, segregation, systemic discrimination, and more recently, wanton acts of gerrymandering and voter suppression, black Americans have always had to do more to get the same slice of the American Dream that comes to many with little or no effort.

For many years, at least we could see we were making progress. But that has not been the case of late. For some time now, America has been losing ground on multiple fronts. We have lost sight of our aspirations and the truths we hold dear. As is often the case, when we forget to be our best, we give in to our worst impulses. These are the shades of "white supremacy" still lurking in the dark waters of the American psyche. In the absence of the beacon that was— at one point— the American Dream, many cannot resist the lure of imagining a return to a time when their essential worth as human beings was guaranteed by the color of their skin or the accident of their birth. Such thinking embodies the worst aspects of humanity.

Yet we cannot forget these people are also our brothers and sisters. We cannot forget that only by aspiring together can we rekindle an American Dream that includes everybody. During his life, Dr. King referred to keeping "our eyes on the prize." We must do that today.

We have made some progress in 250 years. We no longer exterminate whole peoples; we no longer have slave markets; and gay people can marry whom they love. On the other hand, our government still separates families; they put children in cages; and as of last week, a black man can still be murdered in slow motion by law enforcement officers in the presence of a dozen witnesses while cameras are rolling.

**We are not finished as a nation and we are not complete as human beings until all of us are safe.** If one of us is sick and cannot receive treatment, then our country is sick. If a black life or a brown life is somehow "less than" a white life, then all our lives are tarnished with shame.

It should go without saying— since "all lives matter"— but sadly, in the summer of 2020 in the United States of America, it still must be said **"Black Lives Matter."**

I've heard that talk is cheap and that actions speak louder than words. I disagree. Language is everything. It is only through language that we can orchestrate and contextualize complex actions. It is language that makes aspiration possible, and it is only through collective aspiration that we can build a just and equitable society that values every life.

Such aspirations only become real if we toil in their presence with a free and open heart, sharing with all people the gifts we have received. It is a choice we each must make every day of our lives: a choice between the intellectual laziness of bigotry, greed, fear, and anger … and empathy, grace, generosity, and love.

# Fran Stewart

"Be the change you wish to see in the world" and someday—maybe within our children's lifetime—no one will need ever say again

<u>"Black Lives Matter."</u>

On behalf of the people of the Atlanta Shakespeare Company,

Jeff Watkins, President & Artistic Director
The Atlanta Shakespeare Company at The Shakespeare Tavern® Playhouse

~~~

**In love with justice**

**Thursday 6/4/2020** – There's nothing wrong with money. I like money. I like not having to worry about where my next meal is coming from. I like feeling financially serene.

But am I in love with money?

Nope. That's why I've always believed in tithing. Ten percent of my income goes to others—to organizations that carry on the work I'm unable to do myself and/or to individuals who have inspired me.

The funny thing is that the times I've had the most financial worries in my life are the times I haven't been tithing. Give some away and more will flow back.

It's like the old story that asks which wolf (the mean one or the kind one) will win. The answer is: the one I feed.

I spoke at an elementary school once a number of years ago about the joys and challenges of being an author. One of the students asked me if I was rich.

Although I had to think about my answer for a few seconds, it didn't take too long for me to understand what I needed to say. "Yes," I told him. "Not because I bring in a lot of money, but because I spend less than I make. That makes me rich."

What about you? Are you in love with money? Or are you truly rich?

~ ~ ~

**The Youngest I'll Ever Be**

**Friday 6/5/2020** – Today, right now, I'm the oldest I've ever been.

At the same time, right now I'm the youngest I'll ever be from now on.

Feels like a new lease on life, doesn't it?

~ ~ ~

**My London Trip**

**Saturday 6/6/2020** – Every once in a while, I rummage through old photo albums. I came across this picture I took back in the 70s on a trip to London. I can remember wanting to capture the Mary Poppins-ish view of the old chimneys and the Griffin statue in the middle of Fleet Street outlined against the sky—but I didn't want any electric wires or phone poles in the picture.

# Fran Stewart

The only way I could accomplish that was to step off the curb (kerb in London), crouch down, and point my camera upwards.

I waited for a lull in the traffic, looked to my right to be sure nobody was barreling around the slight curve, got into position, took my picture, and rose to find a truck (lorry) waiting for me to get out of his way.

The driver leaned out his window as he drove past and called, "You should have taken a picture of me, lovie!"

The street was his domain, not mine. He could so easily have shouted, "Stupid American tourist" or "Get outta the road, dummy!" Instead, he chose a kinder approach.

How I wish I'd had the presence of mind to raise my camera and snap a picture of his waving hand and his broad grin before he withdrew his head into his window and disappeared from my sight.

All these years later, I still remember his kindness.

And I'm extremely grateful he didn't run me down!

~ ~ ~

**Infinity**

**Monday 6/8/2020** – My MasterMind partner and I use the infinity sign as an indication that something we've been visualizing is still in process, although we certainly don't plan on those items taking forever to come to fruition.

One of the long-term projects I'm working on is the publication of these Facebook author page posts into book format. Have I already shared this with you? It's something I think about so often, but I'm not sure whether or not I've voiced it to many people outside my immediate circle of family and close friends.

It's the same sort of thing I did with my beekeeping blog, turning those 600 days of postings into a six-volume memoir set, 100 posts per volume. These FB posts will be different, though. After all, I post daily except for Sundays. That means more than 300 posts per year – and I've been doing this since 2014.

The good news (if you can call it that) is that FB won't let me go back and retrieve quite a few of my posts. I'm missing a big chunk of 2014, quite a bit of 2015, and all of 2016. In 2017, fortunately, I started saving each post (and the matching photo) in a separate document, so the last couple of years are intact.

There's still a LOT of work to be done before I can send these documents to my wonderful formatter. Darlene is the one who originally published all of my books (except for the ScotShop Mysteries). She designed all my covers, and she's formatted all these books for the revised editions I've published through My Own Ship Press.

What I'm saying is, don't hold your breath waiting for these FB memoirs of mine. They may be a long time coming. But—I certainly hope!—they'll be well worth waiting for.

~ ~ ~

**chickadee nest**

**Tuesday 6/9/2020** – My cats (rescues every one of them) have always become indoor cats. 100%. I would never consider an outdoor cat. Not as long as I can give my indoor cats a good life, with lots of toys and climbing trees and scratching posts. Every day I brush them and play with them.

There's an outdoor cat in our neighborhood, though, who has decided that my wildlife friendly yard makes for a perfect buffet. He's a very friendly cat (to people), but he's an absolute terror where smaller living things are concerned.

Over the years he and his humans have lived next door, he's killed numerous birds from my yard, as well as squirrels, chipmunks, mice, and who knows what else.

Over the past month I spent a lot of time sitting on my front porch watching a pair of resident chickadees flying in and out of one of the birdhouses, creating one of their intricately layered nests. Then, for a long time, I didn't see any chickadees around that house at all.

They had it completely ready for eggs – but then they disappeared, most likely down Cousteau's gullet. Here's a picture of the nest they built. The bottom layers are mosses, then straw and cat hair. Yes. Cat hair. When I brush Fuzzy Britches, I put her golden and white hair out in a special holder on the front porch where all the small birds take from it to line their nests.

# Fran Stewart

The depression you can see in the middle of this picture is a deep hole where the eggs were meant to nestle. Only no eggs ever ended up there.

I know it's the circle of life (and death). But I'm not happy. Even wearing a bell, Cousteau has a huge advantage. Two years ago, bluebirds built a nest in this same box, but he killed the parents, and the babies that had already hatched starved to death before I realized the parents were gone.

I'm feeling very sad today.

~ ~ ~

**cross number puzzle book**

**Wednesday 6/10/2020** – Do you like number puzzles as much as I do?

A whole bunch of years ago, I found a marvelous number puzzle book called "Sit & Solve Cross Number Puzzles" by Henry Hook.

I worked every puzzle in the whole book. Then I erased every page and started over again. I think I'm on my fourth (or is it fifth?) run-through. The answers have gotten a bit embedded in the pages, but most of them are still too fuzzy for me to be sure of. So I re-work each clue and re-enter each answer.

On this one, for instance, you can see that if you multiply 8-Across by 2, you'll get the answer to 19-Down. And so on. Of course, you have to have solved 8-across before you can get there.

I have a LOT of fun doing it. I figure it has the potential to keep me entertained for another ten or twelve years at least. As long as I don't erase holes in the pages.

 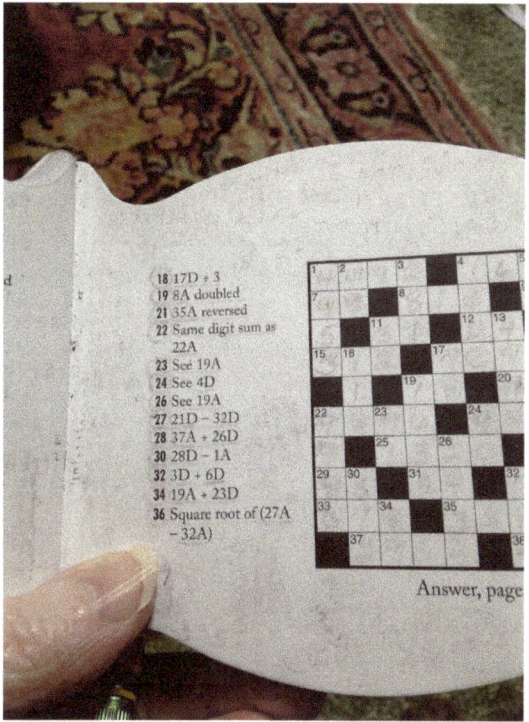

~ ~ ~

**Learned from a book**

**Thursday 6/11/2020** – I believe in sequels. I believe in complexity. I believe in hanging in there regardless of how dark things may sometimes seem. And I believe there's a crummy side to the best of us and a good side to the worst of us.

Thank goodness I started reading early. It's served me well throughout my life. Emily Dickinson said, "There is no frigate like a book."
How very true. Words are the wind that fills the sails of the ships I travel in every single day.
Especially during these times of social distancing, books take on extra importance. I pity people who say they don't like to read. How on earth can they travel? Where do your frigates take you?

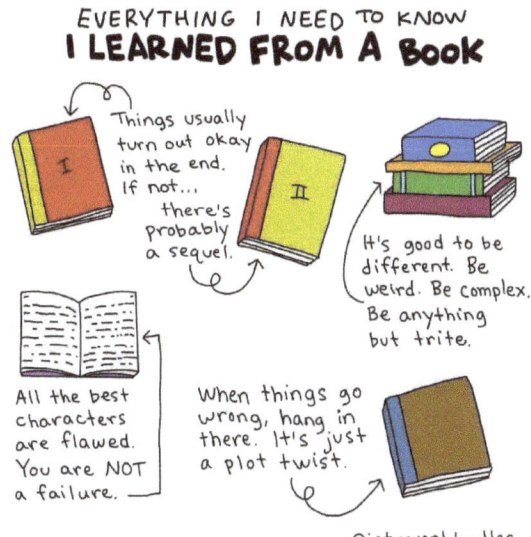

Fran Stewart

## Grateful for the Problems You Don't Have

**Friday 6/12/2020** – I don't have a whole lot to say about this message. Except to note how very true it is.

Well, come to think about it, I DO have something to say. Years ago, I read a book by Sarah Ban Breathnach called *Simple Abundance*, in which she recommended keeping a gratitude list. At the end of each day, she instructed, sit down and write a list of "Five things for which I am grateful."

After about six months of keeping such a list, I realized that nothing related to my job (for which I commuted three-plus hours into and out of midtown Atlanta each day) ever showed up on my lists. That realization changed my life. Nine months later (like birthing a new baby) I was able to quit that job and enter on a new adventure.

Gratitude is powerful indeed.

What are you grateful for today?

> **Happiness comes easily when you stop complaining about your problems & start being grateful for all the problems you don't have.**

~ ~ ~

## Fuzzy Britches on blue fleece

**Saturday 6/13/2020** – I started this week of posts by complaining about a killer cat. I'd like to finish the week thanking Fuzzy Britches for being the sweet soul she is. When I'm hurting, she cuddles with me and has been known to lick a whole gallon of tears off my face.

She wandered into my life a number of years ago with one back leg injured (probably by a collision with a car). All my free cats end up costing a lot in vet fees. But although the vet said she'd probably limp for the rest of her life, she healed completely. She also decided that the world out there isn't nearly as comforting as the world in here. I accidentally left my front door open one day, and came back in to find Fuzzy curled in "meatloaf position" on the floor about ten feet from the door, watching to be sure no chipmunks came inside.

Thank you, Fuzzy Britches.

~ ~ ~

**Squirrel Repeller**

**Monday 6/15/2020** – So, a little background here. If you've read these posts of mine for any length of time, you know I've had an ongoing disagreement with the squirrels and grackles and other creatures who think they own the rights to my bird feeders.

I finally decided to feed the little birds on my front porch, so I put up a cage that prevents squirrels from getting into the seed. Each morning I open the spring-loaded lid, add a scoop of "Nesting Blend" seed from Wild Birds Unlimited, close it back up, and watch the titmice and chickadees and Carolina wrens and countless other feathered creatures come to the feast.

But one of the squirrels decided to take on the challenge. She hung from my porch rail, hooked a little paw over the edge of the recycled-cardboard bowl, and somehow or other chewed a hole in it so the seed spilled out.

Then I tried putting the bowl on a heavy plastic plate.

Didn't work. Despite the rocks holding it down, she managed to upend the whole thing.

Now, I've graduated to a china plate that holds the plastic plate that holds a replacement cardboard bowl – from which I cut off the pointed corners so Mrs. Squirrel cannot reach in and grab those edges.

Think this will work?

If not, I'll try something else. I can be just as persistent as any squirrel.

# Fran Stewart

~ ~ ~

**tree holding moon**

**Tuesday 6/16/2020** – I love the way all of nature is interconnected. Any time I change one thing in my yard—say I move the birdfeeder poles to a different location—the grasses [HA! the weeds] readjust and spring up in a different configuration. The chipmunks may dig a new entrance hole to their underground burrow. The frogs find a new path to hop to the birdbath that lies conveniently flat on the ground just so they can get into the water easily.

It's all about flexibility. As long as I don't clear-cut the whole yard, as long as I don't spray poisons, as long as I'm careful where I step so the lizards are safe sunning themselves on my paving stone pathway, we all manage to live together peacefully.

If I (or rather the unknown photographer) were to move a few steps to the left or a few steps to the right, this tree would no longer be holding the moon. But right where I am, right now, is perfect.

~ ~ ~

### Ceiling shadows

**Wednesday 6/17/2020** – When the twilight fades enough that I need some lights on in order to read, I try to remember to look upward, both to see the blue light of a rainy evening coming in through the skylights and to see the intricate shadows from the ceiling lights and fan.

Isn't it amazing that (if we will only open our eyes) we can see art everywhere?

~ ~ ~

### You Can't See Me

**Thursday 6/18/2020** – I love this photo. Aside from the funniness of a giraffe apparently hiding behind a bare truck, I do wonder how the tree feels having that metal (or is it plastic) screening/webbing around its lower fourteen or fifteen feet.

What if a taller giraffe comes along?

What if the tree grows so much that its girth needs to increase beyond the confines of its wrapping?

What if the mechanism for holding up that wrapping fails and the whole thing falls down? Would animals get stuck in it? Would the tree have lasting scars?

What if . . . What if . . .

Those two words are music to a writer's ears.

Just think of all the stories that come about when we answer the *what if's* in our lives!

~ ~ ~

**Juneteenth**

**Friday 6/19/2020** – Time to celebrate the second declaration of independence.

Here's to all the people who fought and suffered and died for freedom's sake.

Barack Obama
@BarackObama

On Juneteenth, we celebrate our capacity to make real the promise of our founding, that thing inside each of us that says America is not yet finished, that compels all of us to fight for justice and equality until this country we love more closely aligns with our highest ideals.

**pre-dawn walk**

**Saturday 6/20/2020** – This was my view a couple of months ago on my early morning walk. Only two other houses in my neighborhood had lights in the windows. One of the lighted windows was in the nursery of a family with their first baby.

That got me to thinking about what we teach our children when they are tiny. If we turn on a light when we enter a nursery to feed our child, are we teaching the baby that mommy brings light, and that loneliness happens in the dark?

That doesn't seem very fair. When I rose to feed my children (forty-some-odd years ago) I went into their room in the dark, sat with them in the dark, nurtured them in the dark.

When I was nine, I remember asking my mother to leave my curtains open at night. That was the year we lived in a third-floor apartment where my bedroom window looked out on a thick stand of tall pine trees. She refused, saying that if I woke up when the moon shone in my window, I'd think it was a burglar's flashlight, and I'd get scared.

That said a lot more about my mother's fears than it said about mine.

I wish I'd been disobedient enough to get up and open my curtains.

I hope I gave my children an appreciation of the beauty of the night. I've never thought to ask them about it, though. Maybe—someday—they'll read these stories of mine.

# Fran Stewart

## Solstice at Stonehenge

**Sunday 6/21/2020** – Although I usually don't post anything on Sundays, this morning I have to share with you what I did yesterday afternoon and last night. The English Heritage Society live-streamed the summer solstice sunset and sunrise from Stonehenge.

In England, sunset was at 9:26 last night and sunrise at 4:51 this morning, which translated to 4:26 and 11:51 (both PM, both Saturday) here in my time zone. So I set a couple of alarms and tuned in to watch.

The first thing that struck me was the silence, except for the sound of the wind across the Salisbury plain. They had four or five cameras going. Several of them were fixed, and one (or two?) could pan across the stones. Every so often a bird would land on one of the lintels. Other than that and the camera changes, nothing moved. (Okay, I'll admit there were four or five times when a quiet employee passed in back of the far stones—but there was no disruption to the peacefulness, except for an occasional motorcycle passing by.)

At several points, the camera person walked into the middle of the henge and pivoted, so we could see the stones all the way around it.

Nobody spoke, because, after all, what was there to be said? For thousands of years, these stones have pinpointed the summer and winter solstices every year. Seeing the sky colors fade before sunset and brighten before sunrise felt like a journey to me.

I had to be grateful that Stonehenge is in England. If it were here in the United States, there would be a theme park built around it, most likely. There would be scads of lighting, eerie music, and an emcee giving the play-by-play. "Look at that, folks! It's getting darker!" "Look at this now. Can you see how the sun's about to peek over the horizon?" And there'd probably be fireworks, too.

Baloney.

The elegance of this experience was that I could feel I was there by myself, witness to the flow of time. AND, at the same time, I felt a connection to the thousands of people who were watching it with me.

Sunset was fairly cloudy, so there was no instant where I could say, "This is it." Just some birds winging their way across the sky.

Most years there are huge celebrations at Stonehenge. This year, though, because of the pandemic, Stonehenge is closed to the public. Hence, the silence.

That made this a once-in-a-lifetime experience.

I'm so glad I didn't miss it.

~ ~ ~

### Toothbrush Model for Writing

**Monday 6/22/2020** – I had to share this with you. I brush my teeth in the shower. And I write the same way.

"Huh? What do you mean, Frannie?"

I'm glad you asked.

Last February, at a meeting of my Atlanta NLAPW group, I read this essay from my book *From the Tip of My Pen: a Workbook for Writers*. Molly Read Woo videotaped it and posted it online.

It's called "Confessions of a Time Saver – A Toothbrush Model for Writing."

This system works whether you're writing a novel, a mystery, a memoir, or a research paper. It also works as a general principle for how to approach life.

Go ahead. Give this a try.

And let me know how it turns out.

~ ~ ~

### Do Not Feed the Fears

**Tuesday 6/23/2020** – There's so much fear swirling around us nowadays, it seems important to mention that what we feed is what grows.

Another way of saying that is the old computer programming term: GIGO – or, to unravel the acronym: Garbage In, Garbage Out.

Today, only good stuff goes into my mind. Today I will feed hope and beauty and sincerity and consideration.

Will you join me ((virtually))?

# Fran Stewart

~ ~ ~

### Stormtrooper helmet

**Wednesday 6/24/2020** – Don't you love it how looking at the world from a different angle gives you a whole new perspective?

Somewhere or other (unless I loaned it to someone) I have a book called *A Soprano on Her Head* by Eloise Ristad. I think I've probably mentioned the book before in these posts, but since I can't recall whether I really did or whether I just thought of doing it, I'll tell you about it again.

Ristad makes the point that when we try without success to master a skill, we might need to stand on our head—to go about the task in a completely different way, with a completely different attitude. Say there's a soprano who cannot reach a particular note. She tries and tries, but because she doesn't truly think she's capable of that impossibly high note, her body tenses as she approaches it. Consequently, she can't manage it.

When Ristad coached a woman like that years ago, she finally (with some exasperation) said, "Okay. Get down on the floor and do a head stand."

Then she ran her upside-down pupil through the same exercise, leading up to the note, which the woman sang with no effort whatsoever.

Now, if I tried to stand on my head every time I get stuck with something, I'd probably be spending the rest of my life in the chiropractor's office. But you get the idea. When we concentrate on a *solution* rather than on what we perceive as a *problem*, we're more likely to get the result we want.

So, turn that storm trooper's helmet upside down! Go ahead! You'll be amazed at what you find. (And my inner editor wants to put an apostrophe where it's needed on that first line.)

~ ~ ~

## How to Cook Umber

**Thursday 6/25/2020** – I couldn't resist yet another punny meme.

I'm sure all my artist friends will appreciate this one.

I, for one, have never tasted umber, either raw or burnt. Can anyone enlighten me?

If not, I'll just wait for evening when I can sit out on the porch and appreciate the fireflies. (Or do you call them lightning bugs?)

~ ~ ~

## Ridiculous Example

**Friday 6/26/2020** – If only people would THINK before posting some of these ridiculous statements that float around the Internet, burrowing into our brains and numbing them.

Here's an example I received a couple of days ago:

# Fran Stewart

=========

> *This year, 2020, the whole world is of the same age. It only happens once every 1000 years.*
> *Calculate:*
> *Your age + your year of birth = 2020*
>
> *This is true for everyone living today!*
> *Very strange....experts cannot explain it.*
>
> *Go figure yours and see if it is 2020.*

=========

Go figure indeed. First of all, whoever wrote this either has no idea about the way math works OR knows quite well and wanted to see how many folks he could make fools of. I would guess it's the second of those two scenarios.

Secondly, any time I see an email that assures me something happens only once every thousand years, I pretty much know it's a hoax.

In the third place, it doesn't take an expert to figure out that ANY time you add your age to your year of birth, you're going to get the current year—as long as your birthday has already occurred that particular year. If your birthday hasn't happened yet this year, then you'll get LAST year as an answer.

Go ahead. Figure that out.

And then please stop sending me these stupid emails.

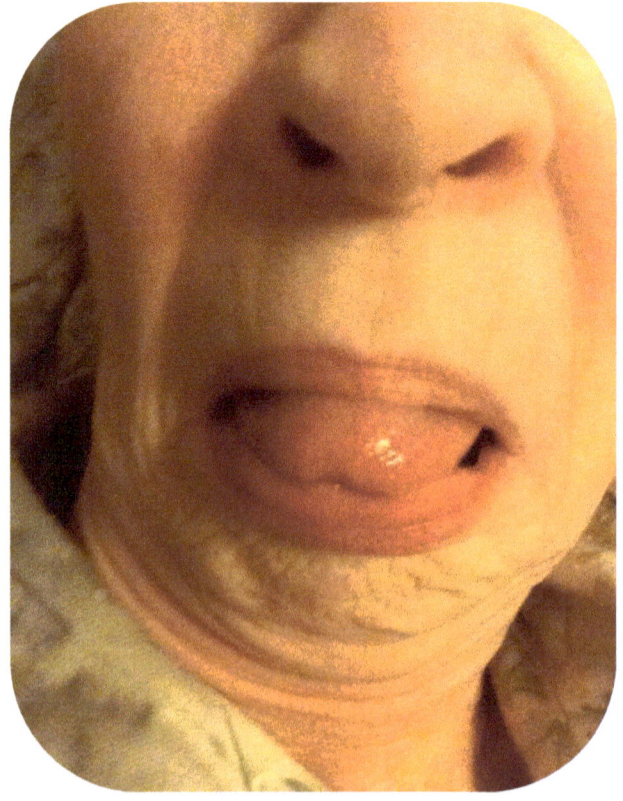

~ ~ ~

### Attempted Murder

**Saturday 6/27/2020** – It looks like I'm devolving into a rut. A good rut, I guess. The rut called "End the Week with a Funny Photo."

I enjoy it. I hope you do as well.

~ ~ ~

### Ruth Bader Ginsburg

**Monday 6/29/2020** – [**A Later Note:** Of course, now, as I compile this book, the amazing, notorious RBG is gone, but I've chosen to leave this post just as it was first written.]

Quick – Who's the Chief Justice of our Supreme Court, and how many other members can you name?

In case you're wondering, here they are:

> Chief Justice John Roberts
> Ruth Bader Ginsburg
> Elena Kagan
> Sonia Sotomayor
> Stephen Breyer
> Samuel Alito
> Neil Gorsuch
> Clarence Thomas
> and Brett Kavanaugh

Why on earth can't we all name all nine of these people? They have the ability to drastically change the way our lives are ordered.

When we elect people who hand out lifetime appointments, we have to understand that we're collaborators in the long-range effects of those appointments.

The next person elected as POTUS will quite likely appoint a replacement for Ruth Bader Ginsburg.

It's just a thought.

P.S. This is a photo of one of my favorite tee-shirts.

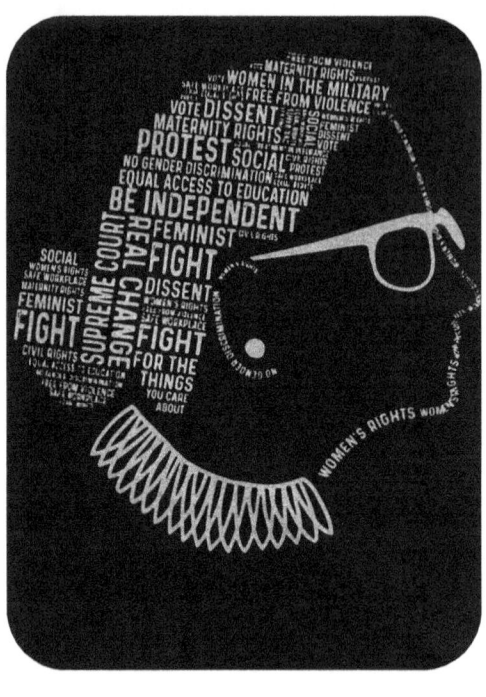

~ ~ ~

**Honeymoons and Telephone Lines**

**Tuesday 6/30/2020** – Before we end this month that traditionally has more weddings than any other month, I thought you might be interested in something I read only recently:

The derivation of the word *honeymoon*.

Here it is:

It was the accepted practice in Babylon 4,000 years ago that for a month after the wedding, the bride's father would supply his son-in-law with all the mead he could drink. Mead is a honey wine and because their calendar was lunar based, this period was called the honey month, which we know today as the honeymoon.

Now, is this true? I doubt it. Babylon? 4,000 years ago?

It's much more likely to be what my dictionary says:

        16th century. Affection wanes like the moon.

How depressing.

Let's have a happy photo instead.

Fran Stewart

# July 2020

## The Dance for Today

**Wednesday 7/1/2020** – What's the dance for today? The 183/183 (!)

Why?

I'm glad you asked.

Today is the 183rd day of 2020 and there are 183 days left to go in the year. This 183/183 combo happens only during Leap Years, so it'll be another four years before we can do the 183/183 dance again.

What are you waiting for? Wave your arms around and celebrate!

~ ~ ~

## Passiflora Incarnata

**Thursday 7/2/2020** – *Passiflora incarnata* is the host plant of the Gulf Fritillary Butterfly, a little bright orange creature with silvery streaks on its wings. One year I had 27 chrysalises on the siding of my house, just above a prolific passionflower vine that a passing bird must have planted when it pooped as it flew past.

I even had a chrysalis right beside my front door. I was lucky enough to watch that one being formed, and then, several weeks later I was once again on my porch at exactly the right time, and I watched the long and arduous process as the butterfly emerged from its cocoon. It was one of the defining moments of my life, for I realized that I had been in my own personal cocoon for a very long period, and it was time for me to emerge.

I feel as if that year was when I finally woke to the possibilities of truly taking responsibility for my own life and making a difference not only in my life, but in how I could interact more positively with the lives of those around me.

A wake-up call indeed.

Thank you, Mama Nature.

~ ~ ~

**Pack the Essentials**

**Friday 7/3/2020** – No, I'm not planning a vacation any time soon, but it occurred to me that this advice applies to all the other times of life.

Pack only the essentials.

This is a good time for me to clean out my closet of all those clothes I don't much like, the ones that don't fit well, and the ones I just never get around to wearing. Out they go to a charity shop.

It's a good time to clean out my kitchen cabinets. Yes, I'm ashamed to say I have a tall can of Martins Ground Mustard in there. Martins store brand spices were available at the Martins Grocery Store in Vermont where I lived and shopped more than 25 years ago. How embarrassing. Out it goes to the garbage.

Books I'll never want to re-read, CDs I'll never play again, dishes I'll never use. Out they go to find new homes where they'll be appreciated.

I'm even considering getting rid of some of the (less than stellar) artwork on my walls.

Packing only the essentials feels good. Won't you join me in this effort?

only pack essentials when going on vacation

~ ~ ~

**Kissing Booth**

**Saturday 7/4/2020** – Ending the week with laugh. Have a safe and healthy weekend. I'm starting off this Independence Day by reading the Declaration of Independence, the way I always do on the 4th. I hope you'll join me in that. This afternoon I'll read the U.S. Constitution. Again, be my guest to do the same.

And, of course, please laugh along with me at this kissing booth!

## Tower Raven

**Monday 7/6/2020** – Good morning. There is something about a face-to-face greeting that just doesn't quite come across on a phone call. That's why I'm using Zoom so much more lately. There's nothing that can compensate for not being able to see minute facial cues during a conversation. That's one thing that's so disconcerting about wearing a mask.

Do I wear a mask when I choose to go out?

Of course.

Do I wish I didn't have to?

Of course.

Will I wear a mask anyway?

Of course. Need you even ask?

On Friday I saw my neighbors walking down the cul-de-sac with their six-month-old, so I stepped outside to say hello. I didn't put on a mask, because I knew I could stay a good six or eight feet away from them and knew they would respect that. It was lovely to have the human interaction without a camera and monitor in the middle, but I still felt a bit of an undercurrent of concern. What if the breeze shifts in my direction? I kept backing up. We finally ended our visit with me a good twelve feet away from them.

At least with Zoom I can get "closer."

As close as this raven from the Tower of London.

# Fran Stewart

~ ~ ~

## No Matter What

**Tuesday 7/7/2020** – I am so unbelievably fortunate, sometimes I wonder how the heck I got here.

Why fortunate?

Because I have a friend like this, someone who understands that sometimes I just need to vent. Someone who will listen without judgment, someone who will empathize (even if I'm being unreasonable), someone who knows me well and cares for me enough to hold that umbrella until I get to where I can see the sun again.

She's listened to me cry, and she's cried along with me.

She's listened to me howl with laughter, and she's joined in the glee.

She's listened to my occasional rants and, once I've settled down, has quietly offered another possible perspective.

Thank you, Darlene. You mean the world to me.

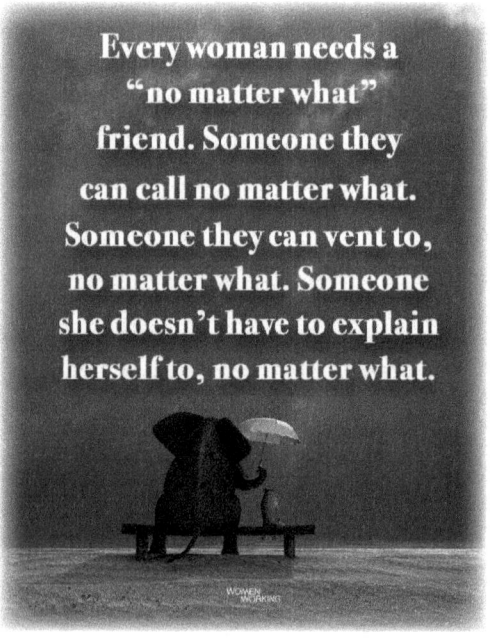

~ ~ ~

## Not Always What You See

**Wednesday 7/8/2020** – You might want to take a look at my current website just to see what a mess it is (before it disappears).

Yes, that's what I said. The new Fran Stewart.com will be up within the next couple of days and you might want to compare the old hopelessly outdated site to the new one. The old site is the shrunken leaf. The new site will be the huge carrot below ground. [I probably didn't need to explain that...]

I hired someone (melanielatrelle.com) to design a new site for me – one that I could manage myself. I know you may think of me as a mystery writer (and the new site will certainly allow you to easily find the newly-revised versions of my books), but the focus of the site will be on the online memoirs classes I'm going to be conducting.

You see, I've migrated into a new phase in my life, where the importance of these classes has overshadowed the satisfaction I once got from writing a good mystery with some real meat to it.

Melanie had taken several of the memoirs classes I taught in local libraries, so she understood just how much these classes mean to me.

Be sure you go to the home page of franstewart.com and sign up for my newsletter so you'll be one of the first to see this new creation. Do it now so you don't miss out!

I think you'll really enjoy it. And I hope you'll enroll in one of the classes. This Friday at 11am I'll be speaking on the Doug Dahlgren Internet Radio Show on Artist First Radio (ArtistFirst dot com) about memoirs. If you feel like you need more info before enrolling, give a listen!

There's a big carrot in there somewhere!

~ ~ ~

**Live Streams**

**Thursday 7/9/2020** – I have one of these in my back yard. A live stream. U̶̶̶̶̶̶̶̶̶̶̶̶̶̶̶̶̶̶̶̶̶̶̶̶̶̶h, I don't even bother to answer my (silenced) phone when I'm out there. It's e̶̶̶̶̶̶̶̶̶̶̶̶̶̶̶̶̶̶̶̶̶̶ listen to the gurgling. I've shared photos of my live stream before here on these FB ̶̶̶̶̶̶̶̶̶̶̶̶̶̶̶̶̶̶̶̶̶̶̶̶̶̶̶̶ of those pictures in case you missed it the first time around. This one shows the cre̶̶̶̶̶̶̶̶̶̶̶̶̶̶̶̶̶̶̶̶̶̶̶̶̶̶ imagine how lush it is when the leaves appear.

People have always needed live streams. I feel sorry for those who don't even ̶r̶e̶a̶l̶i̶z̶e̶ ̶h̶o̶w̶ ̶m̶u̶c̶h̶ they're missing.

Back in the early 70s I read a newly published book by Elaine Moran called *The Descent of Woman*. I've re-read it a couple of times since then and have always been impressed by her cogent arguments that human beings developed as they did because of the influence of water as the place where mothers retreated to in order to protect themselves and their children. Water is built into our psyches. I'm not talking about visiting a beach with throngs of other people sunning themselves, playing frisbee or tossing around a beach ball. I'm talking about the quiet realization that water soothes the soul.

Do you have a live stream in your life? I certainly hope so.

~ ~ ~

**Letting My Hair Down**

**Friday 7/10/2020** – I don't know why I've posted so many pictures of my hair in recent months, but here's yet another one.

I twist my hair up on top of my head at night and fasten it with two extra-long bobby pins to keep the wispy strands from tickling me so much. This also keeps Wooly Bear from getting her paws tangled when she sleeps beside my pillow.

When I take out the pins in the morning, my hair falls down. This photo shows the result after the removal of the first pin. Still one to go.

Now, if I could just twist up my built-in biases
and let go of them that easily. One pin, two pins ... all gone

p.s. Great news! My brand-new website is live now.
Check it out: FranStewart.com.

~ ~ ~

**VelCrows**

**Saturday 7/11/2020** – I have hordes of grackles and starlings that decimate the contents of my bird feeders and scare off the smaller birds. With THEM I have an ongoing battle.

I also have a bunch of crows that regularly visit my bird feeders. I like crows. I like their raucous "caw, caw, caw." I like the way they strut around. I like that they clean up the spilled seed under the feeding posts.

So, the crows are welcome to hang around, no matter how they manage to do that.

'Bye till Monday.

~ ~ ~

**Clean bug**

**Monday 7/13/2020** – This seems like a good week for a bit of laundry-room philosophy.

Last weekend I did the laundry (big accomplishment). After I'd taken all the clothes out of the washer, I noticed a brownish speck left in the bottom, so I reached down to remove it. It was a little bug. This little bug—the one in the photo.

It surprised the heck out of me by walking up my finger and across my palm. I took it outside and transferred it to a nearby shrub. How had it lasted? Now, admittedly, I do all my wash loads using cold water. And a very mild detergent. No bleach. No fancy additions.

But still, that was a lot of water and a lot of agitating for a little fella like this to go through and manage to survive. Can you imagine the poor little bug during the spin cycle?

A good analogy, I thought, for these times we're living through. No matter how much we get thrown around by wash and rinse cycles, we CAN come through it. But then, I probably didn't need to make that point. You'd already gotten it, hadn't you?

Tomorrow I'll have another laundry story to share with you.

~ ~ ~

**Used Dryer**

**Tuesday 7/14/2020** – An awful lot of my posts here begin with, or at least contain, the words "A long time ago…" Well, here's another one, now that we're spending a week talking about laundry.

A long time ago in what seems like another lifetime, my then-husband and I went looking for a used dryer. The local women's shelter (where I volunteered part time) had been given a brand-new dryer, so they wanted to get rid of the old one.

"Doesn't work very well at all," the director warned us. "Won't dry things worth a darn."

Hmmm. I took one look and could tell what the problem was – but they already had a new dryer in place, so we hauled off their old one.

The lint filter (that looked just like the one in this fuzzy picture taken from the internet) was so clogged with dried on lint that I had to take a screwdriver to scrape the stuff off. Several years' worth of lint. Cruddy stuff. It's a wonder it hadn't combusted, but the lint had dried so much it wasn't dust-like. More rock-like.

No wonder the clothes stayed wet.

I know you can probably tell where I'm going with this.

How much mind-lint do we carry around with us? We're often too lazy to look at our outdated attitudes and say, "Somebody needs to clean this out." Still, nothing's going to turn out right if we're too squeamish, too nervous, too downright scared to challenge the way things HAVE been and change them into the way they SHOULD be.

That old dryer worked beautifully for a lot of years. All it needed was for somebody to gouge out the outmoded careless treatment it had been receiving.

I'm ready to check out the nasty corners of my life, the places where I've stood by when something ought to be said, the places where I've stepped aside saying, "This is wrong. People ought to do something about it," without recognizing that "those people" are me, myself, and I.

Where's your lint piling up? Want to join me in some deep cleaning?

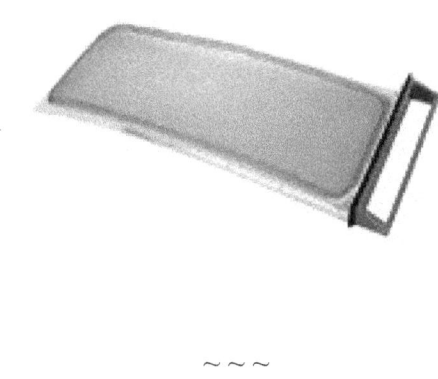

~ ~ ~

**Lint Traps**

**Wednesday 7/15/2020** – When on earth did they stop making washing machines with lint traps?

Eight or nine years ago, my old washer died. Thoroughly dead. Unfixably dead. Completely dead. So, I went washer shopping.

I looked through model after model on the showroom floor and was struck with one undisputable fact—not a single washer had a lint trap.

You remember filter-flow lint traps, don't you?

The point of all this is that we seem to have gotten to the point where we want to sanitize everything. Not to the point of actually getting rid of the garbage, but of merely hiding where we're stuffing it.

You see, your laundry (mine as well) still has a lot of lint. It's just that we no longer have to reach into the filter and remove the yucky stuff. I'm not really sure just where it goes now. Maybe, like Monday's bug, it's still there, but distributed throughout the clothing so we don't see it.

Wouldn't it be healthier for us to see our garbage? That's the point of the #MeToo movement, the Black Lives Matter movement, the wear-a-mask-to-protect-others movement. What "right" does anyone have to spew their violence, their sadism, their misogyny, their microbes around? We need a flow-through device that will not only let us recognize our garbage, but then do something about it. We need to reach into our own filters and remove that messy, toxic lint.

# Fran Stewart

We need to believe women so we don't end up with more perverts on our Supreme Court; we need to recognize that until Black Lives Matter, no life will matter; we need to be willing to protect the most vulnerable in our society; we need to see that no amount of shouting (or tweeting) will turn lies into truth.

Now, the question is, what am I going to do about it? And what are you going to do about it?

~ ~ ~

### Believe Me

**Thursday 7/16/2020** – I've been reading *Believe Me: How Trusting Women Can Change the World* edited by Jessica Valenti and Jaclyn Friedman. It's a series of essays written by women—some of them well known, some not. All of them have points of view worth considering. I've read only to the marvelous 4th essay, called "Listening Will Never Be Enough."

We've spent the week so far talking about dirty laundry. At least, I've been talking about it. I hope you've joined in the conversation on some level.

These Facebook posts of mine comprise a large part of my personal memoirs—the stories of my life. They include what I'm laughing about, what I'm thinking about, what I'm crying about.

Right now, I'm crying about our country. An insidious virus—and I'm not talking about COVID here—has ravaged the USA, and indeed the entire world, for hundreds (thousands) of years. I'm talking about the tendency of human beings to see anyone not like ourselves as other, as alien, as somehow not quite equal. When we view people like that—whether we're talking about women, Native Americans, African Americans, Latinos & Latinas, people who are LGBTQIA—any time we view people as "other," we're tearing away a bit of our own humanity, and we stoop a bit farther down as a result. The Constitution says that we are all created EQUAL. This doesn't mean we were all created the SAME. It means that we should all be treated equally under the law regardless of how different our skin colors, our birth languages, our genders might be.

For once, let's stand tall. Let's stand up to the bullies, the haters, the self-righteous, the ones who are out to line their own pockets no matter what the cost to the rest of us.

Let's take a stand.

~ ~ ~

**The Same Bird**

**Friday 7/17/2020** – The same bird. What a novel thought. This post isn't exactly about laundry, but it's about cleaning up messes. Today and tomorrow I'd like to suggest two good solutions.

How about a change to the structure of the Senate and the House of Representatives? I may have mentioned this before somewhere in these years of postings, but if so, it deserves repetition.

How about if the seats in those two houses of Congress were rearranged so everyone had to sit alphabetically? No more of this "my side of the aisle" garbage.

What if they actually had to talk to each other?

What if they had to (gasp!) listen to each other?

Wouldn't it be easier for them to work together if they weren't so entrenched in believing that there were two different birds in those rooms?

It's just a thought. But I think it's a good one. What about you?

# Fran Stewart

~ ~ ~

**Women Leading Countries**

**Saturday 7/18/2020** – In the world I grew up in, women did the laundry. In those years I never heard about a man starting the washer.

There was "women's work," and there was "man's work." Not much thought was given to the fact that while the men were away fighting in the war, women had been back here doing the men's work as well as the women's work. And making it all work.

When I was writing the last four books of my Biscuit McKee Mysteries, somewhere in there I had the women who were sorting through Biscuit's attic find a trunk full of uniforms that went back to the tattered remains of some from the Civil War. They got to talking about how often wars occur—usually about every 25 years.

Now, though? We've been at constant war for a lot longer than any other war has gone on in the history of this country. So long—and so far away—that practically nobody thinks much about it anymore. Except perhaps the families that are torn apart by the deaths, the horrific injuries, the effects of PTSD. We're warring in our own streets, too.

I'd say those are messes that need attention, but nobody's been doing any laundry for years. Let's think about the fact that wars are generally started by men. Let's talk about the fact that the tweetership of this country is doing nothing to protect "We the People" and everything to protect his own financial interests, backed up by a Congress too intimidated to stand up to him.

I'm fed up. I'm taking a stand. Not a rant, but a stand. I hope you'll join me.

~ ~ ~

**A Lot More "Me"**

**Monday 7/20/2020** – After last week, it seems a bit anticlimactic to go back to non-political posts. But I'm willing to do that, as long as I remember—and I hope you will, too—the things I wrote about last week.

Meanwhile, here's the news I wanted to share with you. I've been working closely with Melanie to revise my website so it will concentrate on my work now, which is bringing you classes to help you write your memoirs, the stories of your life.

Melanie is NOT someone who just designs a site, tells you good luck, and disappears. She's teaching me a lot about focusing what I say and how I say it so that I end up helping the most people in the best possible way.

Here's my new look. It's a lot more ME than my previous sites have been.

# Fran Stewart

~ ~ ~

**In Loving Memory 7/20/20**

**Tuesday 7/21/2020** – Yesterday, a warm, funny, gentle, staunch, brilliant, loving man of integrity left this life. Judge Ramón Al_____panic judge to sit on a Gwinnett Count___

After he was sworn i_____ss while maintaining the integrity of th_____ant to find a good balance to allow peop_____. I want to provide people with a very po___

I knew Ramón prima_____t to her now as she goes through the step_____, perhaps a year from now, when we c_____ebrate his life.

In the meantime, all I_____yers to help Drew get through the comi___

Ramón Alvarado, res___

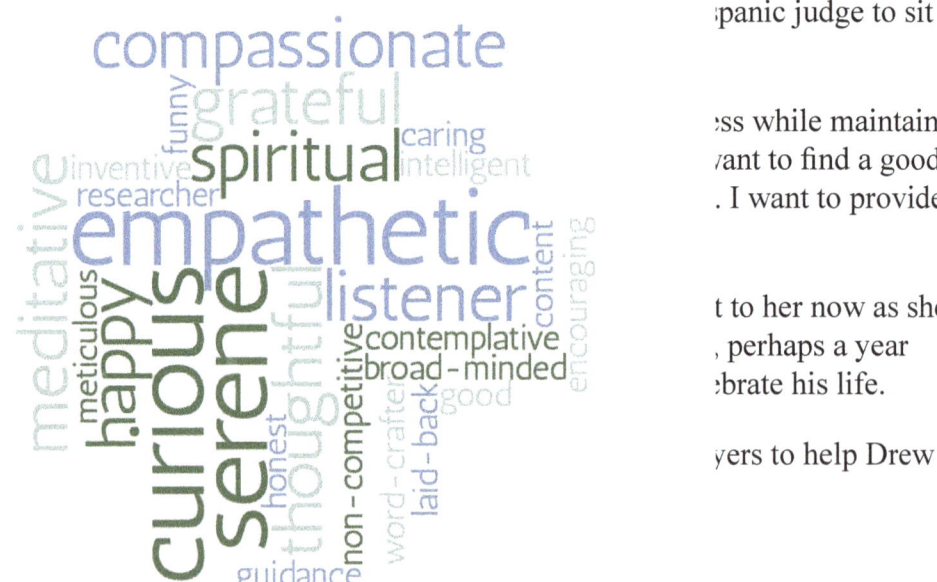

~ ~ ~

**Word Bubble**

**Wednesday 7/22/2020** – And—to continue our thoughts from Monday—Melanie created what she calls a "Word Bubble" for me. I'd like to share it with you.

Think about it in terms of your own life. What positive words would other people use to describe you? What positive words would you use to describe yourself?

If you're having a hard time thinking of those words, maybe it's time for you to take one of my classes. You see, when you begin to write the stories of your life, you can begin to put your life into perspective, to make sense of it. That's what I'm good at helping people to see. That's what I'd love to help you with.

Just something to think about. You can sign up on my website.

### When You Have Lost Things

**Thursday 7/23/2020** – Nowadays, with COVID-19 still raging, I've been thinking a lot about the value of friendship. It's easy to take people for granted when you can get together for casual lunches, movie nights, sitting and talking through an evening. Now, though, when sitting in a café, enjoying a film, shopping together, or sharing conversation over a glass of wine may put your life at risk, we have to redefine just what holds friends together.

It was never the lunches or the shopping. It was the connection we felt to that person.

Today, now, it is more important than ever to keep those connections alive. Today, now, it's imperative that we reach out to each other to offer encouragement, friendship, even just a smile. How? you ask. Well, there's Facetime, Zoom, and Skype. Or even just the sound of the smile in your voice during a phone call.

Now. Today. Time to reach out. That's what I'm doing. Will you join me?

### Never Was a Dress

**Friday 7/24/2020** – I'm fortunate to have known a lot of powerful women. It's important to recognize that their superwoman capes were there whether we recognized them or not.

And I'm not talking only about the obviously powerful women, but the ones also who have persistently gone about the work they were called to do regardless of the impediments our society and our culture placed in their way.

Time to assume your capes, my friends! Time to recognize the capes that are already there.

How about acknowledging the powerful women in your life? How about acknowledging your own power?

~ ~ ~

**Sneaky Tree**

**Saturday 7/25/2020** – Okay. Let's get back into the habit of the Saturday morning laugh. Of course, laughter is good more than just once a week, but I try to bring out the chuckles each Saturday just as a good way to end the week.

I'll be back on Monday. Or maybe I'll have one more laugh tomorrow. Who can tell?

~ ~ ~

**Sunday 7/26/2020** – Couldn't resist this one. I wonder what the architect of this building must be feeling as he sees this picture on social media.

The Spread of COVID-19 Is Based On Two Factors:
1. How Dense The Population is
2. How Dense The Population is

~ ~ ~

## Two Factors

**Monday 7/27/2020** – I'm so glad that many people are using common sense. Our county schools, for instance, have finally announced they will not be opening their doors this fall. Our county libraries have gone back to curb-side service only. My favorite birdseed store, Wild Birds Unlimited of Suwanee, will not let customers in the door unless they're wearing a mask (and wearing it properly).

No matter how dense POTUS 45 is, no matter how politically-minded the governor is, no matter what stupidities are floating through the air, there are still a great number of people who are choosing to use their minds. Thank goodness.

Yesterday I spoke with a friend who said, "I'm not sure cases are spreading as much as they say they are. It's just that there's a lot more testing." You have to be kidding me. Tell that to the thousands upon thousands of families who've had someone die of COVID or COVID-related complications.

Whether or not we know concrete numbers has no effect on the explosion of viral elements from a person's mouth when that person breathes or talks or coughs or sneezes or sings.

I get it that people are frustrated. I get it that they're tired of the restrictions that are necessary. I get it that folks want to get back to "normal," whatever form that might take. What I don't get is the number of people who are willing to expose others to danger just so they can try to get "there" a little faster.

I wear my mask and limit my trips out into public to protect you. Will you please limit your trips and wear your mask (properly) to protect me?

~ ~ ~

### 9 Blueberries and 11 Blackberries

**Tuesday 7/28/2020** – Here's a picture of my first harvest of blueberries and blackberries back in early June. Recently, though, a friend of mine gave me a big bag full of blueberries. Her bushes are overflowing, while mine have just about petered out. All through the month of June and half of July, I harvested a handful or two of berries each day, which was just enough for me to enjoy, but my friend's bushes are considerably older, taller, and more prolific than mine, so she had plenty to share. Thank you, Mikki!

Every other day since she gave them to me, I've been pouring out a big portion into a bowl. I then take all the ones that aren't fully ripe yet, put them in a different bowl, and cover it with a clear glass plate. I eat the ones that are left in the first bowl. Overnight the others ripen completely, so I can eat them the next day.

Are you aware that blueberries are red when they're green? Only in the English language.

I wonder if there are such oddities in other languages. I'm sure there probably are, but I'm not aware of them.

If you know of any, would you clue me in, please? Meanwhile, I have some fully ripe blueberries and blackberries calling my name…

~ ~ ~

### Toxic Positivity

**Wednesday 7/29/2020** – I'd like to recommend a marvelous book called *There Is No Good Card For This* by Kelsey Crowe and Emily McDowell. It says many of the same sorts of things as today's picture, but branches out into a lot more topics. Chapter 7 in particular is what they call an "empathy directory." There

# Fran Stewart

are cheat sheets that tell you the DOs and DON'Ts – good responses and bad ones to illness, divorce, miscarriage, infertility, loss, unemployment—all of which are situations that you or your friends might come up against without warning.

Just think about it. Say you're facing a major trauma, and someone says to you, "Just think happy thoughts." How, I ask you, is that of any help whatsoever?

Remember, when someone in your life is hurting, it's not about YOU. It takes courage (and empathy) to step out of our comfort zone when someone we know is challenged. Get a good book ahead of time so you'll be ready. Or at least read this chart.

~ ~ ~

**CBC News – Crushed Glass Replaces Sand**

**Thursday 7/30/2020** – I love news like this. Sand is considered a non-renewable resource. Glass is basically sand that's been processed. So here's a woman who asked, "Why can't I use crushed glass in place of sand in the soil mixtures for growing grapes on top of four city buildings in Montreal?"

And then she did it!

The use of crushed glass takes a lot of wasted bottles and jars out of the dumps and puts them to good use. The first harvest, according to this report from CBC News, netted 100 bottles of perfect rosé.

I'd like to propose a toast to this woman and her ingenuity.

And if you ask why I insist on using the term "dumps" rather than "sanitary landfills," I'd like to explain that these mountains of garbage ARE dumps—places where we dump the things we're too non-thinking or non-caring to try to reuse or recycle. Better yet, I try to reduce, so I don't have so much to reuse or recycle. And then I have a lot less to dump.

Want to join me in this way of living?

~ ~ ~

**Bookstores are Sacred Ground**

**Friday 7/31/2020** – I miss roaming through bookstores. I miss finding treasures I hadn't expected. I miss that feeling of anticipation walking up and down the aisles, knowing that some as-yet-unknown author awaits the touch of my hand on the spine of their book. I miss striking up casual conversations with people who've picked up a book that looks interesting.

When there's a book I want to buy, I can order it from my neighborhood bookstore. I can go and pick it up when they let me know it's there. I'm not willing, though, to put my life at risk doing the wandering-around I used to do.

I look forward to the day—probably a long time hence—when bookstores (and all stores) will be fully open for those sorts of interactions. I want to walk on their sacred grounds.

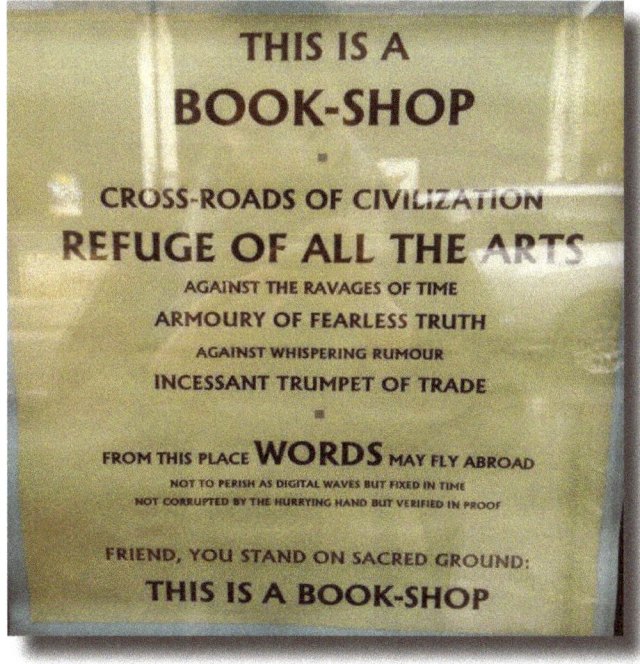

# Fran Stewart

## August 2020

### CATegories

**Saturday 8/1/2020** – It's time for the Saturday laugh.

And just in case you freak out, I'd guess that the CAT 5 picture was photoshopped. Looks to me like the kitten on the left was photographed lying on its back and then pasted in against a blue background. It has a suspicious black shadow stretching down its right side. And the one on the right may have been photographed standing on glass—see the way the front paws are splayed?

For the other four—blow dryers? Or large fans on a hot humid day?

What do you think?

~ ~ ~

### English is Hard 2/27/2019

**Monday 8/3/2020** – I'm reading a fascinating book right now. *Why We Sleep* by Matthew Walker Ph.D. His premise is that most of us are sleep-deprived, and he backs up this premise with information gathered from decades of meticulous research.

I think everybody should read it. Especially Chapter 7.

What does this have to do with "English is Hard" (where, you may have noticed, one of the lines is repeated)?

I'm glad you asked.

One of the topics he covers is how important sleep is to language acquisition. The long hours of sleeping that babies and young children engage in is vital to the way they learn their language—and it's why learning other languages is easier for children than it is for adults.

Just an idea. Think about it. Read the book.

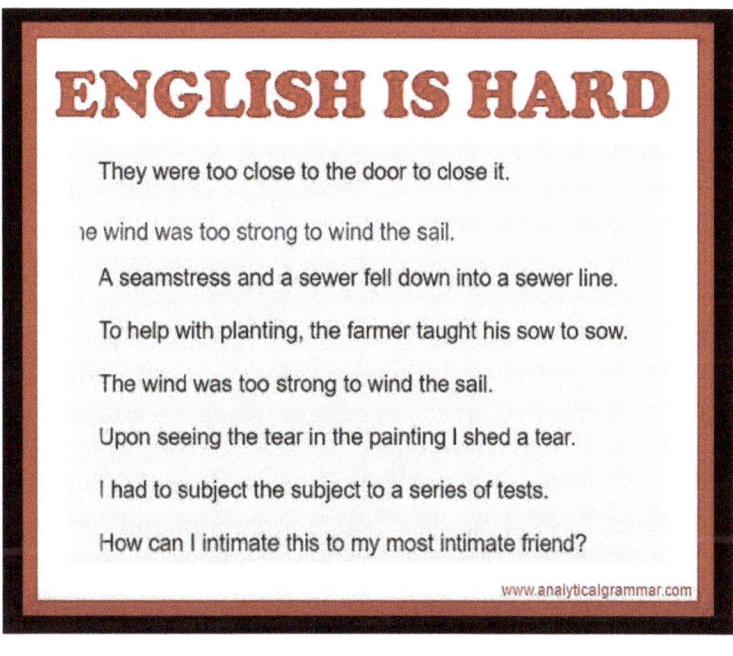

~ ~ ~

**Three Simple Rules**

**Tuesday 8/4/2020** – Common sense. Unfortunately, it's not so common.

You'd think these three rules would be embedded in each of us. You'd think we'd pay attention.

But how many times have I stood back and wished for something without taking even a tiny baby step toward it? How many times have I not asked for what I needed? And how many times have I stayed in one place because it felt easier than walking into an uncertain future?

'Nuff of that! Let's go beyond wishing. Let's actively ask. Let's step forward.

How about it?

*I know I showed this same quotation back on page 42 but it's worth talking about again.*

"Three simple rules in life. 1. If you do not go after what you want, you'll never have it. 2. If you do not ask, the answer will always be no. 3. If you do not step forward, you will always be in the same place."

~ ~ ~

**Life from My Side**

**Wednesday 8/5/2020** – Did you ever notice how seeing someone else's point of view can enlarge your own life? That book I mentioned a couple of days ago, *Why We Sleep* by Matthew Walker, talks about the ways in which we contribute to the drastic problems facing our young people today.

How?

I'm glad you asked. He devotes a large segment of the book to the reasons why school start times contribute to traffic fatalities, substantially lowered reasoning ability, and almost non-existent good judgment on the part of teens. This isn't just his opinion. It's backed up with years of sleep studies and clinical trials.

His arguments are very convincing. The biological rhythms of people's sleep times (when they get sleepy and they're wakeful) vary during different periods of life. Teens, it turns out, have a much later "gotta go to sleep" time than adults. Consequently, their bodies are geared to a much later "gotta wake up" impulse. This is a biological imperative. Teens are not lazy. They have a different internal clock. <u>The final hours of sleep are the time when the brain processes reasoning ability.</u>

So what do we do to our teens? We wake them before their brains get that vital information and put them on school buses (or—worse yet—let them drive) in the pre-dawn hours so they can reach school in time for a ridiculously early first class.

Read the book. It's a totally different point of view. Then think twice before you call a teen lazy just because he can barely open his eyes at 6AM or she seems to be zoning out at 7AM.

### Rosalind Franklin's

**Thursday 8/6/2020** – The funny thing, which I found out only recently, is that Rosalind Franklin was working completely independently from Crick and Watson. Yes, those two men received a Nobel prize for their discovery of the helical structure of DNA, and Rosalind Franklin didn't, but only because she died before the award winners were named. Had she lived, she most likely would have received a Nobel prize as well for HER discovery of that same structure.

So this meme may be funny, but it's not accurate.

> scientist: "does everyone here know what Watson and Crick discovered?"
> me from back of room: "Rosalind Franklin's notes"

### Black Girls Code

**Friday 8/7/2020** – My son recently did an online presentation about the two years he's spent living in a retro-fitted van—the fun, the challenges, the sights, the goofs, as well as practical to-do lists (and don't-do lists). People who signed into Zoom to watch were encouraged to donate whatever amount they chose to give to the woman who hosted the event—and most of the proceeds went to an organization Eli chose called BlackGirlsCode.com. Here's the vision statement from their website:

> To increase the number of women of color in the digital space by empowering girls of color ages 7 to 17 to become innovators in STEM fields, leaders in their communities, and builders of their own futures through exposure to computer science and technology. To provide African-American youth with the skills to occupy some of the 1.4 million computing job openings expected to be available in the U.S. by 2020, and to train 1 million girls by 2040.

I'm proud of him for choosing to support such an effective group, one that takes concrete steps each day to increase the chances of girls in a highly competitive field.

# Fran Stewart

~ ~ ~

**Focus Too Hard**

**Saturday 8/8/2020** – My friend Kathy Pate gave me a cat toy last year. It's a squishy, bumpy little purple thingie with a lot of small holes in it and one big hole. The big hole is where the treats come out if you bat it around until the hole is pointed downward.

Fuzzy Britches will spend long minutes at a time sniffing the little holes. She can smell the treats inside. She pushes the thing around delicately, seldom managing to get it upside down so an elusive treat will fall out. Occasionally she's successful, but she hasn't quite figured out that a good solid POW on the side of the thing will send it careening across the floor dumping out goodies as it rotates.

The trouble is, cats do not learn by watching humans. I can bat the thing around all day long, but she never gets the concept. She keeps brushing it gently with her paw, enjoying the scent, enjoying the periodic (but maddeningly infrequent) treat expulsions.

Do you think she's focusing too hard on the problem?

Is that a lesson for us?

'Bye till Monday

If you focus too hard on the problem..

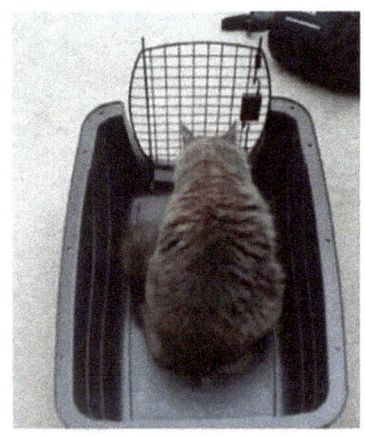

..the solution can often evade you.

~ ~ ~

**Moon Behind Pines**

**Monday 8/10/2020** – In the memoirs classes I teach, we talk quite a bit about just why our stories are important. They say a picture is worth a thousand words, and I can't disagree with that, but at the same time, a picture without words is simply a picture, to be interpreted a different way by each and every person who sees it.

If I show you this lovely photo of a full moon behind a stand of pine trees, you might be reminded of a quiet walk you took on a camping trip with your family when you were twelve, while I might recall the way my mother refused to let me have my curtains open at night. I've shared that story with you before, so I won't repeat it here.

Three days from now, if you and I looked at this same picture, you might remember a date you went on that turned out to be the most boring time imaginable—and the only thing that saved your sanity was the beauty of the moon that night. Three days from now, I'd recall a long pre-dawn walk I took last month when the full moon stopped me in my tracks. It was bright enough to cast a shadow, and I had one of those ah-ha moments when I realized that, no matter the differences between us, the shadows we cast are the same color.

So, the thousand words (the story) that a picture is worth depends entirely on who's looking at the picture and when they're looking at it. I'd really like it if we'd all get around to writing our stories. If you want help writing yours, check out franstewart dot com.

### Self-Propelled

**Tuesday 8/11/2020** – As I was taking my morning walk the other day, I noticed an errant passion-flower vine (also known as a maypop) in a neighbor's yard. Sure enough, a little farther on, there were some Gulf Fritillary butterflies hovering around someone else's front yard garden.

Those fluttery wings—orange and black on the top, silver and black on the undersides—reminded me of the time a number of years ago when the birds in my yard must have pooped out some maypop seeds. The maypop is the host plant for Gulf Fritillaries. I had the vines growing all over the place and ended up with more than two dozen chrysalises on the siding of my house. I know I've mentioned those chrysalises before in these posts, but it's such a lovely memory. Time to revisit it—and this picture brought it all back.

### Our Impact

**Wednesday 8/12/2020** – In getting these daily FB posts of mine ready for publication in print form, I came across a post from several years ago where I showed a picture of a waterfall and talked about the impact of splashes. Sometimes you can stand on the edge of a pool and feel the water drops from a distant fall – and sometimes the splash is so tiny that you can only see it from where you stand.

But the waterfall is still making its—well—its splash.

In that old post of mine, I talked about how I'd heard from people who had been affected by the social issues I talked about in my Biscuit McKee mysteries—and who thanked me for making information available so they could find information or help.

I made a splash. It feels good to know that.

Think about the splashes you make each day.

~ ~ ~

**Meet the Person**

**Thursday 8/13/2020** – Yesterday I talked about the impact we make on those around us. Today it makes sense to talk about personal responsibility.

Unlike yesterday's waterfall that flows out from us whether we're aware of it or not, the decisions we make each day—each moment, in fact—are like the banks of that river. They guide which way the water flows. Those banks are ours to care for. We can shore them up with good responsible actions and decisions, or we can let them run amok and be eaten away by the water that flows through our daily life.

Like all analogies, this one has its weaknesses. I know that. Still, I think the picture it draws is a pretty good one. When I step up to the mirror today, I'm going to see the person responsible for my life, every step I take, every bite I eat, every decision I make.

Let's start a movement, shall we?

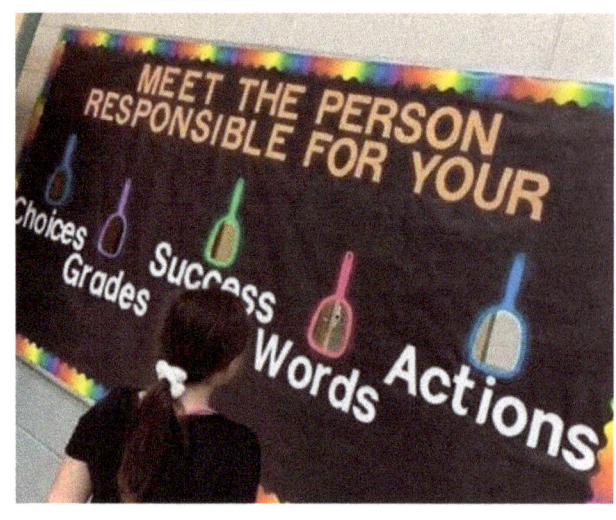

~ ~ ~

**Indoor Plant**

**Friday 8/14/2020** – Have I ever told you about my indoor plants? Or, rather, the lack of them?

I've found over the years that one of the troubles of having indoor cats is that they like to munch on foliage. And then they generally throw up the results.

My answer to this? Get rid of all the indoor plants.

That worked for a lot of years, but then I got a bit tired of not having greenery around the house. Still, I'd been very happy not to have to clean up partly-digested leaves, not to have to pick up dead fallen leaves, not to have to worry about under-watering or over-watering, and not to be responsible for the low-light, high-light, dappled-light requirements of multiple organisms.

But, there wasn't any green around (except for the living room carpet).

Here was my solution. It's not too prickly, but it's prickly enough to discourage munching. It takes one ounce (30 cc) of water just once a month. It sits happily on my sideboard. It grows steadily, but V-E-R-Y slowly. And it hasn't dropped a single leaf in the two years it's lived here.

My idea of the perfect indoor plant.

## Walkie Talkie

**Saturday 8/15/2020** – I don't know about you, but I could use one of these regular Saturday jokes right about now. I've been sending out sympathy cards—four losses in the past month of people I knew well.

But a neighbor brought me a freshly-picked tomato from her garden; another neighbor asked me for help gathering figs from her backyard (and let me take bags of them home with me); someone I haven't talked with since last year called for a catch-up chat. Also, the hummingbirds regularly buzz around my head before they perch on the feeder above the bench on my front porch; the local bookstore told me they're ordering more of my books because they're selling out of them; and Fuzzy Britches seems to have figured out how to get her cat treats out of the roll-around toy.

All in all, life is easy-peasy & happy-wappy. And I'm a lucky-ducky.

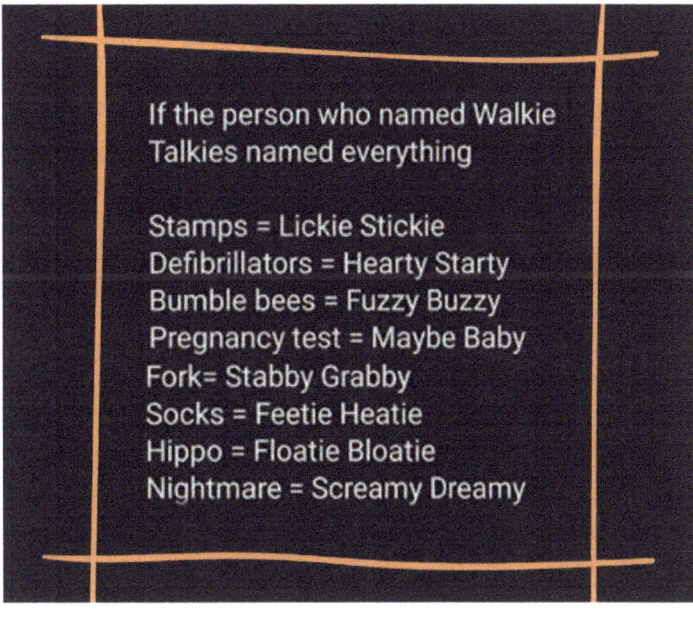

~ ~ ~

## Immigrants

**Monday 8/17/2020** – Last week I had the honor of listening to a virtual presentation by a woman who will remain anonymous—you'll see why after I explain.

She's from China. She's an artist, a very fine artist, and the first part of her Zoom talk focused on her artwork. I was blown away by the exquisite detail of her seascapes and the delicacy of her more traditional Chinese paintings on silk.

After she'd wowed us all with her creativity, she spoke about her family. She, her husband, and their small children live in the USA, but her extended family are still in China. She spoke about the constant repression of the Chinese government and mentioned that she was afraid the Chinese government might find a record of this presentation of hers. If they did, she said, they would take it out on her family still living in China since she was making negative comments about the Chinese government. The people hosting the Zoom talk decided not to make a recording of the event available to anyone.

She had spoken about China's one-child rule that went into effect in 1979. She spoke of the many abortions that relatives of hers were required to have in order to avoid having a second child.

Although the US-born listeners were appalled at the dictatorial nature of that law (and so was I), I did wonder about a disturbing parallel. That government chose to tell women that they could not have multiple children, even though in an agrarian society, multiple children are generally needed to work the land and to support the parents in their older years.

Here, we have a government that seems determined to tell women that they must have children they don't want, even if those children would be born into a life of poverty, even if they were conceived through rape, even if the mother wants to prevent bringing a child into a home where there is violence, even if bearing that child would sentence the mother to a constant conflict with her work responsibilities, even if the birth of the child would endanger the life of the mother, even if the child would be born with severe medical conditions.

When prohibition reigned in the US in the 20$^{th}$ century, organized crime blossomed, and practically nobody who wanted booze had to do without it, but a lot of people were blinded by rotgut. Nowadays, restrictive laws will not prevent abortions. It will prevent safe abortions among women who cannot afford to travel to obtain one. When will we learn that we cannot legislate morality?

Keep your laws off my body.

~ ~ ~

**Potato Harvest**

**Tuesday 8/18/2020** – Remember when I showed you my plastic trash can potato gardens? I started out with three. The deer ate one of the plants all the way to the ground. I moved them onto my fenced-in back deck; They all three withered from lack of sun. They all three died. There were no green shoots left.

The other day I decided to dump out the dirt—and look what I found!

Please don't laugh. My potato harvest may have been small. This isn't a dinner plate they're on—the largest potato is less than three inches long. Still, they grew even when their lifeblood—the green leaves above them—were slowly giving up. And they stayed nestled in the gentle soil just waiting for me to look below the surface.

I'm thinking there may be other areas in my life where I'll have to look below the surface impressions to find real value.

What about you? Any hidden treasures you've yet to find?

~ ~ ~

**Silly**

**Thursday 8/20/2020** – Maybe it was silly of me, but I sat down yesterday to write my usual post, and began to wonder if it even mattered. I also wondered if anyone would even notice.

The same way I've sometimes wondered how long it would take someone, anyone, to find my body if I fell down the stairs and croaked.

So, I waited until after 9AM, loaded my dead vacuum cleaner into the trunk, checked the website to be sure the repair place was still there ("Now open," it said, "from 9AM to 5PM"), and headed off to get the repair work ordered.

Got there and pulled into their parking area. Not only were they not open—they were GONE. As in nothing left inside the expansive front windows.

Talk about falling downstairs and having nobody notice. I have no idea when they stopped doing business. I've passed by the shop any number of times over the past few months, but my Dyson was working just fine. Didn't need to check on them until I REALLY needed to check on them.

So I drove home with my vacuum cleaner still in the trunk to find a message from someone asking if I was okay. "Haven't seen your post today," she told me. I guess somebody DID notice.

I called her and we had a great chat.

Even if my carpets are messy, life is good.

# Fran Stewart

*A few of the comments that came in response to this POST:*

**ELI:** Awwww, this is such a touching story. Love you so much, Mom!

**LINDA:** Yep, you're needed & wanted. Sorry about the Dyson. I finally gave up & got one a couple of years ago. Love that it gets the cat hair. Hope yours gets repaired.

**PETIE:** Missed you and look for you all the time! Hugs & kitty kisses!

**MELANIE:** Aww I love this Fran!

**LEA:** I went to your page looking for yesterday's post-three times! 🧡

**JONNINE:** Some of your posts are thought provoking. I enjoy your posts

**MARCIA:** Missed your post.

**KATHY:** I always enjoy your posts. 🧡

**DARLINE:** Miss you!

~ ~ ~

### Easiest Way

**Friday 8/21/2020** – Like many of us, I've found the time during the COVID lockdown to do a lot of sorting. Even after all the efforts I've made during the past number of years, I still have an awful lot of STUFF sitting around my house, in my drawers, and in my closets.

Now, though, I'm left in a quandary: what to do with it.

I'm not willing simply to throw away perfectly useable items. But to the best of my knowledge, consignment stores and thrift shops aren't accepting donations now. A garage sale is out of the question. I've thought about simply leaving things out on the curb, but with so much rain recently, that's not an option—and anyway, there's not much traffic in our quiet cul-de-sac.

So I'm keeping my stuff for now. Maybe I could just put it all in the guest/sewing room (since I have no guests and precious little reason to sew anything except face masks).

Hmmm … Something to think about.

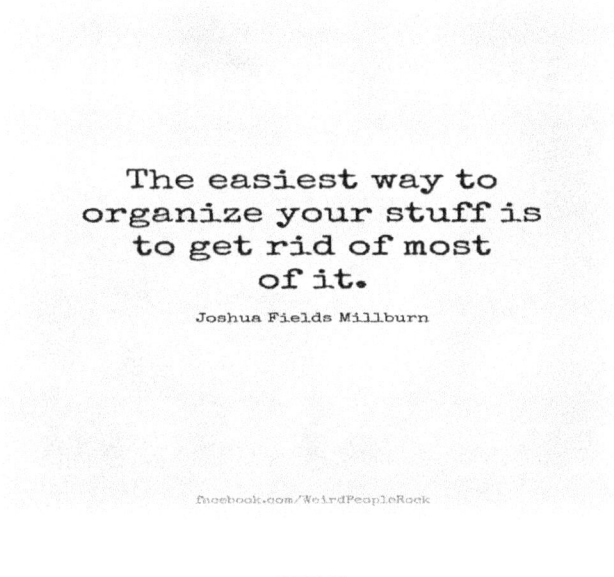

~ ~ ~

**Matching Socks**

**Saturday 8/22/2020** – Let's talk a bit about socks, shall we?

In one of my Biscuit McKee mysteries (I don't recall which one) I have Biscuit (the librarian) mention that she feels like she's in high fashion if her socks match her turtleneck. Talk about putting myself in my books!

A number of years ago, I went into Atlanta for a Board meeting at the Shakespeare Tavern, and found an acquaintance there who wore two different colored tennis shoes. One was bright orange and the other bright yellow. On top of that, she had on a bright yellow sock with the orange shoe and a bright orange sock with—you guessed it—the yellow shoe.

I loved the whimsy of it, but it seemed like way too much trouble to go to just to get dressed. Also, and more importantly I suppose, I don't have that many pairs of shoes.

I love Bombas socks, and I do splurge a bit to buy them, but all those colors they come in? Nope. I bought three pairs of white and three pairs of black. That's good enough for just about anything.

Maybe today, though, I'll put on one black one and one white one. Just for the whimsy of it.

p.s. You may remember, though, how happy I was when my daughter knitted me a pair of socks striped in shades of lavender/gray/purple. Love them! And wouldn't trade them for anything. They match, and go with just about every shirt I own.

~ ~ ~

**Sweet Autumn Clematis**

**Monday 8/24/2020** – Yesterday morning, just pre-dawn when I started taking my walk, I noticed a whiff of something wonderful, but couldn't place a name to the smell—until I came back down the hill. There was just barely enough light to see the cloud of white blossoms that had erupted overnight at the top of the Gingko Biloba tree. (And just barely enough light to take this picture.)

A couple of years ago, the Sweet Autumn Clematis I'd planted to serve as groundcover decided to go aerial, and I let it (not that I had much to say about the process).

As you may notice, the blossoms to the left of this photo have climbed even farther up into the Washington Hawthorne. At first, I mistook that lighter area as brightening sky behind the trees, but no—it's nothing but a mass of flowers.

Just then a downdraft brought the glory of the scent plummeting into the cul-de-sac, and the rest of my walk was doubly pleasant as a result.

Smelled anything wonderful lately? If not, do drop by for a (physically-distanced) visit.

~ ~ ~

**Relative Importance**

**Tuesday 8/25/2020** – What's important to you right now? Internet, obviously, since you're reading this post. I'm fairly dependent on it as well, particularly since I teach my memoirs classes entirely online now.

For me, sweatpants (which I pretty much live in now) are way higher than coffee (which I gave up completely after I read *Why We Sleep*. I remind myself of the early-morning news anchors who used to be said to go on-camera with ties and suit jackets on top and pajamas bottoms or shorts on their lower limbs where they couldn't be seen.

The car? I love my car. Even when it sits in the garage most of the time.

Shaving? Good grief. One of the lovely things about getting past menopause two decades ago was that hair stopped growing in those areas I used to shave regularly, so the pandemic made absolutely no difference to me on that front.

I wonder what we'll be considering important a year from now.

Sure do hope our democracy is still intact in 2021.

Fran Stewart

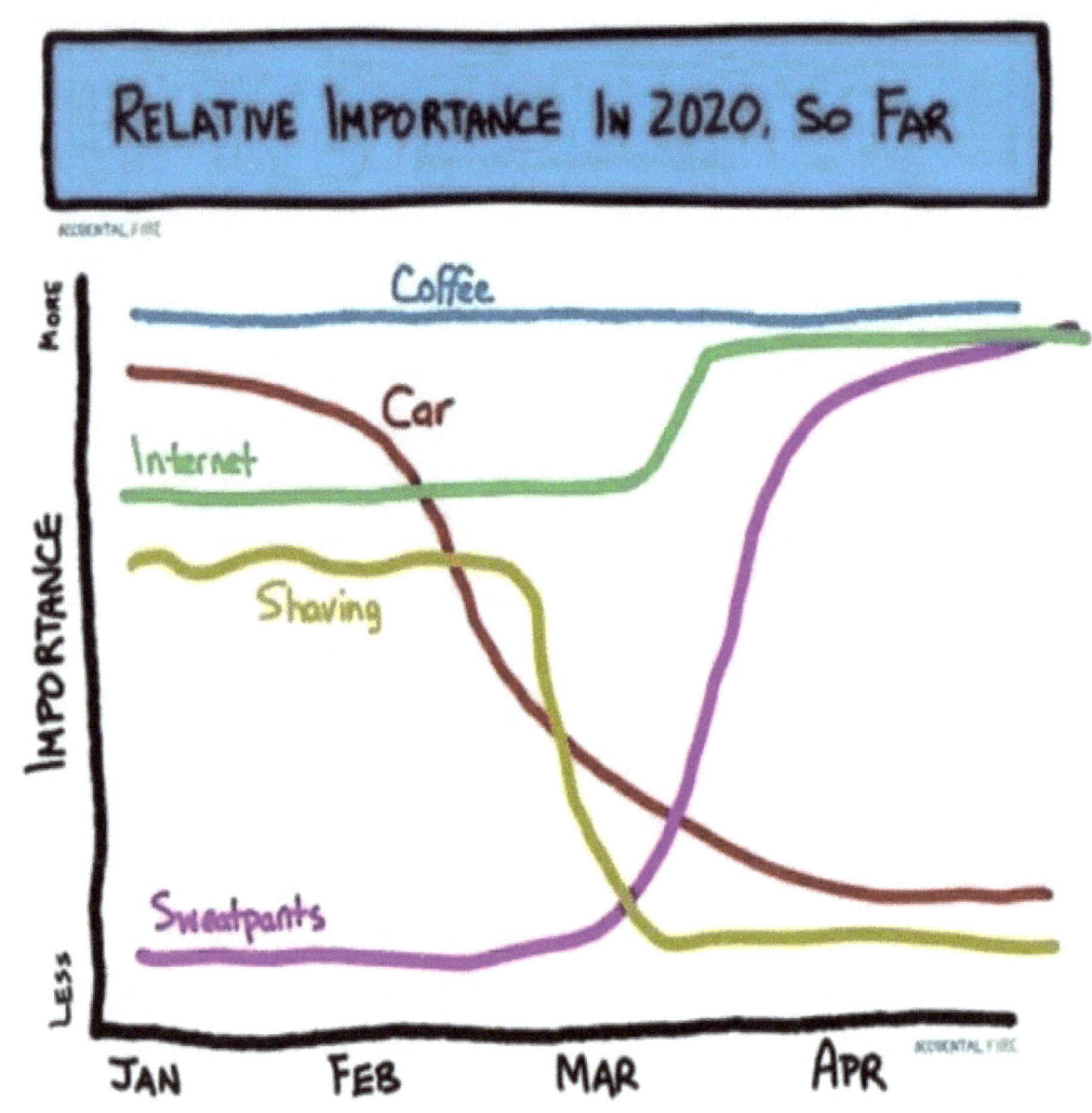

# September 2020

## Terra Rescue Eco Engines

**Wednesday 8/26/2020** – I'm always appalled when I drive through neighborhoods where every front yard is a flat green desert of wildlife-unfriendly grass. I shudder to think about all the wasted water, all the horrific weed-killers and pesticides, all the gas-guzzling lawn-mowing.

I'd like to recommend landscaping with groves of trees—not just one lonely isolated specimen.

It's something to think about.

~ ~ ~

## Stick Figures

**Thursday 8/27/2020** – This gives new meaning to the term "stick figures," wouldn't you say?

In all my not-very-artistic life, I've drawn exactly one stick figure that seemed to say something. I call it "Insouciance." It lives inside one of my kitchen cabinets, where it's attached to the door so I can chuckle every time I reach for a plate (or the catnip, which for some reason or other I keep next to the salad plates).

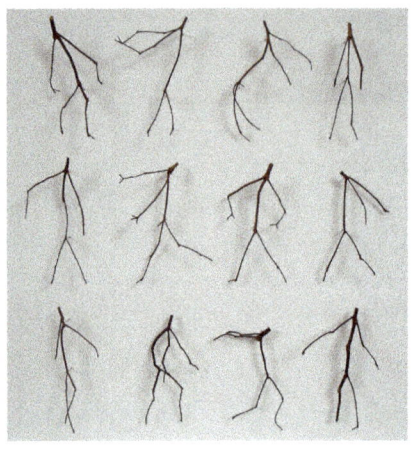 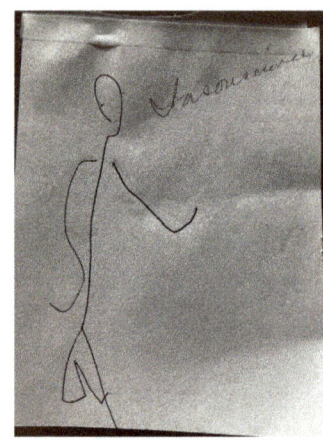

~ ~ ~

**Public Transport**

**Friday 8/28/2020** – I still remember the first time I ever used a bus. I'd enrolled in a summer school course that was held down in the middle of Colorado Springs at Palmer High School. We lived far beyond walking distance, so I had to take a bus. My mother had given me two nickels and a dime that morning—for fare going and returning, and for lunch. I hauled myself up the stairs and deposited my nickel. As I headed back to find a seat in the crowded vehicle, the driver called out to me: "Young lady, you owe another five cents!"

I wore a monochromatic outfit that day—most of my outfits were monochromatic—but I'm sure my bright red face more than made up for the lack of sartorial color.

Who would have guessed a bus ride cost as much as the lunch I wasn't able to buy that day?

> Time to remember the best
> voting advice I have heard -
> Voting isn't marriage -
> it's public transport.
> You are not waiting for "the one"
> who is absolutely perfect.
> You are getting the bus.
> And if there isn't one going
> exactly to your destination,
> you don't stay at home and sulk -
> you take the one going closest
> to where you want to be.

### Third from the Left

**Saturday 8/29/2020** – Here I go again, posting a photo I think I've already used before. (Isn't it amazing, by the way, to see what someone can do with Photoshop, adding a cat to a meerkat lineup?)

Did I already post this? I don't know. I'm the kind of person who seldom remembers the punchline of a joke. The good news is that every time I hear a repeat of the same old joke, I can laugh anew, because I've forgotten how it ends.

Reminds me of the time I went to re-read one of my earliest Biscuit McKee mysteries that a book club was reading—they'd invited me to attend via Skype—and although I remembered "whodunnit," I couldn't recall exactly how.

Wasn't it Sherlock Holmes who said he never bothered cluttering up his brain with information he was unlikely to need?

What do we choose to forget? Or what can we simply not remember?

p.s. Although I don't usually post on Sundays, I'll be sharing something with you tomorrow that I think you'll enjoy knowing.

### Today in history: Aug. 30

**Sunday 8/30/2020** – This gem from the CBC (that would be Canadian Broadcasting, in case you don't know):

> **1901:** British engineer Cecil Booth patented the first commercially produced vacuum cleaner. His gigantic creation was mounted on wheels and parked outside the houses being cleaned. One of its first jobs was to clean the aisle carpet of Westminster Abbey for the 1902 coronation of King Ed-

ward VII and Queen Alexandra. The King was so impressed that he ordered vacuum cleaners for both Buckingham Palace and Windsor Castle.

I must admit, I wonder if the vacuum cleaner was one of those machines invented by a woman but patented by a man.

I couldn't find a photo of the horse-drawn contraption—or rather, I found a number of pictures, but they weren't copyable. Search for "first vacuum" if you want to see it.

~ ~ ~

### Sleeping Later

**Monday 8/31/2020** – You may (or may not) have noticed that lately my posts don't show up as early in the day as they used to. That's because I used to get up at 4:30 every day.

It's amazing how much I could get written or otherwise accomplished before dawn. But life changed (or rather, I decided to change) when I read *Why We Sleep*, a book I've mentioned several times in these posts. Now. I'm going to bed slightly later and waking quite a bit later. Hence, the later posts.

Last night, though, as I lay in bed reading for a few minutes before turning out the light, watching the lightning flashes brightening the room, listening to the rain and the thunder, an enormous KA-BOOM practically lifted me off the mattress—and all the power in the cul-de-sac went out.

I'd already unplugged the computer, as I do anytime a thunderstorm arrives, but I went around the house with a flashlight to check. After all, years ago, some friends of mine had a fire in their house because of a lightning strike. All seemed to be well. But by the time I'd combed through all the rooms, there were bright lights outside, and a neighbor was texting me to ask if I was okay.

I could see a power truck just two doors up the street. Couldn't believe how quickly they'd gotten here. One of the workers was shining a light up the power pole at the edge of my property, so I went out to ask what was going on. "Lightning struck that pole up the street, ma'am. I'm just checking to be sure your pole is fine. We'll have the power back on shortly."

Okay. So I went and sat down on the front porch bench and watched the show. After all, I was WIDE awake by this time.

The truck finally left. A few minutes later, the power went on. I went upstairs, back to bed, and KA-BOOM. Closer, louder, scarier.

By the time I got back outside, the truck was back, this time snuggling up close to the pole in my yard.

Out I went into the rain, again. "Sorry about this, ma'am. When the power went back on, it blew your transformer. We'll have the power back on shortly."

Sit on the porch, watch the show, wait for the power. Turn out all the lights, Good night.

Thank you to the Jackson Electric linemen who were out in the pouring rain and who worked so efficiently. I truly appreciate you.

# Crystal Clear

~ ~ ~

**Closing the Book**

**Thursday 9/3/2020** – My sleep pattern, which I had so recently perfected (sort of), got screwed up with the lightning strike brouhaha Sunday night. Not only did I end up taking a LONG nap yesterday, I stayed up, like the person in this picture, way too late, reading. Then I woke up way too early and went back to the book for quite a while.

You know what, though? It's a really good book, so it was time well spent.

What was I reading?

I'm glad you asked. It's a book I've read before, but I thought I'd re-read it just for the fun of it. Let's see now, what's it called? Something with Pink in the title. Oh yeah, *Pink as a Peony* by—uh, somebody named Fran something-or-other.

## Fran Stewart

~ ~ ~

### What's Free?

**Friday 9/4/2020** – I love that old song, "The Best Things in Life are Free." In case you don't know it, here are the lyrics:

> The moon belongs to everyone;
> The best things in life are free.
> The stars belong to everyone;
> They gleam there for you and me.
> The flowers in spring, the robins that sing,
> The sunbeams that shine, they're yours, they're mine,
> And love can come to everyone.
> The best things in life are free.

Remember to add kindness to that list.

~ ~ ~

### Mathematical Limerick

**Saturday 9/5/2020** – Okay, folks. You know I love this sort of thing, so here's your Saturday chuckle. Go ahead, read it out loud as you follow the math.

A limerick:

$$\frac{12 + 144 + 20 + 3\sqrt{4}}{7} + (5 \times 11) = 9^2 + 0$$

Doesn't look like a limerick to you? Try this:

> A dozen, a gross, and a score
> Plus three times the square root of four
> Divided by seven
> Plus five times eleven
> Is nine squared and not a bit more.

~ ~ ~

**Muzzled Humans**

**Monday 9/7/2020** – Good dogs.

Wish everybody would learn from them.

Fran Stewart

~ ~ ~

### Freedom for Everyone

**Tuesday 9/8/2020** – I love this letter to the editor. After all, most everybody manages to survive food poisoning, right?

It's something to think about.

> **Freedom to not wear a mask**
>
> Welcome to the Freedom Cafe!
>
> We trust you to make your own choices if you want to wear a face mask. And, in the same spirit of individual liberty, we allow our staff to make their own choices about the safety procedures they prefer to follow as they prepare and serve your food.
>
> We encourage employees to wash their hands after using the bathroom, but understand that some people may be allergic to certain soaps or may simply prefer not to wash their hands. It is not our place to tell them what to do.
>
> We understand that you may be used to chicken that has been cooked to 165 degrees. We do have to respect that some of our cooks may have seen a meme or a YouTube video saying that 100 degrees is fine and we do not want to encroach on their beliefs.
>
> Some servers may wish to touch your food as they serve it. There is no reason that a healthy person with clean hands can't touch your food. We will take their word for it that they are healthy and clean.
>
> Water temperature and detergent are highly personal choices, and we allow our dishwashing team to decide how they'd prefer to wash the silverware you will put in your mouth.
>
> Some of you may get sick, but almost everyone survives food poisoning. We think you'll agree that it's a small price to pay for the sweet freedom of no one ever being told what to do – and especially not for the silly reason of keeping strangers healthy.
>
> Kathony Jerauld
> Amador City

~ ~ ~

**Not What We Bought**

**Wednesday 9/9/2020** – In the memoirs classes I teach, sometimes we talk about writing our own funeral service. You know, what would we like to have people read or sing or recite? Do we want coffin notes (little pieces of paper with messages each attendee writes), or would we rather keep it all very dignified?

That last option would NOT be my choice. I want a party!

Maybe I've mentioned this before, but I periodically think it might be a good idea to hold my wake before I'm dead. After all, it might be fun to hear what people think of me. I think, though, that we could consider such an event only if we truly thought our life had been of some benefit to others.

If you'd asked me thirty or forty years ago, I wouldn't have dared open up that can of you-know-what.

But now? I know I've tried a lot harder to live a life of some significance—not only to myself, but, more importantly, to others. I *have* built. I *have* shared.

So, in a couple of years, once this pandemic is over—would you like to come to my wake? And if you have one for yourself, I'd love to attend it. Be sure to let me know.

p.s. There are still a couple of spaces available for the memoirs class I'll be starting this coming Sunday (9/13 at 2PM eastern). If you'd like to begin telling the stories of your life, head to my website (franstewart dot com).

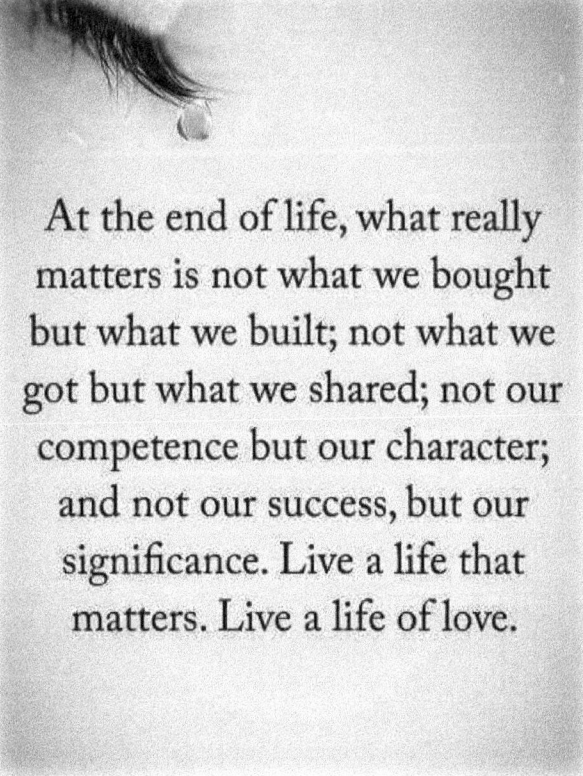

### Run Away from Home

**Thursday 9/10/2020** – With so many of us wanting to run away from home during this pandemic, here's the best way to do it without risking ourselves or compromising others.

It doesn't matter what your art form is. Twyla Tharp (whom I was fortunate enough to see perform at the Fox Theater in Atlanta a number of years ago) chose dance. You might choose music—whether you make a recording or simply sing in the shower. Your art of choice might be painting or sculpture or whittling or graphic design or doodling on an empty envelope. You might fiddle around with writing a novel or a treatise on ecology or—here's a thought—your memoirs.

If that last one is your choice, check out my website and sign up for a class to help you get started. The next class begins in three days.

### Remember

**Friday 9/11/2020** – I wonder if my parents ever felt sad that so many people seemed to have forgotten about December 7th.

One of the things I remember the most, though, about September 11th was the number of people who missed their ride, who were kept home by a sick child, who felt lousy enough to call in and take one of their sick days, who changed a meeting place or time at the last minute.

I remember the pain and the anguish, but I also remember the miracles.

~ ~ ~

**Move Over**

**Saturday 9/12/2020** – Saturday end-of-week giggle time.

Why do I generally try to post a giggle moment at the end of each week?

I'm glad you asked.

I truly do believe that laughter is a form of medicine. Some of the most positive people I've ever known have been ones who were able to laugh—not just at jokes, but at themselves. Think about it. Do you know people who are always ready to tell a joke at the expense of someone else? You don't think much of them, right? But the people whose funny stories revolve around their own all-too-obvious humanity are the ones who we think of as endearing (for the most part. This is certainly one of those sweeping generalizations that I usually despise).

The funny stories about things I've done or said that were highly embarrassing—I generally save those for my private journals or sometimes to tell the memoirs classes I teach. Some fine day far in the future my granddaughter will roll off her chair laughing when she reads them. Sorry, but you won't get that honor.

At any rate, I don't have a self-deprecating funny story to tell about myself this week, so I thought I'd depend on the leaning tower of Pisa to serve in my place.

Actually, the tower is a good replacement, since you'll notice that the lower you get on the tower, the wider it is. The extra COVID pounds perhaps? <<<sigh>>>

Can I take a picture of the moon?
Pisa Tower: yea sorry

~ ~ ~

**Rest in Peace, Wooly Bear**

**Sunday 9/13/2020** – Wooly Bear went over the Rainbow Bridge earlier this summer, but I simply couldn't face letting you know about it until now.

She brightened my life for a number of years, and I still feel her presence occasionally. I miss her bright eyes, her inquisitive personality, her leaps of joy, her boundless enthusiasm, and her loving snuggles.

~ ~ ~

**The Power of Friction**

**Monday 9/14/2020** – The power of friction. That's right I said *friction*, not *fiction*. And no, this isn't going to be a physics lesson—it's going to be a grammar lesson.

If you've been paying attention to these posts, you will have noted that I talk about puzzles every so often. I think I've probably mentioned them more since some of us (not enough of us) started self-isolating because of the COVID-19 pandemic.

That's because I've been reverting to them more often.

Just for the heck of it, I bought a bunch of puzzle books from Penny Dell Puzzles. One of them contains nothing but what they call "Quotefalls."

You can see how I've started to work on #3. Really, English only has just so many ways of combining letters into words when you have no more than 4 letter choices per column.

In #4, my first thought was that the first word was "TO," but it could just as easily be "IF." And the first word in the second line could be SHE, SOW, THE, or TOW, depending on what the rest of the sentence turns out to be. But—are you with me, here?—there aren't many English words that end in the letter "i," which is what would be left over if you used two of those four words on lines 2 and 4. That means the i has to go in the first line (IF).

And then the second word must be LAUGHTER: that's about the only thing that fits given the letter choices. Unless you think OULRGEN is a viable word …

So, our sentence, using the reasoning that says verbs fit in certain places and nouns in certain others, begins "If laughter were really the best medicine …" and so on. I'll leave it to you to figure out the rest of the quote.

And where, you may ask, does "friction" fit into all these meanderings of mine? Well, it doesn't, I guess. When I started writing this post, I must have had something in mind, but I obviously meandered off that path.

It's a puzzle. Have fun!

p.s. And yes, I generally use a pen rather than a pencil when I'm doing a puzzle.

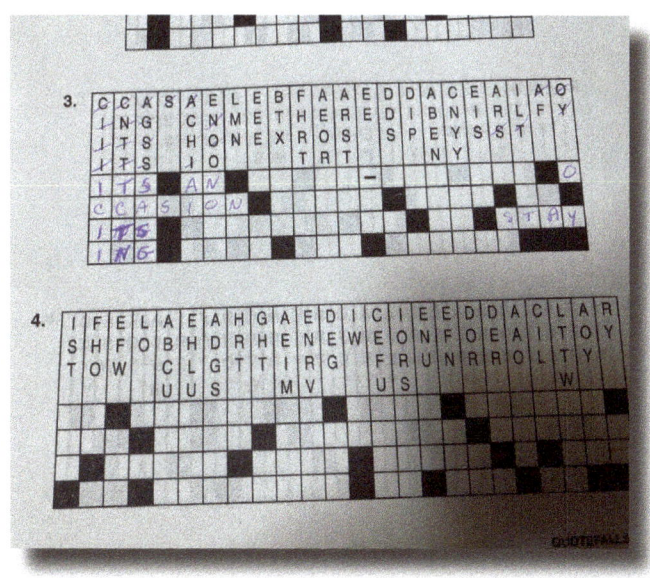

# Fran Stewart

~ ~ ~

## The Only Time

**Tuesday 9/15/2020** – There was only once in my life when I had one of those "glamour shots" taken. Back in June of 2018 I told you that someday I'd share it with you.

I'm not sure why that day is here, now, today. But it is.

I hardly remember who this person is anymore.

~ ~ ~

## The Emptier the Wagon

**Wednesday 9/16/2020** – This is definitely something to keep in mind. It rather reminds me of that line in the New Testament about clanging cymbals. I was talking with my son last week about the restrictions of living in a van (which he's been doing for more than two years), and he said that he will not buy or otherwise acquire any item at all unless he already has a place designated for it to "live" in his van.

When your square footage is severely limited, you have to think about such things.

Well, that sort of limitation applies to other things than just physical space—but it works the other way around. I try to choose carefully what I put into my mind and heart, not because those spaces are limited, but because they are limitless, and I want them chock full of only the finest thoughts, the highest emotions, the dearest connections. I want my mental and emotional wagon as full as it can be, even as I'm trying to pare down on the number of unnecessary "things" in my physical space. When I speak (or write) I want to do so softly and encouragingly.

What about you? If you're a regular reader of these posts of mine, I'd imagine that you never waste much time clanging, bragging, or belittling. What a great way to be.

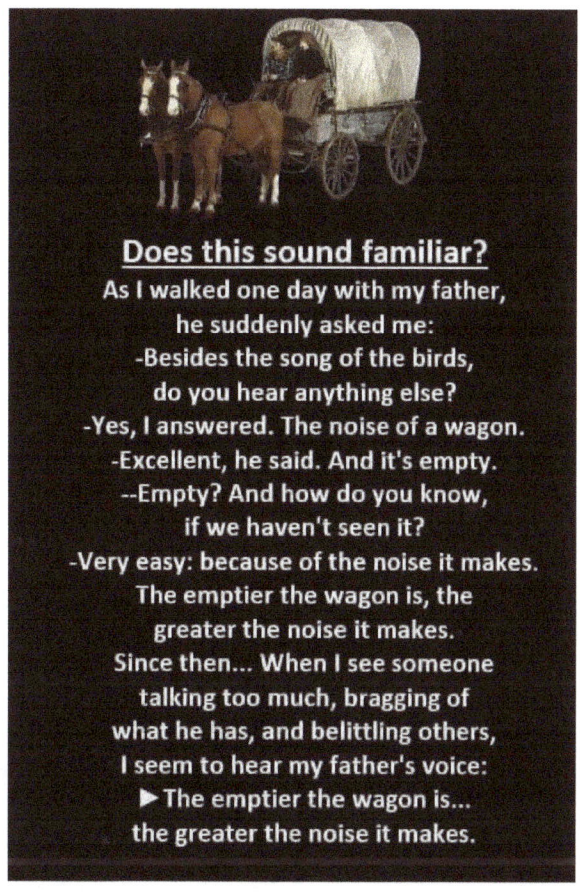

~ ~ ~

**Mirror**

**Thursday 9/17/2020** – I'd imagine that now, six months into the pandemic, most of us are looking for a change. But the little bird here is right. My outer circumstances may indeed change, but if I haven't looked within and changed what's in my mind and heart (see yesterday's post), then all the outer change—and all the individuals I may have wanted to "make me happy"—won't do a bit of good.

I need to think about this. What's the one thing I can do today to brighten my day? Maybe it means taking a step to brighten someone else's day. It's funny how the sunshine we spread spills over onto us. Maybe I could go a little farther on my morning walk—because doing something to help shed those extra pounds I've gained would certainly brighten my day.

Then again, maybe I'll make some fudge.

## Fran Stewart

~ ~ ~

### Closet Confessions

**Friday 9/18/2020** – There was one day last week when I decided all this self-isolating had to be good for something, so I decided that since Wooly Bear is no longer here to climb all over my various shelves, I could easily rearrange everything. Fuzzy Britches simply never ventures into my closet, so I didn't need to worry about that.

So, I took EVERYTHING (except for a hair clip or two) out and piled it all on my bed, cleaned thoroughly—Wooly Bear hair was all over the place—and then was too pooped to do anything else.

I slept downstairs that night.

What sort of projects have you gotten yourself into (but not out of)?

~ ~ ~

### Ruth Bader Ginsburg

**Saturday 9/19/2020** – I cried yesterday when I heard of RBG's death. She has been such a stalwart defender of humanity throughout her many years on the Supreme Court, and I have always held her as a role model.

The world is a drearier place without her. Once she was asked how many female justices there should be on the Supreme Court. Her answer: "Nine." She was right.

God help us through the next four months as the one-issue folks try to ram through a nomination.

I'm wearing my green RBG shirt as a sign of mourning today.

 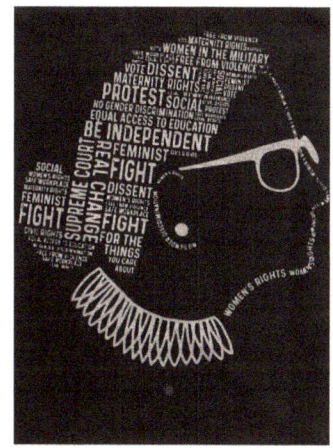

~ ~ ~

**I Will Not Remain Silent**

**Sunday 9/20/2020** – When Justice Scalia died in 2016, also an election year, Senate Leader Mitch McConnell refused to act on Obama's nomination of Judge Merrick Garland to fill the opening, saying it was too close to the election. The seat remained vacant until after Trump's surprising presidential victory in the electoral college (even though he hadn't received a majority of the popular vote). McConnell now says he will move to confirm a Trump nominee to replace Justice Ginsburg.

One of the men on Trump's short list recently recommended that the U.S. military be called out to quell protesters–and that they be allowed to shoot the protesters.

I am appalled at the lack of integrity in both our legislative and executive branches.

~ ~ ~

**Porch Frogs**

**Monday 9/21/2020** – Three or four years ago I had a crummy birdbath that teetered on a thin metal pole. One of the local free-roaming cats (NOT one of my indoor cats) decided to jump up on it, which bent the support pole and cracked the plastic bath bowl.

I set aside the bowl, pulled out the hopelessly messed-up pole, wondering why I'd ever bought such a chintzy thing to begin with, and went to buy a new one. That afternoon, it rained, and the plastic bowl ended up with a small amount of water in it, all the way up to the crack.

There was also a little frog in there.

A couple of days later the frog was gone, so I took the bird bath inside, sealed up the crack, let it air out for several days, then put it back outside with a rock in the middle to give birds something to perch on.

Rain. Full of water. Frog.

# Fran Stewart

Happy. Made me remember the nights I fell asleep as a child listening to the booming sounds of bullfrogs on my grandparents' farm. Of course, this isn't a bullfrog ...

Since then, I've regularly had frogs (usually only one at a time) find my little mini pond.

A couple of weeks ago there were three frogs in there, but when I stepped closer to take a picture, the two little ones jumped out into the weeds I let grow high around it (to camouflage it a bit and hopefully discourage the cat).

The next day, I stepped out onto the porch to fill the bird feeders, and somebody jumped away from my foot and landed next to a shriveled-up leaf. Thank goodness I hadn't stepped on her!

Do you love frogs as much as I do?

My niece Erica commented: Have I told you the story of Scott and me with the tadpoles? No? Well, Dad sent us out to the pasture to the windmill to clean out algae growing in the stock tank. We worked for an hour or so when we took a break and sat on the edge of the concrete.

There was mud all around with deeper pockets of water in the cow tracks. Gradually I noticed that the water was...moving. I pointed it out to Scott and told him to stick his hand in there to see what it was. After recoiling in horror he told me to stick MY hand in there. We compromised and got a shovel that we dipped in the mud hole and we came up with a BUNCH of tadpoles. Obviously we couldn't let them die!! But how were we to get them back to the farm?

I sent Scott back to the house for a bucket or something. While he was gone I finished cleaning the tank and assessed which puddles had tadpoles. He finally returned with a glass gallon jar. We filled it with our new friends and off we went to the corrals. There was another stock tank there where our little buddies would be safe.

A couple of days later we went to check but they were all gone.

About a month later it rained, and we stepped outside - a farmer thing - and we heard the frogs singing. Dad listened a moment and said, "Where'd those damned frogs come from?" Scott and I glanced at each other behind him and stayed quiet. And that glass jar? It was the one mom used to make sun tea. I washed it really well!

~ ~ ~

**Warning Signs**

**Tuesday 9/22/2020** – I posted this back on July 4th in 2019. I think it's time to post it again in case you didn't see it the first time—and in case you did see it but have just forgotten about it:

= = = = = = = = =

**7/4/2019** – I've been reading a number of documents lately, one of which has been an eye-opener.

In 2003, political scientist Dr. Lawrence Britt wrote an article called "Fascism Anyone?" It was published in the Spring 2003 issue of *Free Inquiry* (page 20). He studied the fascist regimes of Hitler (Germany), Mussolini (Italy), Franco (Spain), Suharto (Indonesia), and Pinochet (Chile), and found they all had 14 elements in common. He calls these the identifying characteristics of fascism. You may Google them, but I'd like to list them here in accordance with the Fair Use terms of the copyright laws.

The 14 characteristics or fascism (© 2003 *Free Inquiry magazine*) are:

1. **Powerful and Continuing Nationalism** Fascist regimes tend to make constant use of patriotic mottos, slogans, symbols, songs, and other paraphernalia. Flags are seen everywhere, as are flag symbols on clothing and in public displays.
2. **Disdain for the Recognition of Human Rights** Because of fear of enemies and the need for security, the people in fascist regimes are persuaded that human rights can be ignored in certain cases because of "need." The people tend to look the other way or even approve of torture, summary executions, assassinations, long incarcerations of prisoners, etc.
3. **Identification of Enemies/Scapegoats as a Unifying Cause** The people are rallied into a unifying patriotic frenzy over the need to eliminate a perceived common threat or foe: racial, ethnic or religious minorities; liberals; communists; socialists, terrorists, etc.
4. **Supremacy of the Military** Even when there are widespread domestic problems, the military is given a disproportionate amount of government funding, and the domestic agenda is neglected. Soldiers and military service are glamorized.
5. **Rampant Sexism** The governments of fascist nations tend to be almost exclusively male-dominated. Under fascist regimes, traditional gender roles are made more rigid. Opposition to abortion is high, as is homophobia and anti-gay legislation and national policy.
6. **Controlled Mass Media** Sometimes [the] media is directly controlled by the government, but in other cases, the media is indirectly controlled by government regulation, or sympathetic media spokespeople and executives. Censorship, especially in wartime, is very common. [**2020 Note:** The press (as in freedom of the press) is the only industry directly mentioned in the Constitution.]
7. **Obsession with National Security** Fear is used as a motivational tool by the government over the masses.
8. **Religion and Government are Intertwined** Governments in fascist nations tend to use the most common religion in the nation as a tool to manipulate public opinion. Religious rhetoric and terminology is common from government leaders, even when the major tenets of the religion are diametrically opposed to the government's policies or actions.

9. **Corporate Power is Protected** The industrial and business aristocracy of a fascist nation often are the ones who put the government leaders into power, creating a mutually beneficial business/government relationship and power elite.
10. **Labor Power is Suppressed** Because the organizing power of labor is the only real threat to a fascist government, labor unions are either eliminated entirely, or are severely suppressed.
11. **Disdain for Intellectuals and the Arts** Fascist nations tend to promote and tolerate open hostility to higher education, and academia. It is not uncommon for professors and other academics to be censored or even arrested. Free expression in the arts is openly attacked, and governments often refuse to fund the arts.
12. **Obsession with Crime and Punishment** Under fascist regimes, the police are given almost limitless power to enforce laws. The people are often willing to overlook police abuses and even forego civil liberties in the name of patriotism. There is often a national police force with virtually unlimited power in fascist nations.
13. **Rampant Cronyism and Corruption** Fascist regimes almost always are governed by groups of friends and associates who appoint each other to government positions and use governmental power and authority to protect their friends from accountability. It is not uncommon in fascist regimes for national resources and even treasures to be appropriated or even outright stolen by government leaders.
14. **Fraudulent Elections** Sometimes elections in fascist nations are a complete sham. Other times elections are manipulated by smear campaigns against or even assassination of opposition candidates, use of legislation to control voting numbers or political district boundaries, and manipulation of the media. Fascist nations also typically use their judiciaries to manipulate or control elections.

Copyright © 2003 *Free Inquiry magazine* Reprinted for Fair Use Only.

If you don't know what "fair use" means, I suggest you Google it.

= = = = = = = = =

~ ~ ~

**Why Ships Sink**

**Wednesday 9/23/2020** – Almost two years ago (January 7, 2019), I posted this photo along with a quotation from Archimedes.

Today, with the pandemic still in full swing, I think this saying is particularly apt and appropriate for a repeat.

Recently I've spoken with several friends about the things that we miss the most. Lunch with friends, yes. Long talks and walks with friends, yes. Casual encounters at almost any time of the day, yes. But what I miss most is the hugs.

My son told me during a phone call this past week that he's touched only four other people in the last three months. That got me to thinking. In the past six and a half months, since March 13th, I have not touched a single other human being. During that same time only five people have touched me (and they were all wearing gloves and masks and face shields): my hygienist, my dentist, my eye doctor, my cardiologist, and the nurse who hooked me up for an EKG.

Still, I haven't let that loss—it IS a real loss as far as I'm concerned—get inside me and weigh me down. Instead, I'm buoyed up by the caring concern of folks who've reached out through emails, messaging, Zoom, FaceTime, phone calls, comments on these posts of mine, and (gasp!) letters. I'm also buoyed up by the times I've reached out to others through those same channels.

I hope I never again take a casual touch on the arm or shoulder for granted.

P.S. This doesn't exactly apply, but it has to do with water:

> Ginsburg wrote memorably in 2013 that the court's decision to cut out a key part of the federal law that had ensured the voting rights of Black people, Hispanics and other minorities was "like throwing away your umbrella in a rainstorm because you are not getting wet."

**Comment from Susan Derderian:**

Dear Fran, you have made me cry. You put into words what I have been thinking: that in the last 3 months, I have hugged my son only twice: Mother's Day & my birthday (which also came with a kiss on the cheek). And we live in the same house. Touch is SO important. It has caused me to despise this pandemic in waves. 😢😢😢 But!!! We can still "touch" each other in words & gestures & video chats & phone calls. We WILL beat this thing. 🙏🙏🙏 Stay safe, plz.

~ ~ ~

### Hugo and Pavarotti

**Thursday 9/24/2020** – I used to have a cat that loved music, especially the sweeping intricacies of Rimski-Korsakov. He'd snuggle up to the radio. He was sweetly non-judgmental when I played the piano, too, for he'd either put his head against the sounding board next to the pedals, or he'd jump into my lap and rest his chin on the keyboard.

He adopted me when his person moved to Asia for a year. Naturally, I changed his name to Rimski.

That's why I'm a sucker for videos of animals listening to music.

Like this one of a dog in Cork named Hugo. If you want to check out his duet, do a search for *dog reaction to Pavarotti*. It's priceless.

~ ~ ~

### Eli's View of the Oregon Fires

**Friday 9/25/2020** – When I first looked at this photo from my son last week, I thought it was a sunrise over a foggy mountain.

But it wasn't. This is his view of one of the Oregon forest fires.

He's safe, thank goodness, and in his moveable house (his van) he's been able to skirt the wildfires throughout his travels through California, Oregon, and Washington. He has a phone app that gives him up-to-the minute info on where the fires are, so he can avoid them.

Wherever you are as you read this, please stay safe.

Crystal Clear

*Photo Credit: Eli Reiman*

**From Eli's FB page on 2/24/2020:**

WHY I LOVE VANLIFE:

A friend asked this recently, so here are my thoughts... Van life is the haiku of living. It requires efficiency and precision, and out of the profound constraints, great creativity can blossom. Having lived in a large and expensive house, I remember endlessly searching for things, digging thru piles of detritus, and often buying another of something simply because I could not find it. Now I know exactly what I have, and where each thing lives, and can find things in the dark with my eyes closed. The space constraints of 72sqft force me to consciously consider every single thing which I purchase, as it requires a home, and may require getting rid of something. I reminisce in embarrassment about my Amazon addiction and relentless gluttonous purchasing, which I am happy to have ended cold turkey. I feel good generating less trash.

In the realm of resources, vanlife is my form of activism. I am (mostly) self contained, and have enough solar for my minimal needs and thus no power bill. My propane bill is less than $10 per month, and have a similar water bill for drinking and showering (less than 1 gallon per shower). I have a composting toilet, thus waste no water there either. Since I carry all my water by hand, I have learned to be extremely efficient in how I wash my dishes. I think the world would be better off if we all had similar constraints.

I love that I have been able to purchase my home and am debt free. This would not have been possible for me when I was living in the bay.

There is a certain joy and confidence which comes from having built my house with my own hands and completely understanding it down to the last screw, and knowing that if something breaks, that I can fix it again.

My friends and family are distributed around the country, so I have the flexibility to spend quality time with them on a regular basis, especially my parents, to whom I have made a commitment to spend more frequent and higher quality time with.

In the realm of adventure and exploration, vanlife suits my passions, as I have two paddleboards on my roof, and have paddled many of the lakes and rivers all across the country and have surfed from Florida to Washington. One of the aspects which I like best is that it affords me a slower pace of exploration. I am in no rush, and thus can visit all of the out of the way places neglected by most travelers who want to check

# Fran Stewart

the big highlights off their list. I have carved out enough space for my other hobbies like slack lining, scuba, and OneWheeling, and even have a space for my 88-key weighted keyboard.

And as we continue to move further into uncharted territory of environmental devastation, I am so glad to have the flexibility and security that arises from having a solid reliable 4WD fortress where I can move away from wildfires and hurricanes and other environmental pressures.

Finally, this is such an incredible country, and planet, which we inhabit. In the same way that I have witnessed the global coral reefs die off during my 17-year diving career, I envision that many more natural wonders will be destroyed by our incompetence and unwillingness to change. So I want to try to visit as many of them as I can, and document them and share their majesty with all who will listen in hopes that they will be inspired to help preserve them.

I could go on at length, but will stop there. Thanks for listening!

~ ~ ~

**If You Leave**

**Saturday 9/26/2020** – Here's your Saturday chuckle.

Isn't it amazing the difference one little letter can make?

~ ~ ~

**A Sunday Sort of Thought**

**Sunday 9/27/2020** – I know. I know. I don't usually post on Sundays, but this thought came to me yesterday as I was going through my old FB posts to get them ready for print publication.

More than a year ago, I quoted this poem, which is attributed to Carol Coombs, in a post about the myth of being too busy.

> "Importance"
> I've mending I must do, and beds to make.
> I should not sit and watch the red sun set
> Behind the hills of afternoon, nor take
> This time to dream when I have work. And yet
> Supposing that I go at duty's call
> To make the beds and sweep the floors? What then?
> These things have no real value after all.
> Tomorrow they must all be done again.
> I have too many of such tasks to do.
> Therefore, I shall forget them, every one.
> And I shall sit and feel the rising dew
> And watch the haze around the setting sun.
> And I may find time for the housework too,
> When this, the more important thing, is done.

I remember discussing the poem once with my sister, Diana. In doing so, I made the big mistake of referring to the Mary and Martha story from somewhere in the New Testament. Diana got her britches twisted royally.

"Mary may have been admirable in a lot of ways," she said, "but nobody would have been fed, and nobody would have had clean clothes or a place to sleep if Martha hadn't taken on the responsibility of doing the housework, the cooking, and all the rest. It's so easy for people to sit back and philosophize while the rest of us do the work to keep the world going."

It's something to think about. Now, copy this link: https://www.youtube.com/watch?v=Xcwi4Z104UI

## Hurricane Side Effects

**Monday 9/28/2020** – When the tail end of Hurricane Sally came through the Atlanta area a couple of weeks ago, the ground got so soggy from the drenching rain that one of my birdfeeder poles began to list dangerously.

Luckily for me, I was able to wait for the rain to change from a downpour to a regular-pour before I went out to reset the pole. I still got wet, but not quite drenched the way I would have been if I'd braved the storm earlier.

Here are the before and after pictures. Can you see the cardinal sitting in the nearby tree wondering what the heck happened to his peanut feeder—and the tufted titmouse in the second photo peeking from behind the squirrel baffle asking if it's okay to come out now. I'd appreciate it if you'd ignore the highly invasive Japanese Stiltgrass that has taken over that side of my yard.

p.s. You may want to skip my post tomorrow if you have arachnophobia. I plan to post photos of a couple of gorgeous spiders in my back yard.

## Golden Orb Beauties

**Tuesday 9/29/2020** – Well, I couldn't get a well-enough focused photo to show you the two marvels in my back yard, so I imported a couple of pics and some info from the Internet, but they don't even begin to show the brilliant metallic-looking gold of the dots on the spiders' bodies.

# Crystal Clear

The two in my backyard have constructed closely spaced webs. Talk about community cooperation, here and there the webs are actually interwoven. The supporting strands reach from my back deck to a tree that's a good 8 or 10 feet away, and the strands of the web are golden. Such a lovely sight.

I need names for these two and am open to suggestions. "Goldie" is already taken for a spider in the yard of a friend of mine.

In these two photos, by the way, you can see the much smaller, brownish males. My beauties, too, have a couple of those males on their webs. I go out and check on them every morning (and on various other occasions during the day). It's almost as good as when I had those two beehives on my deck. Only trouble is—these spiders don't buzz.

Hello there!
I know I am a **BIG SPIDER**, and I look scary, but I am very beneficial!

I am an *Argiope aurantia*, or a Golden Orb Weaver. **My bite is not dangerous** and I like to build nice visible webs since I'm primarily daytime active. I will even shake my web at you to make it extra obvious if you get too close! **I eat aphids, flies, wasps, mosquitos and many other harmful bugs.** So please don't kill me. We may not ever truly be friends, but I will help out around the garden if you let me stay there.

Fran Stewart

~ ~ ~

**Cupidity Magnified**

**Wednesday 9/30/2020** – Last Sunday, I listened to one of the video essays that Beau of the Fifth Column puts out each day in which he pointed out the stupidity and greed of the Florida governor's decision to open the state without any COVID restrictions. Beau lives in Florida, by the way, so he has all the more reason to be concerned about this.

I was particularly struck by one of his (satiric) comments that went something like this:

> It's quite all right. We'll be safe here in Florida. After all, most people only visit for a week. They'll mingle in all our packed restaurants and tourist attractions, and then they'll go home and get really sick there, and overload their own states' healthcare systems.

In other words, "My end just rose 200 feet."

Whether you're talking about climate change or about COVID, are those 200 feet really that reassuring?

*When people say climate change isn't happening because it's snowing where they are...*

**THE SHIP CAN'T BE SINKING**

**MY END JUST ROSE 200 FEET**

# October 2020

## "Because We Don't …"

**Thursday 10/1/2020** – This makes me happy that I never go to these places.

This makes me sad that so many people whom we consider to be essential (after all, they're cooking and serving our food, right?) are without essential health care.

p.s. If you pay any attention to the times of day that I post these daily musings, you may have noticed that my schedule is completely askew. Why? I have no idea. Thank goodness nobody has to use me to set their internal clock, because I'm not too dependable a model nowadays.

~ ~ ~

## Chess Skills

**Friday 10/2/2020** – I'm certainly no expert at chess, but three things come to mind when I look at this artistic chess board:

> 1. I should think it would take a lot more brain power to play here than on a regular board,
>
> 2. The players will probably have to stand up to make some of their moves, and
>
> 3. Whoever set up the pieces didn't know that the queen is always supposed to stand on her own color.

p.s. For those of you who are interested, the winners of the "Name the Spiders" contest are Lea McClellan Ray ("Legs") and Marcia Dunscomb ("Ora"). I'm sure these two beauties appreciate the names (and so do the spiders!)

~ ~ ~

**Old Lang Sign**

**Saturday 10/3/2020** – Should aulde acquaintance be forgot …

Maybe I should have saved this for New Year's Eve, but it was too good to pass up.

~ ~ ~

### Relativity

**Monday 10/5/2020** – I'm in just about 100% agreement with this little graph.

If you delete shaving altogether and substitute herbal tea for coffee, you'll see what my life is like—especially the sweatpants.

And to think I bought a Tesla last December just so I could travel around the country visiting friends and family. Best-laid plans, eh? [**And an added note:** In preparing these posts for print publication, I realize I used this same chart back in August. Thanks for being patient with such repetitions.]

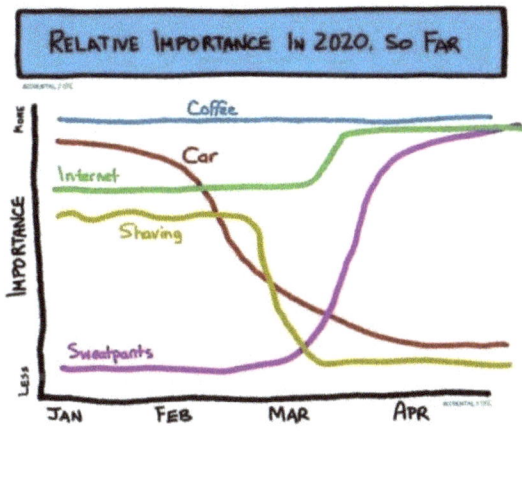

~ ~ ~

### Relative Sizes

**Tuesday 10/6/2020** – While we're talking about relativity, exactly nine years ago, I posted the following little essay on my beekeeping blog, and I thought it was still particularly apt. So here it is. (And if you'd like to read all those essays, you might want to head to my website https://www.franstewart.com/books to find them easily assembled in print form. This essay is from *BeesKnees #4*.)

### Day #359 Earth to Antares

Someone sent me one of *those* emails recently. You know the ones I mean. They're characterized by multiple exclamation points, ENORMOUS fonts, usually in a bolded CAPITALIZED bright red, along with a *shake-your-finger-in-my-face* narrative that tells me:

> how little I understand,
> how little I can think for myself,
> how ungrateful I am for all the riches life offers,
> and what horrible things will happen if I don't forward the message immediately.

# Fran Stewart

I hate those emails.

Every once in a while, though, one shows up that has something interesting in it. And I steal those ideas for my blog.

The email I have in mind had this series of pictures of various sized balls. The first shows a teeny Pluto, a slightly larger Mercury, a bigger Mars, a still larger Venus, and a great big Earth.

In the next picture, Earth is dwarfed by Neptune, and the sizes moved progressively up through Uranus and Saturn to an enormous Jupiter.

In the 3rd picture, Jupiter is miniscule compared to the Sun.

In the 4th, the sun, Sirius, and Pollux, each in greatly increasing sizes, are nevertheless insignificant when compared to Arcturus.

# Crystal Clear

And of course, Arcturus isn't even a 100th the size of Betelgeuse, which is about half the diameter of Antares.

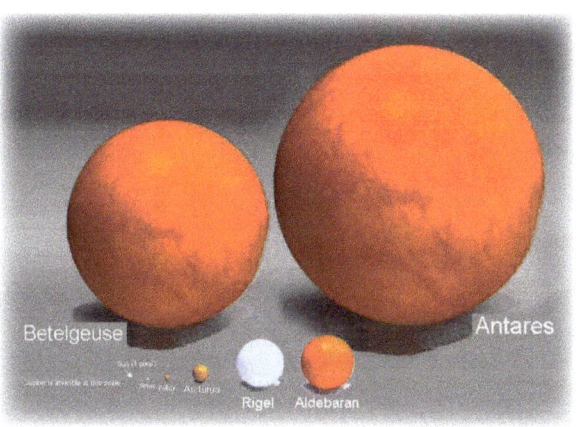

Antares, incidentally, is more than a thousand light years away from earth, barely a hairsbreadth away when one considers the limitless span of the Universe.

The email ended by telling me that I ought to feel horribly humble in the face of all this HUGENESS (that's my word, not the email's).

On the other hand, miniscule fleas caused the Plague that devastated Europe, killing the major bulk of the population, and the great big people were powerless to do anything about it.

People may be able to grow to be six or seven feet in height, while a honeybee never reaches much more than about half an inch or so, yet the honeybee is responsible for pollinating 1/3 of our food products. Without all those teeny bees, we'd be in deep doo-doo.

Relative size has very little to do with relative importance. I think we all have our role to fill, whether we are a bee, a planet, a star, or a person who sends emails. And it is *what we do with our lives here and now* that gives us value—not how little we are, or how big either.

**BeeAttitude for Day #359:** *Blessed are those who take themselves with a grain of salt, for they shall enjoy a flavorful life.*

# Fran Stewart

~ ~ ~

## Social Dilemma

**Wednesday 10/7/2020** – I'm giving you advanced warning. December 31st of this year will be the last day I post anything on this author page. At the end of that day I plan to deactivate my Facebook account.

Why?

I'm glad you asked.

My daughter suggested that I watch the Netflix documentary, *The Social Dilemma.* In case you haven't heard about it, it features people who founded or helped to expand Facebook, Pinterest, Google, Uber, Twitter, and a number of other social media giants. These men and women all say that their intentions to begin with were good—to bring the world together, to allow easy dissemination of vital information. https://www.thesocialdilemma.com

It didn't work out that way. None of these people allow their children to have cell phones. All of them restrict their children's access to so-called social media. For very good reasons.

I've decided to take my online time back into my own hands.

In the interest of fairness, I'll say that Facebook responded quickly to the accusations in the documentary, saying basically that these were a lot of disaffected folks who were no longer on "the inside."

Still, I think the evidence as presented in *The Social Dilemma* is compelling.

Why not end my FB association right now, today? Well, I'm a writer. I like tidy endings, and the final day of 2020 seems like a good time to wrap this up.

I'll miss you. I'll miss your comments. My son assures me that I'll still be able to receive your messages through Messenger. But, just in case that doesn't work, you can always reach me through the contact page on my website. Leave me your comment and your email address there and I'll email you. I think we could have a better conversation that way than through the little comment boxes on FB. If you're someone who has commented often (I know who you are), we could even have some Zoom conversations.

I may have mentioned before that I'm in the process of putting my FB author page posts into book format. I'll warn you ahead of time: because of the format (8½ by 11, full color with ALL those photos) the books will be expensive—but I'm doing it primarily for my children and grandchildren, so they'll have this legacy after I'm gone.

There will be three volumes (2015-2018 / 2019 / 2020). If you want to know more about them, go to my website and sign up for my newsletter.

For now, though, I still have 72 more posts to look forward to (and maybe a few more if I do an occasional Sunday posting).

I truly appreciate you and wish you well.

# Crystal Clear

~ ~ ~

### Grandma's Diaries

**Thursday 10/8/2020** – I'm in the process of reading the transcripts of my grandmother's diaries that were gifted to me years ago by my Aunt Mary Nell. I've skimmed through them before, especially when I was writing the final four books of my Biscuit McKee mystery series. But I never really *read* them.

Well, now I'm making up for that disservice. After all, I'm teaching online courses about how to write your memoirs—the stories of your life.

One of the things I stress in those classes is the importance of including details. You know what you're writing about, but a hundred years from now, your grandchildren and great-grandchildren won't have a clue.

Consider this entry from 1916, where Grandma says, "An old woman came by."

Huh????? What old woman. How old? What did she say? Why did she appear? How did you treat her? Did you learn anything from her? Did you ever think of her again? Was she selling something? Was she a hobo? Did you have a conversation with her?

And a few lines down from that—"Grand Pa Harrison died Tuesday." What was his impact on your life? Did you like him or loathe him? Did you know any good juicy stories about him? Did he ever make a difference in your life? If so, what was it?

I have to acknowledge that I admire my grandmother for having had the discipline to write every single day year after year, despite the rigors of her life as a farm wife in the early 20th century. She quit writing in her diaries after her third child died. I can't say I blame her, as I can imagine how the light must have gone out of her life as she struggled to care for her remaining children—and to birth another child just a few months after the death of the third. I only wish she'd thought it would be a good idea to tell me more of her thoughts. And tell me about that old woman!

```
                        ...ie & children called t

3    I went to the W.O.W.C. this PM at Mrs Gooch
Campbell called this PM. We picked 2 gallons of scu
PM. I finished up one pillow case.

4    Mr Burns wife & 2 children called this PM. Worke
case this PM, also picked 2 gallons of scuppernong
this AM. An old woman came by.

5    I went down to Papa's today. He came after me. I
of preserves, 3 glasses of jellie, canned 2 quarts o
and made part of my gown. Grand Pa Harrison died Tue
Avice has a big boy, he arrived yesterday.

                ...taken dinner here today. Ossie & Stewa
```

# Fran Stewart

~ ~ ~

## Labyrinths

**Friday 10/9/2020** – [78 more days until the end of these posts. If you don't know what I'm talking about, go back 2 days and read that post.]

There's a big difference between a maze (that you can get lost in) and a labyrinth (where getting lost is impossible but patience is an asset).

Almost twenty years ago I was faced with a medical issue that doctors said required surgery. I didn't want to go through that. I spent months (all the while getting more and more uncomfortable with my body), dithering around—do I or don't I? Should I or shouldn't I? What if I do, what if I don't? What if? What if? What if?

I finally found a book with a listing for the Avila Retreat Center in North Carolina. Called them (these were the days before much internet involvement) and made a reservation. One of the drawing points for me had been that they encouraged silence. It wasn't an absolute rule, but it was requested of guests in order to preserve what I began to think of as the "thought space" for each person there.

The evening of the first day I wandered out through one of the gardens and found a labyrinth they had installed just the year before—a steppingstone path that spiraled inward to the center and then out along a similar spiral.

I walked it once, inward and outward. I walked it again, inward and outward. By that time the light had faded, but as I took the final step out of the labyrinth, I noticed a weed growing beside the last steppingstone, so I bent and pulled it.

The next morning, I was out there again, this time on my hands and knees, weeding as I went. By the end of my three-day stay, my knees were sore, but the labyrinth was completely weeded, and the worry-weeds were cleared from my mind.

I drove home and scheduled the surgery.

I'm glad I did.

All that's left of Avila now is this sweatshirt and my memories. The property was sold a couple of years ago. I hope the current owners or developers kept the labyrinth.

~ ~ ~

**One Night Stand**

**Saturday 10/10/2020** – It's Saturday laugh time. I love this type of play on words. Sightly naughty and absolutely delicious!

### *Le Refuge* in Yellowknife, Quebec

**Sunday 10/11/2020** – Since I have only two and a half more months of these posts to do, I'll probably be posting more often on Sundays, just to extend the fun a bit.

I love CBC News, as I'm sure you realize if you've followed me for any length of time.

Here's a story about a woman who saw an abandoned 5,000-square-foot parking lot and envisioned a chance to feed her community. It took almost 30 tons of soil to cover the lot, but she now has a thriving farm.

What an inspiration! I wonder if the yards of abandoned houses in failing neighborhoods could be transformed into urban neighborhood gardens.

If you want to try a search for this article, use "Parking Lot to Farmland." That should get you there.

~ ~ ~

**Never Too Many – A Kinder World**

**Monday 10/12/2020** – We can never have too many hugs. Now, while hugging (except within symptom-free families) isn't safe, I'm turning to Fuzzy Britches more and more. I don't have chickens or a friendly fish or a pig or an elephant, but I can always watch this video, smile, and feel the hugs.

*To find the video, search for "kinder world share the love"*

~ ~ ~

**Structure**

**Tuesday 10/13/2020** – Back in June of 2019, I posted the poem "*The Chambered Nautilus*" by Oliver Wendell Holmes, Sr., along with some musings about my seventh-grade English teacher. As I was re-reading those 2019 posts, getting ready to publish them in book format, I read the poem to myself out loud and was struck by the meter—which I'd never paid much attention to before.

The first line of each stanza is five stressed beats long; the second and third lines have three main beats each. Then five, five, three, and a final line that is six beats long. He also used a rhyme scheme of a, a, b, b, b, c, c for each stanza.

Can you appreciate the discipline needed to craft words into such a pattern without having them end up sounding forced? When I wrote my award-winning poem *Resolution*, I used a pattern of 3, 3, 5, 9 for each stanza. I didn't rhyme the poem, but depended on the internal rhythm and a certain amount of alliteration to carry you along to the final … uh … resolution.

For way too long a time, free verse has reigned supreme in the realm of poetry, and there are many who will defend it, but I think free verse is pretty much a lazy approach – not that there's no rhyming, but that there's no internal structure, rather like a body without a spine. I blame it all on Walt Whitman and his *Leaves of Grass*, one of the most self-involved poor excuses for poetic endeavor I've ever read.

# Fran Stewart

Can you imagine what a mess this chambered nautilus would have been in if she'd constructed her shell in free verse format instead of this highly structured, well-disciplined miracle?

~ ~ ~

**Blue Planet**

**Wednesday 10/14/2020** – Yesterday I watched a short video from NASA that had an astronaut explaining how to poop in the space station. He said that was by far the question astronauts are asked the most often. It was an informative video (with a pee-simulator to demonstrate the vacuum properties of the collection system). You have to be extra careful when everything floats.

The poop place is located quite close to the dome—through which they can watch our blue planet revolving underneath/above/beside them. Directions like up and down have very little relevance in zero gravity of course. I wonder how hard astronauts-in-training have to work to revise their thinking about over/under/up/down.

Sort of like how I had to retrain myself when I moved to Vermont and heard people talking about going "down east." Every New Englander knows that the state of Maine is *Down East*. It makes sense from Vermont. After all, the Green Mountain State has a higher elevation than the Pine Tree State. But how on earth can people in Boston or Connecticut talk of traveling down east when they have to head north to get there?

Very confusing. Just like wondering whether the potty place is under the dome or over the dome.

p.s. Sad news – Legs ate Ora. In case you're a new or only occasional reader of these posts of mine, Legs and Ora each had a big beautiful web – and the webs, spun from brilliant golden silk, were close together and parallel to each other. They also ran right across the path that goes past my back deck, making it impossible for me to get to my compost pile. Ora had a distinctive pattern on her body. A few days ago, I went out to check on the ladies and found that part of Ora's unique body was sticking out of a closely woven black spider casket, and most of her web had been taken down (eaten, perhaps?) by Legs.

I know it's the path of Mama Nature, but it's still sad. The well-fed Legs, by the way, has spun a brand-new web, even larger than the one before. It's more than four feet in diameter, plus the length of the supporting strands. Impressive. And it still blocks my path.

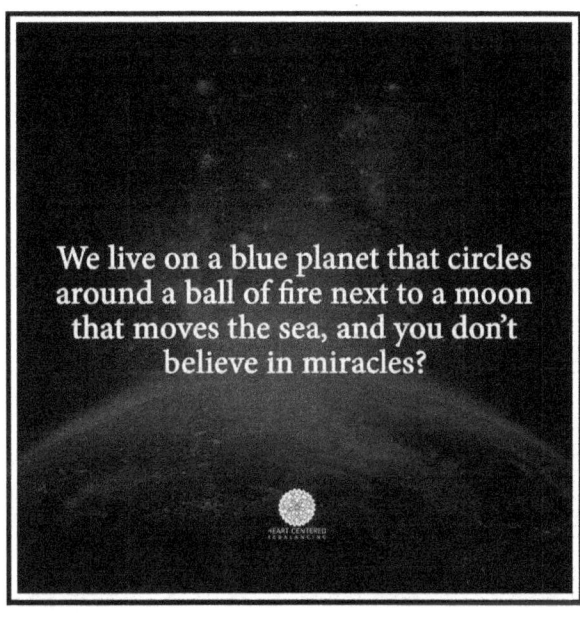

~ ~ ~

**Cowardice, Expediency, & Vanity**

**Thursday 10/15/2020** – "Don't worry about COVID" is a statement coming from expedience (have to get the economy up to par so I can make up some of the 410 million dollars I owe other people), coming from cowardice (don't know how to fix this, so let's just gloss it over), and vanity (didn't hurt me too much, so why should I be concerned about anybody else?)

"Don't worry about COVID" is not right. Now is the time for all of us to consider how much our action (or inaction) affects other people. The news on NPR this morning said that Europe is having a surge of cases—because people got complacent. We can't afford that.

I wear my mask whenever I go out. I wash my hands frequently. I believe in the findings of the scientific/medical community. I do these things because they are the right things to do.

I hope you do, too.

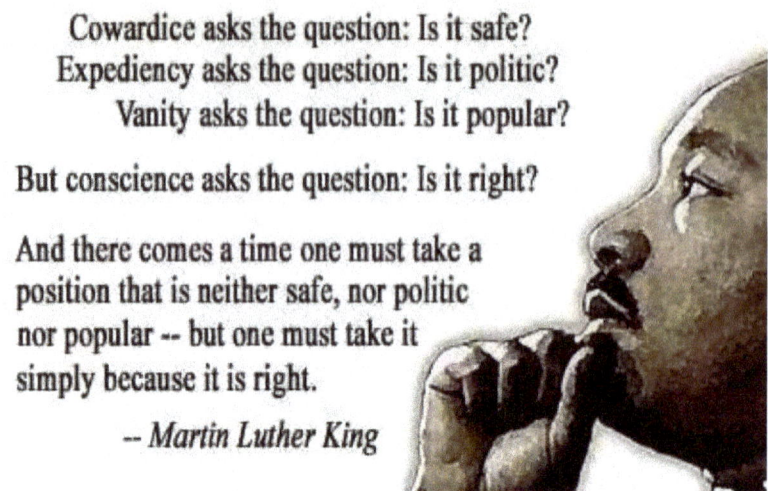

> Cowardice asks the question: Is it safe?
> Expediency asks the question: Is it politic?
> Vanity asks the question: Is it popular?
>
> But conscience asks the question: Is it right?
>
> And there comes a time one must take a position that is neither safe, nor politic nor popular -- but one must take it simply because it is right.
> -- *Martin Luther King*

~ ~ ~

**World Food Day / Bad Grannie**

**Friday 10/16/2020** – How will we feed 10 billion people in 2050? That was a question in an email I opened from The Nature Conservancy last week.

I applaud the Nobel Prize committee members who awarded this year's peace prize to the World Food Programme, an organization that has lifted millions of people out of food insecurity. Wars are often fought when food resources are scarce, as everyone scrambles for nourishment of any kind. Feed people, stop wars.

More importantly, they've worked not just to send food to people, but to give them the tools they need to raise or grow their own food. Another good organization for this sort of endeavor is Heifer International.

One year I decided to give Heifer contributions on behalf of my children and grandchildren. Heifer International sent me a selection of gift cards: "In your name, we sent—a flock of chickens, a pair of goats, two rabbits, two guinea pigs, and a working beehive …

All was well until one of my grandchildren looked at his card and said, "They EAT guinea pigs?"

I tried to explain about lack of protein sources and the need for careful use of resources in areas where extensive grazing is not available for larger meat animals.

Nothin' doin' ! ! !  All he came away with was that his gift meant people were eating cute little fuzzy guinea pigs.

<<<sigh>>> I did not get a good grannie award that year.

~ ~ ~

**Concerned Pigeons**

**Saturday 10/17/2020** – I hope if you're ever lying on the floor, somebody will be concerned about you. Just in case.

This sort of reminds me of the time a few years ago when I was headed downstairs, suddenly remembered something I should have done back upstairs, turned, caught my foot on the next tread, and tumbled all the rest of the way down to the main floor.

Nobody was home except me and my cats.

They came and investigated me.

They weren't a whole lot of help.

Fortunately, 1) the floor was carpeted, 2) I'd moved the table at the end of the loveseat about six inches to the right earlier that morning—otherwise my skull would have contacted the corner of it, 3) my bones are strong so I didn't break anything, and 4) I have a wonderful chiropractor who worked me into her schedule.

The only thing I didn't have with me was a camera. And a couple of pigeons.

~ ~ ~

**No matter what**

**Sunday 10/18/2020** – I agree. Everybody needs at least one of these. I'm unbelievably fortunate to have three. (And I know. I know I used this same photo three or four months ago, but it bears repeating. Anyway, I said something different about it back then.)

## 1st Amendment

**Monday 10/19/2020** – Amy Coney Barrett couldn't name all five freedoms guaranteed by the first amendment. That's like interviewing somebody for a job as a maid.

"Do you know what a vacuum cleaner is?"

"No."

Even more telling, I think, is that when asked why all these five freedoms were lumped together in one Amendment, she said she had no idea. That's like asking the maid applicant why toilets and sinks should both be cleaned on a regular basis. "I have no idea."

Now, I'm willing to understand that someone who's been answering questions for a lot of hours might possibly have a brain-fog and forget one of the five freedoms, but Barrett has repeatedly said that her entire judicial philosophy is based on understanding the intent of the Founding Fathers. And yet, she didn't know one of the basic philosophies of our Constitution and its amendments.

Here's a very simple explanation that I learned in a high school civics class ages ago, one which ANY nominee for the Supreme Court should understand:

> Let's say you have **freedom of religion**. But if you don't have **freedom of assembly**, then you can't possibly have freedom of religion since you wouldn't be able to gather to express your religion.
>
> And you may be given **freedom of speech**, but if you don't have **freedom of the press** so that you can publish your beliefs and argue in favor of them, then you don't really have freedom of speech.
>
> And finally, none of those freedoms work unless you have the **right to petition the government for redress of grievances**.

Notice that the first amendment does not give us the <u>right to redress of grievances</u>. It gives us the right to **petition** (in a court of law) whenever the government oversteps its bounds and curtails those freedoms. This was the freedom Amy Coney Barrett couldn't remember. Do you really want her sitting for the rest of her life on the Supreme Court?

Speaking of freedoms, I took my absentee ballot to the elections office and deposited it in the box myself a couple of days ago.

Then I sanitized my hands, drove home, washed my hands, took off my mask, and had a cup of celebratory tea.

Make a difference this year. Vote, yes—but more importantly, contact your senators and ask them to deny a lifetime appointment on the Supreme Court to someone who obviously does not understand how our Constitution works.

p.s. I heard back from one of the senators I'd sent an email to. She completely ignored my comments, instead proclaiming how proud she was to have supported Barrett's nomination. Then she had the gall to *thank* me for having contacted her. "Your comments and opinions," she said, "are a vital source of information to assist me in carrying out my duties as your U.S. Senator from Georgia."

All I can say is—she ain't MY senator.

~ ~ ~

### PW Garden

**Tuesday 10/20/2020** – This is the month that the Atlanta Branch of the NLAPW traditionally holds their meeting at our Stone Mountain Nature Garden. It's such a peaceful place, and I'm delighted to have my own steppingstone with my name on it as part of the path that winds around the place.

This was the first year in a long time that I didn't go there. Doggone it. The risk was too high. I knew we'd be outside. I knew the other Pen Women would wear masks. But getting from the parking area down to the garden itself? Sometimes we meet walkers on the trails that cross our path. Who could know where those people have been or who they've been in contact with?

So, I stayed home this month. These pictures were taken 8 or 10 years ago in the early spring.

~ ~ ~

**Frozen Music**

**Wednesday 10/21/2020** – I have an aversion to the bird-killer buildings that have sprung up all across our cities in the last four or five decades. You know the ones—reflective blueish glass windows cover the entire building, causing confusion to birds who think they're flying into wide open skies only to collide with glass and fall to their deaths.

I once read that beautiful architecture is frozen music. By the same token, couldn't you say that beautiful music is liquid architecture? You just don't get that sort of feeling when you think of dead birds lying on the sidewalks. But the type of liquid music in this photo? Absolutely glorious.

When I see a building like this, I think of overhanging tree branches that interweave above me, as I'm sure the architect intended. When I was in Junior High School Chorus, we sang a song that began, "I know a green cathedral, a shadowed forest shrine / Where leaves above join hands in love …" Loved that song. Loved that thought.

Imagine standing inside this picture. Imagine the peacefulness. Imagine the way your heart must leap as your sight is drawn upward.

Now take a deep breath (if you haven't already). Have a peace-filled day.

### Master vs. Beginner 1/8/20

**Thursday 10/22/2020** – Someone contacted me recently and asked if she could give my contact information to a client of hers who wanted to become a writer.

"What's he planning to write?"

"I don't know. He said he'd lost his job because of COVID and he needed a way to make some money, so he thought he'd be a writer."

Oh dear. There were so many pitfalls in that statement, I didn't even know where to start. If you've been writing like crazy and you want to become a *published* author, I'll be happy to give you encouragement. If you want to become rich with your writing (but you've never written anything before this), then maybe you need to talk to Yoda.

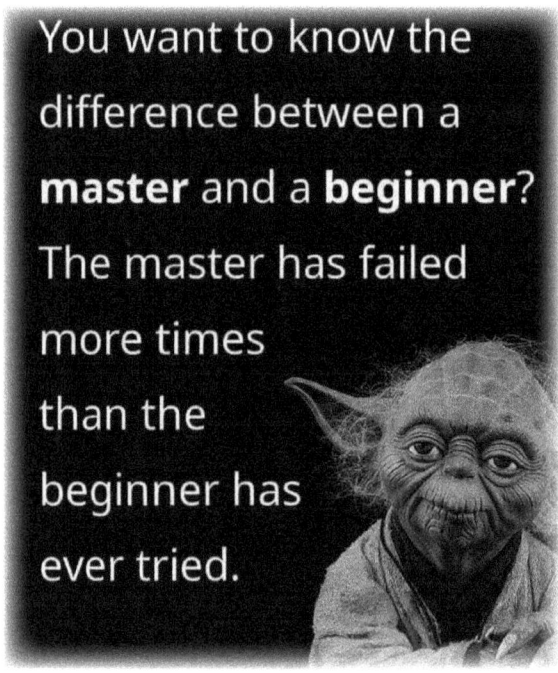

~ ~ ~

### Made from a Tree

**Friday 10/23/2020** – I love being able to listen to Abigail Adams and Ruth Bader Ginsburg, to Maya Angelou and Jane Austen, to Louisa May Alcott and Cokie Roberts. All of these women wrote down their words, their wisdom, their questionings, their doubts.

And all of them are available to me, simply because of the miracle of books.

In the same vein, I love to be able to talk to you through the words I've written. Even fifty years from now, when my body will no longer be here, you'll be able to access what I thought, what I experienced, what I cared for, what I was incensed about, what made me laugh, what made me cry, what I loved.

Won't that be amazing? (And what are you reading today?)

> A book is made from a tree. It is an assemblage of flat, flexible parts (still called "leaves") imprinted with dark pigmented squiggles. One glance at it and you hear the voice of another person, perhaps someone dead for thousands of years. Across the millennia, the author is speaking, clearly and silently, inside your head, directly to you.
>
> Carl Sagan
> *American cosmologist and science communicator*

~ ~ ~

**Best Typo 5/1/20**

**Saturday 10/24/2020** – I've probably shared this before sometime in the last few years, but if I did, I'm not sure when. If I didn't, here it is again for your Saturday laugh.

p.s. You have to read it carefully to catch what the proofreader didn't.

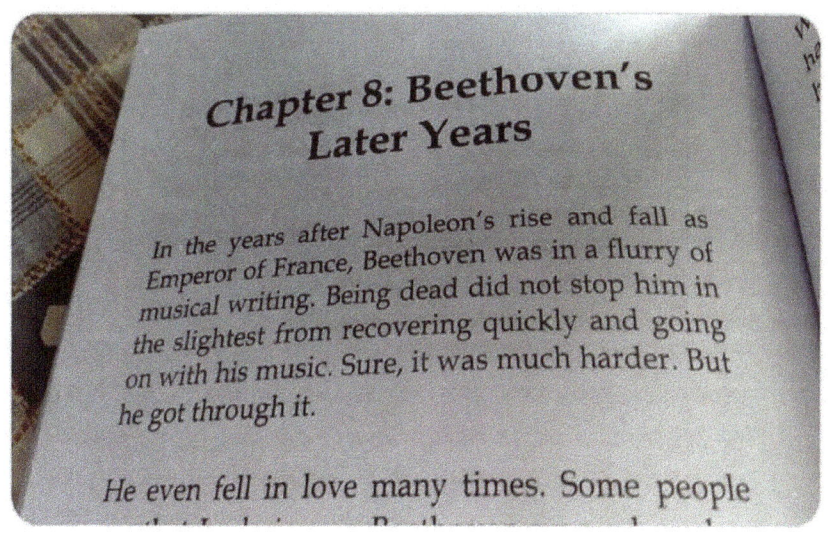

## Reading Goals 2/14/20

**Sunday 10/25/2020** – Since I won't be posting anything come January, I thought I'd share some of my reading goals for 2021 with you. They're expressed beautifully in this meme from Grant Snider.

Whoops! I just realized I don't need to set these as goals. I already do all of them.

~ ~ ~

## Ancient Footprints 10/15/20

**Monday 10/26/2020** – I subscribe to a daily notice from *Smithsonian Magazine*. A week or so ago, they gave a link to an article about footprints found at White Sands National Park that are more than 10,000 years old.

They show that someone walked through mud while carrying a child. At a couple of points on this person's journey, several wooly mammoth prints cross the person's footprints. It occurred to me that most of us now will never leave any footprints for future scientists to find, simply because we usually walk on sidewalks or on paved parking lots. Most of us certainly never walk barefooted through heavy mud.

Here are a couple of brief excerpts from the article:

> "The new paper investigates one specific set of tracks, noting details in the footprints' shapes that reveal how the traveler's weight shifted as they moved the child from one hip to the other. ... At some points along the journey, the toddler's footprints appear as well, most likely because the walker set the child down to rest or adjust their position." ©Smithsonian Magazine

Ten thousand years ago.

There may not be any wooly mammoths crossing our footprints now as there were back then, but for the most part, people haven't changed much at all.

~ ~ ~

**Me, Too 12/14/2019**

**Tuesday 10/27/2020** – There were so many years when I didn't take care of myself. Have you had moments (days, months, years) like that? Don't be afraid to admit it. We all do. Now, though, we can make a new choice. If we've already made it—we can continue it.

# Fran Stewart

Choosing not to bankrupt myself with holiday credit card debt. Choosing to make one extra mortgage payment each year—in case you don't know, that will shorten a 30-year mortgage to only 15 years, savings countless amounts in interest. Choosing to remove myself from the sugar-frenzy of giving out Halloween candy. Choosing to live simply within my means rather than splurging on every new tempting goody being marketed.

Choosing to live without a TV set—why? Mainly because I refused anymore to be bombarded by commercials telling me how broken I was. You don't believe me? Just think about it. "You'll make more friends if you use this deodorant. You'll have more dates if you buy this shampoo. You'll be happy if you buy this toy or that appliance or some-such overpriced nonessential."

Taking care of myself. Won't you join me by saying, "Me, too."

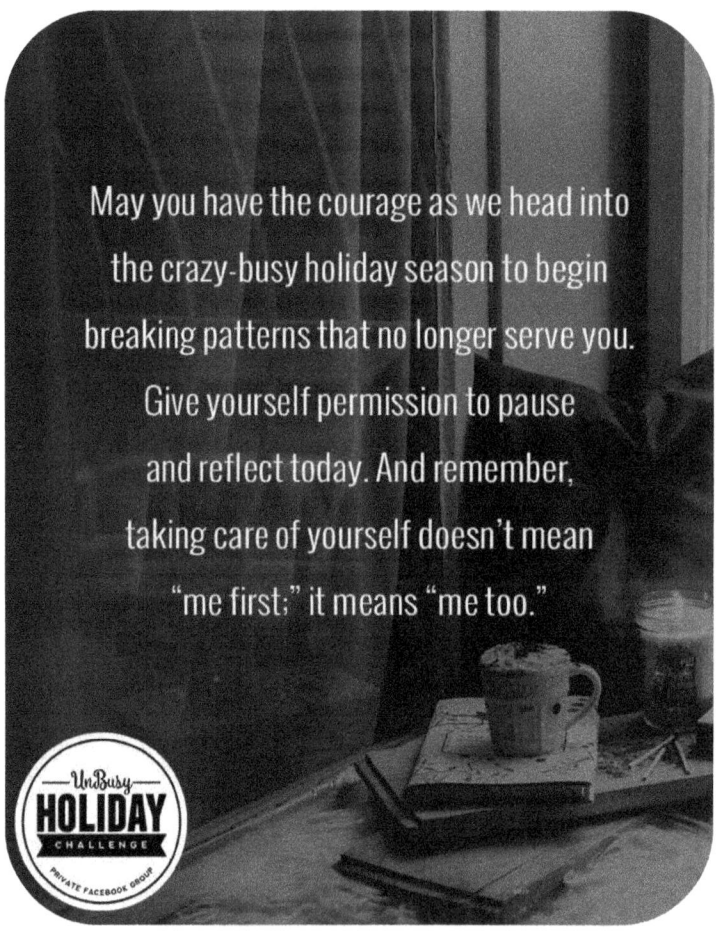

~ ~ ~

### Hug a Cow

**Wednesday 10/28/2020** – There are a kazillion videos out there showing how good it is to hug a cat, hug a dog, hug a chicken or a lion or a baby elephant. But here's one about hugging cows that I saw on the BBC.

Cows have a higher internal temperature than people do, so lying against a cow who's serenely chewing her cud in a field will warm not just your body but your soul.

It's a lovely thought. Now all I have to do is find an amenable cow.

You can do a search for *BBC hug a cow*. That should get you to the story. There's a great video.

~ ~ ~

[**2021 Note**: I know you're going to wonder why the next two entries are printed in red ink. It's because I lost two and a half days of Internet (and all my electricity) to Hurricane Zeke, which roared through here with a vengeance on Wednesday night. When I came back on Saturday, I decided just to skip these two posts (which I'd written in the hopes the power would soon be on) and I took the time to explain what had happened, so you'll read all about it in a couple of pages.

### Centigrade

**Thursday 10/29/2020** – Here's a fun fact for you. Minus 40 degrees Centigrade (or Celsius, if you prefer that name) is exactly the same temperature as minus 40 degrees Fahrenheit. No matter what you call that temperature, I can tell you from personal experience, it's pretty darn cold. You see, a number of decades ago in what now feels like a whole nother lifetime, my then-husband and I went out to spend a weekend at our summer place. In Vermont, those places are called "camps." In the summer, with the lake rippling gently in any passing breeze, we spent a lot of hours simply enjoying the place. In the winter, the lake was frozen so solidly people were safe driving their trucks on it to go ice fishing. We'd spent lots of winter weekends there—the snow was magically brilliant in the winter sunshine. And there was always a furnace so we wouldn't freeze.

Now you have to understand that in the winter we always had to park our car at the end of the unplowed dirt road and hike a mile to camp. And this particular Friday, the temperature was below zero. WELL below zero. Thirty degrees below zero.

We put on extra layers.

We were idiots.

By the time we made it to the camp, the tips of our fingers were frozen. We didn't lose our noses, but it sure felt like we came awfully close.

The coldest it gets here in Georgia is around 10 degrees. Feels like a heat wave.

# Fran Stewart

~ ~ ~

### Painting Rocks

**Friday 10/30/2020** – A bunch of years ago, I arranged for a pretty-much-complete remodel of my house. And then, of course, we had to have a party. The kitchen counter was covered with munchies, and a table under one of the skylights was covered with rocks.

Rocks?????

Yep. I'd taken a whole bunch of beautiful smooth gray river rocks that my sister had given me years before (yes—those rocks made a great present) and got the grandkids to help me paint one side of each of them white. The day of the party, I spread them out on the paper-covered table, along with a huge collection of colored pens and markers. Everyone who walked in the door was invited (after a tour of the house) to sit for a while and decorate a rock. They could take their creation home with them or leave it here or place it in the yard—their choice.

Mikki Root Dillon, a dear friend and fabulous photographer, took this photo of my daughter and two of my grandchildren decorating their rocks. (Well, one of them has finished decorating hers and is taking a picture of it.) Don't you love the way Mikki captured the beautiful sunlight that bounces off the table and illuminates the faces?

*Photo credit: Mikki Root Dillon*

~ ~ ~

**Don't Have Time to Wait**

**Saturday 10/31/2020** – "Welcome back, Fran!" I can hear you saying that. "Where have I been for the past two days?" Well, Hurricane Zeke had fun with our neighborhood (and with a good deal of the southern US). After lying awake most of Wednesday night listening to the high winds buffeting the house, I heard the power go off just before 5AM. Not only lights and no fridge, but no Internet! That was okay because I didn't have a memoirs class scheduled for Thursday, but I couldn't access anyone except via phone.

Lots of branches down, including one on my driveway that was about ten feet long—and came from a tree on the OTHER side of my house! Luckily it missed the room as it blew across.

My daughter came over later that day (after the winds were well gone) and we had a long lovely porch visit. "I know why your power's out, Mom. The next street over is completely blocked off by a huge tree that's knocked down the power lines."

So after she left I walked down to see. OhMyGosh! Talk about huge. The trunk was easily four feet in diameter. Anyway, the power finally was restored at 4:56 this morning. How do I know the exact time? I'd switched a light to "on" in my bedroom and one downstairs so I'd know when the power returned.

# Fran Stewart

Now let's go on to what I'd been planning to write about today. Two things:

1. In case you didn't know, today is a Blue Moon – the second full moon in a calendar month. As far as I know, Blue Moons can occur only during months when there are 31 days. If you've ever known of one during a 30-day month, please tell me when it was. At least I'm completely sure there can never be a Blue Moon during February, since the moon cycles around the earth every 29.5 days.

2. I've been saving this picture since January of 2019, waiting for a day when an eclipse was predicted, but with these posts ready to end in just 61 more days, I don't have time to wait for the sun to cooperate.

So, here it is, for your Saturday laugh—a total eclipse of the cat. Happy Halloween!

# November 2020

## Daylight Savings Time

**Sunday 11/1/2020** – I know this blanket idea would be more appropriate next spring when DST begins again, but since I won't be posting any more after 12/31/2020, I'm sharing it with you now.

And if you don't know what I'm talking about—about not posting, I mean—go back to my post on October 7th.

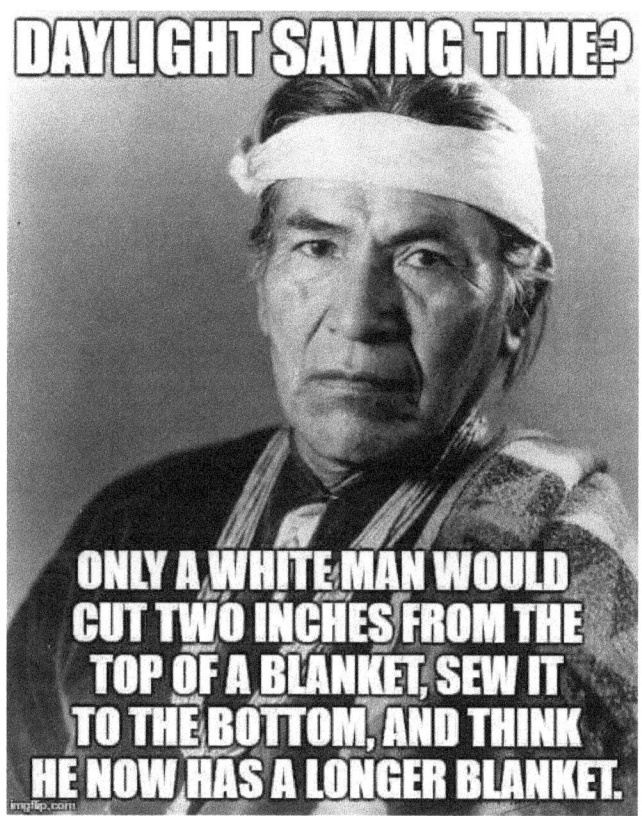

~ ~ ~

## What They Really Need

**Monday 11/2/2020** – I seem to be preaching a lot lately in these posts about living a simpler life, cutting out all the unnecessary extras in our closets, in our pantries, in our lives.

You may have figured out that this is something I truly believe.

Well, here's a lovely thought about the sorts of gifts that are truly worth giving. I think it's particularly apt during this time of surging COVID cases, but at the same time, some of these items aren't possible now, especially if you want to keep yourself and your loved ones free of the virus. Still—think about ways you could get creative. The picture I have (copied from the internet of course) is a bit on the fuzzy side, so I've copied the tiny text here, and I'm showing you only the headline:

# Fran Stewart

Maybe they need help with a utility bill, or a car payment, or the rent.
Maybe they need a kid-free night and could use a babysitter.
Maybe they need a night off cooking and could use a home-cooked meal.
Maybe they need help with gas for their car.
Maybe they need a night out with friends.
Maybe they need a cup of coffee and someone to listen to them.
Maybe they need help making the holidays bright for their children.
Maybe they need help in some other way, but they don't know how to ask, or are too embarrassed to ask.
Maybe you could be the one to give them what they REALLY need, rather than just more stuff.

~ ~ ~

### Non-Political Celebrations

**Tuesday 11/3/2020** – A couple of weeks ago, my granddaughter came over for a visit (masks in place, 10 feet apart, sitting on my front porch). While we were talking, we were interrupted by a flock of about thirty tiny pine siskins that flew around our heads, settled on various bird feeders, partook of the water in the birdbath. They twittered and fluttered and brought us a great deal of joy right at a time when we both needed it.

That afternoon they came back for a short time, and I took this picture of the ones that were, like gleaners in the fields, cleaning up the seeds fallen from the overhead feeder. Their sisters above them were making quite a mess.

If I were a pine siskin, would I be the one making the mess for others to deal with, or the one on the porch cleaning up, but benefitting from the overhead wastefulness? Or maybe a little of both? Which kind of bird are you?

## House Elephant

**Wednesday 11/4/2020** – No, I'm not going to talk about election results this morning. That's because as of this moment, I have no idea what happened yesterday/last night/early this morning. I made a deliberate choice to protect my blood pressure by not listening to the radio at all yesterday, and I haven't turned it on yet this morning.

So, just like my cats, I'm in total ignorance of what's going on—at least for the next half hour or so—until I've had some breakfast. Then I'll check my emails and turn on WABE public radio.

How often do you see a picture like this and say, "I wish I'd thought of that." Now just imagine the trunk … er tail … swishing back and forth.

So, if you ever want to have a house elephant, you can. See? It's simple.

I'm not sure Fuzzy Britches would put up with having me stick some eyeballs on her rear end, though. And her golden rump would never look like an elephant. Oh well, some things just aren't feasible. I suppose I could dye her fur a light elephant gray. Did I ever tell you the story of the time my son (with my help) dyed his sister's Lhasa Apso pink to get back at her for an extremely clever joke she'd played on him. [She'd done it with my help, I must admit.]

I didn't tell you yet?

You'll just have to imagine it (like you're imaging the elephant's trunk).

# Fran Stewart

~ ~ ~

## Doorbells

**Thursday 11/5/2020** – I gave up on doorbells a long time ago. When I bought this house close to twenty years ago, the doorbell didn't work. There were a whole bunch of other things that didn't work as well, and they took precedence over the doorbell—things like the fridge, the washer & dryer, the furnace, one of the toilets, …

So, I spent a lot of time and money fixing things or getting them fixed. It was doable because I'd bought the house fairly cheap "as is." Eventually, though, it was time to tackle the doorbell issue. *Piece of cake*, I thought as I wound my way through the aisles at Home Depot. *This is easy*, I thought as I took out the old doorbell and installed the new contraption—just undo this and attach that and stick on a little cap to cover the wire ends. I've repaired many lamps in my lifetime. It's the same principle.

Ha! For some reason, there's an anti-doorbell genie that lurks inside my walls or under the flooring or perhaps tucked between the rafters.

The lamps always worked, but the doorbell? Nope.

Oh, it rang a couple of times, just enough for me to congratulate myself that I'd hooked it up correctly. But then the problems started. You had to push the button just so—with a little more pressure on the right side than on the left. Until the following week, when you had to push to the left, rather than the right. And the week after that when you had to push it four or five times before it would let out a teensy inaudible squeak. I took the darn thing out and reinstalled it a number of times. Nothing doin' – it was thoroughly unworkable.

But then I found the perfect solution, as evidenced in this sign that covers the outside button. So far, the anti-doorbell genie hasn't had a problem with this one.

~ ~ ~

**Shoulda Been Last Week**

**Friday 11/6/2020** – I know. I should have used this cartoon last Saturday for the end-of-week laugh, but I wanted to do the cat eclipse thing. My son's been a vegan for years (decades, actually), and thrives on a meatless, non-dairy, egg-free regimen. So, what would Shakespeare have done if he'd been a vegan? Can't you just see those three weird sisters hunched over their boiling cauldron?

This reminds me of my own eating regimen. Each Sunday I throw all sorts of stuff into a crockpot. A mixture of beans that I've soaked overnight, some rice so the beans will supply a complete protein, a bunch of whatever veggies I have on hand, a bunch of spices—whatever sounds good—a glurg of olive oil, some fresh-ground pepper. I usually add some dill pickle juice—don't cringe; it provides a certain flair.

Cook it on high for a couple of hours and then turn it to low. That's my noon meal, not only for that Sunday, but for most of the week to come. My evening meal is straight grazing, as I think I've mentioned before in these posts.

Hey, what can I say? It works for me, just as Eli's meals work for him. And these three sisters, too.

~ ~ ~

**One Day …**

**Saturday 11/7/2020** – Two months ago, one of the Saturdays was World Cleanup Day, but that was also the day after Justice Ginsburg's death, and I couldn't face posting my usual Saturday laugh. What I'd been planning to tell you was that every day is cleanup day for me. Whenever I go walking, I carry a bag along with me so I can pick up any trash I find along the street.

# Fran Stewart

The trouble is (and I'll admit right now that it's not uproariously Saturday funny—it's not really even a little bit funny), some mornings I walk in that early morning pre-dawn low-light magical time, a time where it's not always easy to see what's trash and what's Mama Nature. I can't tell you how many times I've bent down to pick up a piece of paper, only to find it's a silvery leaf. (Okay, so it wasn't funny at all.)

'Nuff of that. If we'd just all do our part (or better yet, not create the trash to begin with!) the world would be a cleaner place. I think Justice Ginsburg would have agreed.

Now here's the Saturday laugh.

**BE KIND TO YOUR DAUGHTER, ONE DAY SHE WILL BE IN CHARGE OF YOUR WHEELCHAIR!**

~ ~ ~

### Shakespeare's Haiku

**Sunday 11/8/2020** –William Shakespeare's collected works were first published in 1623, and the world has been considerably richer ever since. Now one of the fairly rare copies of the first folio has sold for more than five million dollars.

Amazing, isn't it, to think that he struggled as a playwright during his life, but now his words are considered priceless, and the printed copies of his words are (almost) priceless.

Shakespeare never wrote haiku, but if COVID-19 had hit 17th-century London, and if his Globe Theater had been forced to close, I would like to think that he might have written something like this 2020 haiku.

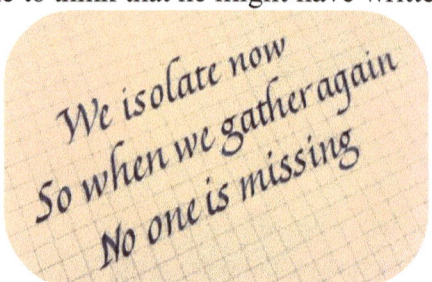

We isolate now
So when we gather again
No one is missing

~ ~ ~

**What is Happening**

**Monday 11/9/2020** – I've received a number of messages bemoaning the fact that I've chosen to deactivate my FB account at the end of this year. If you don't know what I'm talking about, look back at my post on October 7th. Some of these messages came from people who also bemoaned my decision last year to stop writing mysteries and move into this new phase of my life—concentrating on teaching people how to write their memoirs, the stories of their lives.

"What will you do with yourself?" one of these people asked.

Huh? It takes me only a few minutes, seldom more than ten, each morning to choose a photo and write about it. Sometimes I wake up with an idea of what I want to write about, sometimes it's something I've been considering for some time, sometimes it's just the whimsey of the moment. But once those ten minutes are over, I still have the rest of my day ahead of me – 1,430 minutes (less sleep time).

Teaching the memoirs classes online takes a great deal of preparation time, but not a whole day by any means. Reading the monthly book-club book takes some time, but certainly doesn't take weeks of effort. Doing the usual household chores, feeding myself and Fuzzy Britches, going to the library for curb-side pickup of books I've reserved or shopping for groceries or birdseed (about the only three places I go nowadays)—when you add up all the time it takes to accomplish these things, I still have ample time left over.

I'm re-reading every single year of my grandparents' diaries and learning so much about my family. I'd read them (sort of) a number of years ago—scanned them, really. This time I'm reading word-for-word, finding out about how my dad recovered from diphtheria when he was a child, for instance. I'd never known that.

I'm compiling all these FranStewartAuthor posts into a three-volume memoir. If you want notices about when they'll be available, sign up for my newsletter on my website FranStewart dot com. As I write this, the first volume is already available. I'm continuing to write my personal, private memoirs that will someday be available to my children and grandchildren.

And you think I can't find something to do when I'm no longer posting these daily thoughts?

Think again.

## When They're Weakest

**Tuesday 11/10/2020** – Good grief, I've been in a snit off and on for the past couple of days. I finally went back through all the photos (well, a lot of them) on my laptop and found this one that seems to have been written just for me. Just at this moment.

For all my whining, I really should admit that my attitude is up to me. That I can simply refuse to let all my negative thoughts overpower the good in my life.

Wake up, Frannie. Kwitcher bellyaching, as my grandma used to say. Take charge of what's going on in that brain of mine.

Okay. I feel better now.

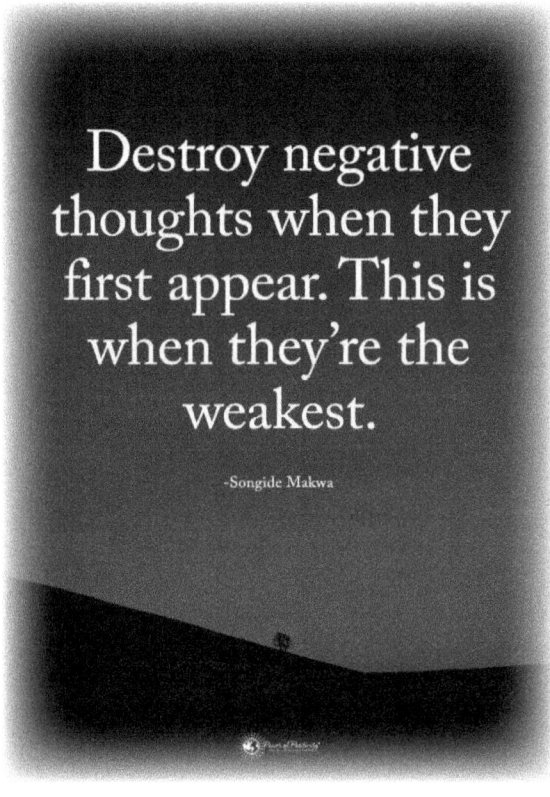

## Leviticus

**Wednesday 11/11/2020** – I'll add only one note to this marvelous meme:

Neither this fellow with the tattoo nor the one who put together the meme understand that Leviticus 18:22 does not forbid homosexuality—it forbids child molestation. You have to read the original language. The

King James version of the bible translated "zachar" as "*male*," but it actually means "*boy*." And yes, the next chapter of Leviticus DOES prohibit tattoos ("you shall not … print any marks upon yourself").

Translations can be dangerous. Just something to think about.

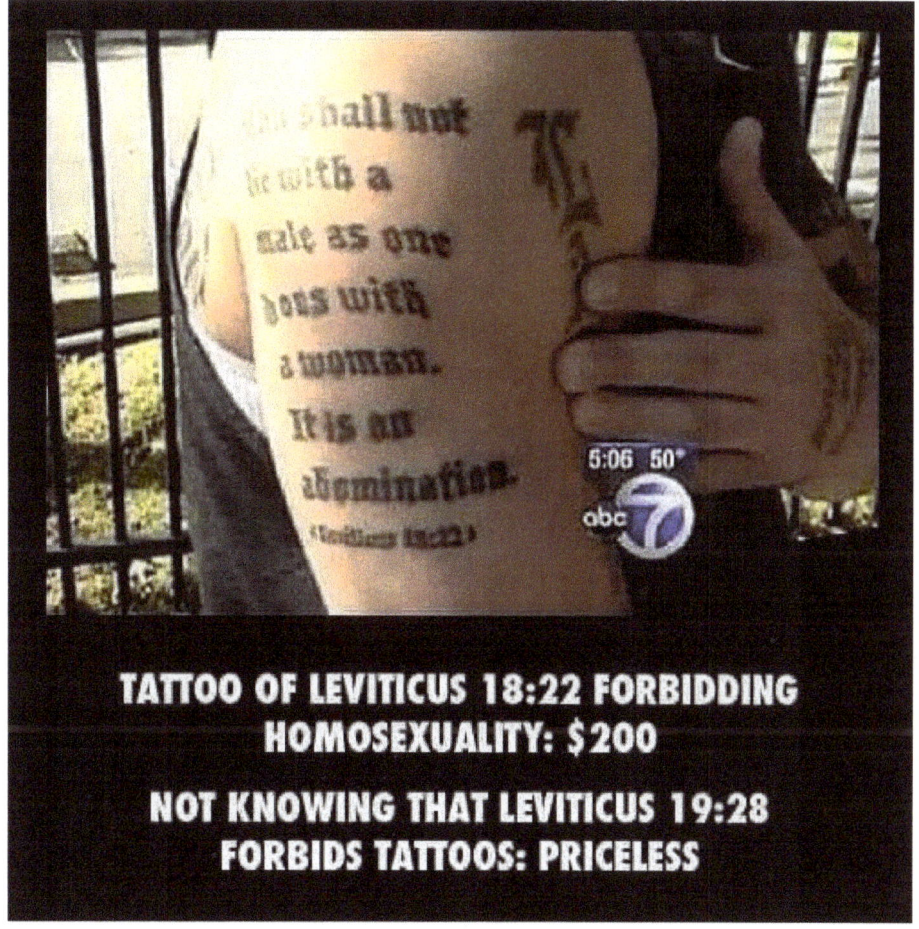

~ ~ ~

**Talking of Tattoos**

**Thursday 11/12/2020** – My son's decided that it's his goal to represent the mosaic of his life visually—all over his body. He started with a couple of meaningful tattoos on his forearms. Then came his shoulders, then a few on his chest. Next came the full-sleeve treatment on both arms. And lots more to pretty-much cover his chest.

His latest tattoo adventure is a listing (in amongst the various arm tattoos that were already there) of the first names of people who have influenced his life. Family and friends, of course, but I was happy to note that on his right wrist, he included Ruth Bader Ginsburg. When I messaged him that in this photo I could see only the first three letters of her name (but I was assuming he meant Ginsberg), his reply was "You can't spell TRUTH without RUT!"

I don't think anyone will make a tee-shirt with that one.

# Fran Stewart

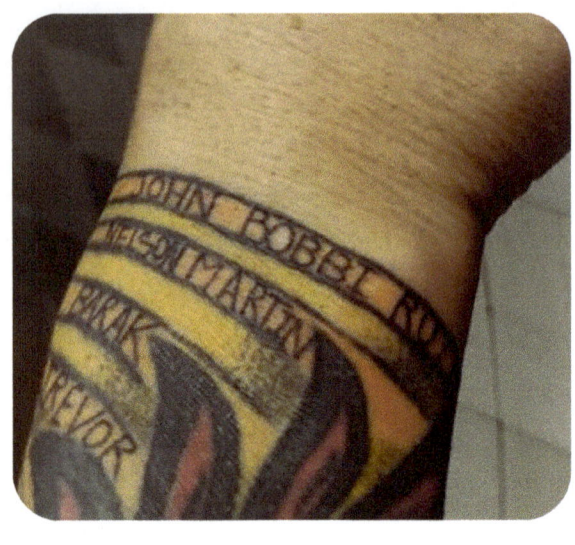

~ ~ ~

**Escher's Skyscraper**

**Friday 11/13/2020** – Did you ever have days when you felt like you were scurrying around on an endless loop that didn't get you anywhere? And every step you took seemed to run you into a solid wall? Sort of like this Escher-inspired skyscraper?

I think it's time for me to stop, take three slow deep breaths and acknowledge that today is a new day. I can make new choices. Good life is still within my grasp. In fact, good life is right here, right now. All is well.

There. That feels better.

"Escher! Get your ass up here."

# Crystal Clear

~ ~ ~

## Translation

**Saturday 11/14/2020** – Back in the early 1970s, my then-husband and I traveled around in Europe for three weeks. We had our Eurail passes, a copy of *Europe on $5 a Day*, assorted maps, two dictionaries (German/English and French/English), and a great deal of optimism.

We also each had one small suitcase. Mine was half-empty, because I planned to buy several items (like a raincoat) while overseas. We wore sturdy walking shoes and clothes that could be mixed and matched.

In a train station somewhere or other, we ran into a couple of other Americans when the woman called out my husband's name at full volume—it reverberated from the I-beams above us. "I can't believe it's you!!!" She and her husband were dragging around seven LARGE pieces of luggage for a 10-day excursion—but that's a story that's better forgotten.

In Germany, we had several memorable meals, after having tried (unsuccessfully) to interpret long-worded menus. I get it that German is a language that strings together a lot of short words to make one long word, but often the results of our piecemeal translations were not only comical, but downright misleading.

There was one menu item in particular that completely baffled us. The best we could figure out was that the word meant "a good collection of something tasty." I assumed some sort of stew. He suggested maybe it was a cheese dish or an antipasto sort of thing.

It was neither. An unidentifiable-to-us cut of meat surrounded by unidentifiable-to-us veggies of some sort.

Makes me appreciate the translation apps that are available nowadays on smartphones.

### Reverse Advent Calendar

**Sunday 11/15/2020** – Here's something to consider for this year. Since 2020 has been, shall we say, a challenge, let's forget about getting, getting, getting this holiday season and instead consider giving, giving, giving.

I'm not talking about giving things that will be quickly set aside, unappreciated and unsung. Instead, how about planning this easy way to fill a food pantry basket?

If you put a few of these on your grocery list each week for the next number of weeks, you can have your box ready to go in time to take it to your local food pantry.

Don't know where a local pantry is? Do a search, for heaven's sake.

# REVERSE
## ADVENT CALENDAR
#### EACH DAY ADD AN ITEM TO A BOX. ON CHRISTMAS EVE DONATE THE CONTENTS TO A FOOD BANK.

December 1 - box of cereal
December 2 - peanut butter
December 3 - stuffing mix
December 4 - boxed potatoes
December 5 - macaroni and cheese
December 6 - canned fruit
December 7 - canned tomatoes
December 8 - canned tuna
December 9 - dessert mix
December 10 - jar of applesauce
December 11 - canned sweet potatoes
December 12 - cranberry sauce
December 13 - canned beans
December 14 - box of crackers
December 15 - package of rice
December 16 - package of oatmeal
December 17 - package pasta
December 18 - spaghetti sauce
December 19 - chicken noodle soup
December 20 - tomato soup
December 21 - can corn
December 22 - can mixed vegetables
December 23 - can carrots
December 24 - can green beans

PASSIONATEPENNYPINCHER.COM

~ ~ ~

## What Didn't I Do?

**Monday 11/16/2020** – A lot of my regrets about things I didn't do revolve around elderly people in my life whom I didn't visit when I had the chance. My grandmother before she died, even though I was on a honeymoon trip across the country and passed within 100 miles of her house. Mother Ebbesen, the woman I've written about before who had rheumatoid arthritis but who created such exquisite embroidery, even though she lived in Denver and I was in Boulder. "It's not that important," I justified. "I can always visit some other time."

Both of these women died before I could revise my thinking.

You know the old saying that what goes around comes around? Well, early last month my granddaughter promised to come visit me so we could sit (masked and ten feet apart) on my front porch. "Next week, Grannie," she said, and I blocked off most of those days except for the memoirs classes I had to teach, so I'd be available whenever she chose to come.

But she never showed up. She was busy, I'm sure. Did I text her and ask where she was? No. Why not? I refuse to guilt her. Maybe because I recognize in her my own unthinking attitude way back when.

What goes around comes around. Now I know how Grandma and Mother Ebbesen must have felt.

To be fair to my granddaughter, though, she did text me two weeks later to ask if she could drop by. I already told you about that marvelous visit, when the little pine siskins graced us with their aerial acrobatics. It was worth waiting for.

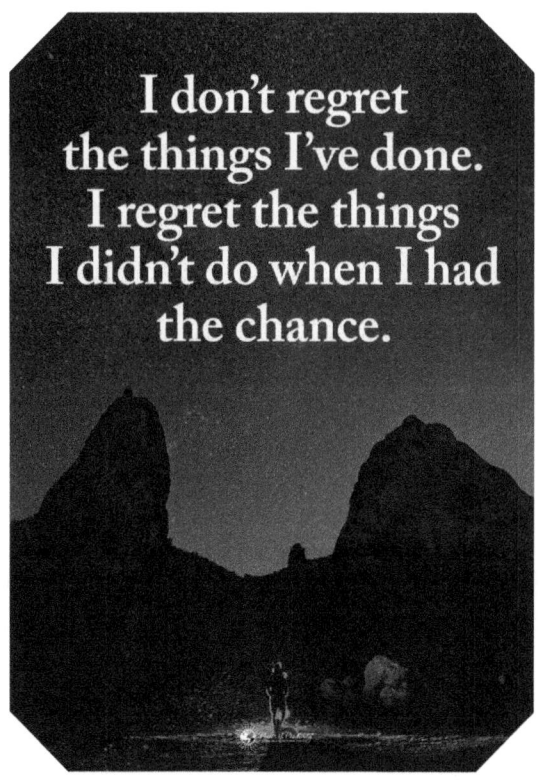

~ ~ ~

### Always Possible

**Tuesday 11/17/2020** – Kindness is one of the unsung virtues. Given a choice between being on the receiving end of a cutting word or a kind one, wouldn't you rather get kindness?

Having in the past been the brunt of a number of jokes told at my expense, I used to bemoan the fact that I never was able to concoct one of those scathing comebacks that we read about so often. Instead, I would meekly swallow my pride and accept the derision.

I wasted a lot of sleepless nights wondering what I could have said. Now, I think my response would simply be, "Thank you for expressing your opinion."

~ ~ ~

### Book Lovers

**Wednesday 11/18/2020** – How many times have you done any of these book-lover kinds of things? I fit every one of these categories. I once saw a bumper sticker that said, "Book lovers never go to bed lonely." Yeah, I agree. You have to understand, though, that I don't limit my reading to bedtime. Evening is a perfect time—and since I don't have a TV set (and I turn off my computer around 6PM every evening)—I get a lot of reading done.

If it's a book on CD, then I can get a lot of knitting done while I listen—sort of a double benefit.

~ ~ ~

**What I Want**

**Thursday 11/19/2020** – I've always considered myself fiscally conservative and socially progressive. Some time ago (last February in fact) I came across this statement that mirrors pretty exactly what I want.

Do you agree? If so, I'm glad. If not, would you like to have a discussion about our points of difference?

> **LET'S SET THE RECORD STRAIGHT:**
>
> I don't want free health care.
> I want my taxes to pay for health care, not war or violence.
>
> I don't want money for nothing.
> I want the opportunity for a good job that pays for at least my basic needs.
>
> I don't expect every election to bring the results I want.
> I just want my vote to count.
>
> I don't want businesses to be unprofitable.
> I want them to stay out of the regulatory and political process.
>
> I don't want the wealthy to pay for everything.
> I want them to pay their fair share.
>
> I don't want open borders.
> I want a path to citizenship for Dreamers and realistic immigration laws that are dignified, humane and fair.

~ ~ ~

**Pay No Attention**

**Friday 11/20/2020** – Maybe this is what your home library looks like, but it's not mine anymore. I've talked a lot in these posts about my drive to simplify my life, to clear out any vestige of excess, to make my home a place where every item in it is needed or loved.

Don't get me wrong. I love books. I love reading. I think people who don't enjoy reading miss out on a lot of joy. But I've also come to terms with the way people who inherit the job of cleaning out a dead person's house frequently revert to the dumpster approach.

Not gonna do that to my daughter! I never want her to have to walk into my house and throw up her hands in despair. So, over the past few years I've cut my book collection down from seven tall wide over-packed bookcases to two. That's right. Two. They're tall, but they're the standard width, and they have breathing room on each shelf.

How did I do it? The same way I clean out my closets periodically. I took everything off the shelves and picked up each book, one at a time. Do I love the writing? Is there a message here I'll want to reread sometime in the next three or four years? Have I opened this book any time within the last five years? Is it primarily for show? Did I start reading it and put it aside out of boredom? Do I have multiple copies of the same book? (I'm sorry to say that I used to buy a second copy when I couldn't find the first one. Turns out the original was buried somewhere behind something in those over-packed shelves.)

As you can tell, I came up with a lot of books that I chose either to give away or take to the used-book place. Nowadays, I use the library a lot. If I buy a book, I think twice before putting it on a shelf. Do I love it? Is there a message … and so on.

Makes life much simpler.

*Photo credit: Tom Gauld / National Library of Scotland*

~ ~ ~

**Why Not?**

**Saturday 11/21/2020** – Did you ever think about the fact that:

$$111{,}111{,}111 \times 111{,}111{,}111 = 12{,}345{,}678{,}987{,}654{,}321$$

You didn't?

Why not?

~ ~ ~

**Identify Their Strengths**

**Sunday 11/22/2020** – I was so fortunate to have grown up going to schools where students were encouraged to think. We were educated. We were never taught-to-the-testing. In fact, back when I was a junior in high school, one of my teachers suggested that I take the PSAT. I'd never heard of it and had no idea it had anything to do with getting ready for college admission.

Okay, so I was kinda dumb (not dumb—merely uninformed) about that sort of thing. But the point is that I took the test with absolutely no test-stress. It was rather fun, in fact. And I did well enough on it. The next year, when I took the SAT, I was equally relaxed. Taking tests turned out to be one of my strengths, but what if I'd been more inclined to working with my hands?

Over the past number of years, I've watched my grandchildren come close to freaking out when faced with life-defining (or so they've been told) tests beginning in *elementary school*.

There's not enough emphasis on trade schools in this country. There's not enough respect for the people who will someday be the ones to repair our toilets or our electrical lines. Let's help children explore their strengths.

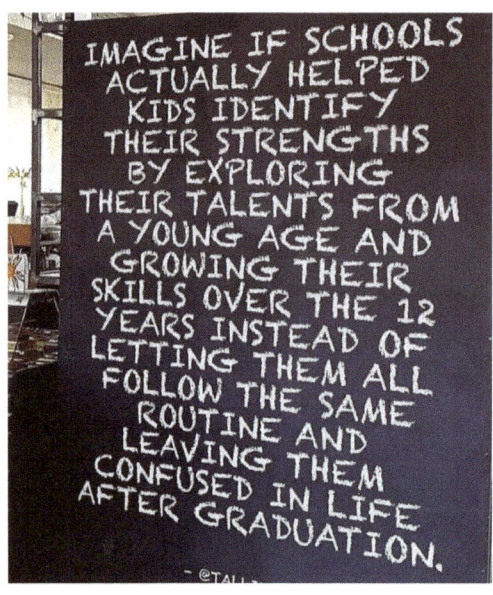

~ ~ ~

**Sit to Save**

**Monday 11/23/2020** – I still find it hard to believe that when I go to grocery store (about the only place I drive to nowadays), there are people who show up either without masks or with their masks down around their chins.

I'm not at risk from anything coming out of your chin, dearie. But what you sneeze or cough or just plain speak out of your mouth and nose could kill me. Would you wake up, please?

~ ~ ~

### Holiday Spirit

**Tuesday 11/24/2020** – What, truly, IS the holiday spirit? Years ago, there were people who complained that banning whale oil production would cripple the American economy. But the whalers found other ways to make a living.

So, now, what if we stopped the insanity of overbuying throughout the year-end holidays. Seems to me that COVID has given us a chance to do just that. Except that most of us haven't. Take a look at the increase in Amazon's profits over the past eight months.

Do we really need all that STUFF? Don't we need, instead, to develop a sense of what a holiday (holy day) should truly mean?

> maybe the holidays don't have to
> pressure you to be jolly.
> maybe they can be here
> to remind you
> that there is light in the darkness.
> that even tho it may take a ton of effort,
> hope can be found.
> if you can even glimpse that,
> you ARE filled with the holiday spirit!
> and if you can't,
> then let others wrap you in love.
> and then
> you'll be cloaked
> in the meaning of the season.
>
> terri st.cloud
> BoneSighArts.com

**Hallelujah Chorus for social isolation – [you can do a search for the video]**

**Wednesday 11/25/2020** – I know this would be a much more appropriate rendition for next Easter, but Thanksgiving is also a good time for a few rousing Hallelujah's isn't it?

And I won't be around on Facebook next April (I've already warned you that I'm deactivating my FB account at the end of this year—see my post on October 7th), so I'm trying to get in all these goodies before I say a virtual goodbye.

~ ~ ~

**The car that prepared it.**

**Thursday 11/26/2020** – Years ago, when I used to go to a Unity Church, I was railroaded into … uh … I mean I was asked to host a Thanksgiving dinner for the singles in the church community who had no family with whom to celebrate the holiday.

As the host, I was supposed to give the blessing at the beginning of the meal. I thanked the turkey for its unwilling sacrifice.

I was never again asked to host anything.

~ ~ ~

**Physical, Not Social**

**Friday 11/27/2020** – I don't like the term "*social distancing.*" I don't want to distance myself from you *socially*. I simply need to distance myself from you *physically*. That six-foot space—which now seems a little close as we're learning more about the distance those deadly droplets can travel—needn't mean we can't be social with each other. It's simply means we shouldn't touch or share our outbreaths.

So, don't talk to me about social distancing. But please stay 10 feet or so away from me.

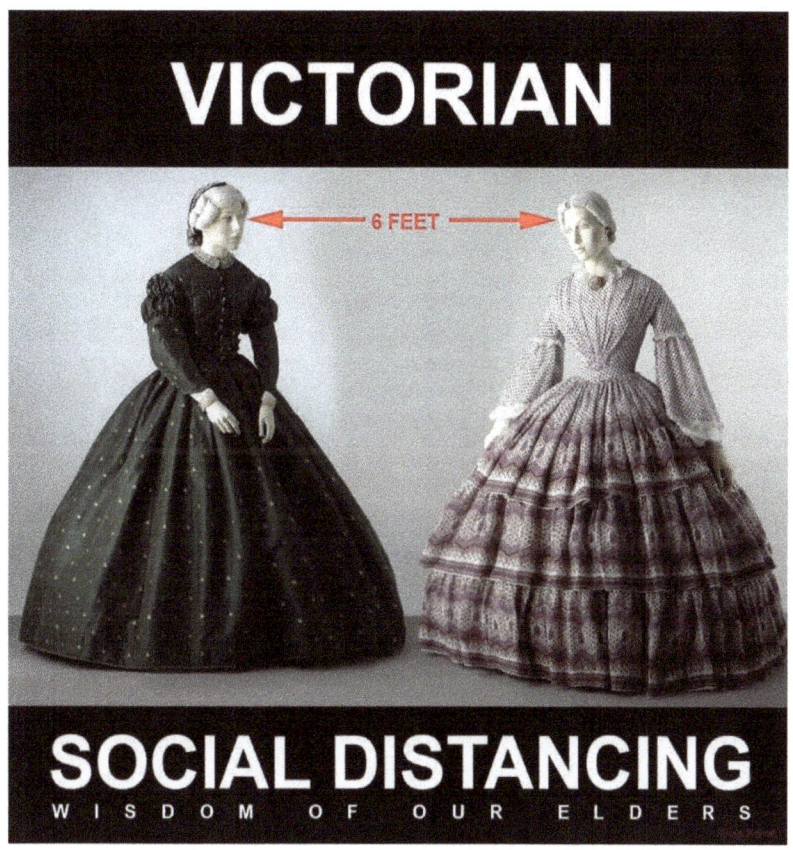

~ ~ ~

**Parentheses**

**Saturday 11/28/2020** – Parentheses are handy things, especially when you consider how confusing life could be without them.

And now that I've started this post with that enticing comment, I can't think of a single example where a mix-up in parenthetics would be funny.

Oh well, at least there's this mug to laugh about.

~ ~ ~

**Yellow Stripey Things**

**Sunday 11/29/2020** – One day last month, when I was on my morning walk, I stopped at a neighbor's house to admire her flowers. It was a cold morning after a cold night, and there were bumblebees curled up in the middle of her marigold flowers. They looked frozen, but when I peered more closely, I could see their little wings quivering.

Bev, my neighbor, saw me outside and came out to chat (six feet apart). "They do that a lot," she told me. Once the sun warms the air, they go about their bumblebee business.

So, if you see a bumblebee curled up and unmoving, don't assume the worst. Assume the best. It's just waiting for a chance to go pollinating for you.

Crystal Clear

# A COMPREHENSIVE GUIDE TO
# YELLOW STRIPEY THINGS

**CARPENTER BEE**
-ACTS LIKE IT'S TOUGH, BUT CAN'T ACTUALLY HURT YOU
-HAS NO CONCEPT OF WHAT GLASS IS
-LIVES IN YOUR FENCE
-FLIES AGGRESSIVELY TO TRY AND SCARE YOU AWAY

**HONEYBEE**
-IS THE BEE THAT NEEDS HELP THE MOST
-EXCELLENT POLLINATOR
-VERY FRIENDLY
-CAN ONLY STING ONCE

**BUMBLEBEE**
-ALSO POLLINATES STUFF VERY WELL
-SO FAT IT SHOULDN'T BE ABLE TO FLY
-WILL LET YOU PET IT WITHOUT GETTING AGITATED
-ACTUALLY A FLYING PANDA

**HOVERFLY**
-WEARS YELLOW STRIPEY UNIFORM TO SCARE YOU
-ACTUALLY CAN'T DO ANYTHING TO YOU
-HANGS OUT IN FIELDS
-FOLLOWS YOU IF IT LIKES YOU

**PAPER WASP**
-LOOKS SCARY, BUT WILL ONLY ATTACK IF PROVOKED
-STING HURTS LIKE THE DEVIL
-WILL CHASE YOU IF YOU SWAT AT IT
-HAS NO CONCEPT OF PERSONAL SPACE

**YELLOW JACKET**
-WANTS YOUR FOOD AND WILL FIGHT YOU FOR IT
-NEVER LEAVES YOU ALONE
-WILL STING YOU JUST FOR THE HECK OF IT
-IS JUST A JERK

**CICADA KILLER**
-LOOKS LIKE SATAN'S NIGHTMARES
-EXCLUSIVELY EATS CICADAS
-CAN STING YOU, BUT USUALLY WON'T
-STILL PRETTY TERRIFYING

**DIRT DAUBER**
-ALMOST NEVER STINGS ANYTHING EXCEPT SPIDERS
-BUILDS NEST IN THE GROUND
-HOARDS SPIDERS IN SAID NEST
-COOLEST LOOKING OF THE WASPS

~ ~ ~

# Fran Stewart

## Doris Day

**Monday 11/30/2020** — It's been one and a half years since the death of Mary Anne Kappelhoff (known to the rest of the world as Doris Day), and that got me to thinking about mortality and immortality. Those of us who remember Doris Day from way back when may have a certain idea of who and what she was. But that was just her screen persona. We may recall her singing "Que Sera, Sera," but that upbeat ditty came nowhere near to expressing the depth of her musical talent. She was a woman who made this world a better place.

The CBC did an obit when she died at 97, in which they spoke of her many feminist tendencies before the feminist movement even began. They went on to say:

"Day was an anti-conformist in one other important way: she stood by her friend and fellow actor Rock Hudson when he was diagnosed with AIDS, during the height of the AIDS crisis, when fear and bigotry were rampant. Later in her life, she founded the Doris Day Animal Foundation and apologized in interviews for having worn fur in films."

Do you ever wonder what your own obit will say? Will it simply list dates of birth and death, those who predeceased you, those who have survived you? Will it list the organizations you belonged to or the places you worked?

Or will it say, "She made the world a better place."

That's the kind of obituary I'd like to live up to.

How about you?

# December 2020

### Singing in sign language: Meet the 1st deaf choir in Newfoundland and Labrador

**Tuesday 12/1/2020** – [This begins the last month of these posts. Enjoy them.] Here's a great start to the month of December.

The entire article is worth reading, but there's a video of it at the very end, so you not only hear the words, but you can see them being signed and interpreted.

Years ago, I took an adult education class in ASL (American Sign Language) and was struck by the beauty of it. I never got very good at it, and with no practice I soon forgot most of it—well, practically all of it. But the remembrance of beauty is still there.

Our "final exam" was for all of us to go out to a pizza place for dinner together. We weren't allowed to speak a single word. I remember how warm-hearted the young woman who took our orders was and how very willing to be patient with us and to meet our needs. When we left, signing "thank you" to her, her face lit up as she realized what we were saying, and she haltingly signed "thank you" right back to us.

If you do a search using the title of today's post, you should be able to find it.

~ ~ ~

### Contronyms

**Wednesday 12/2/2020** – I thought I was fairly conversant about all the different forms of words and word usages. But here was a new one for me: *Contronyms*. Never heard of them. But their definition certainly make sense.

Have you ever thought of this sort of thing?

The next time I go to dust my brownies with a light coating of powdered sugar (extra COVID pounds coming up!) I'll think twice about that word "*dust.*" And then maybe I'll go dust my furniture. Or maybe I'll just eat the brownies …

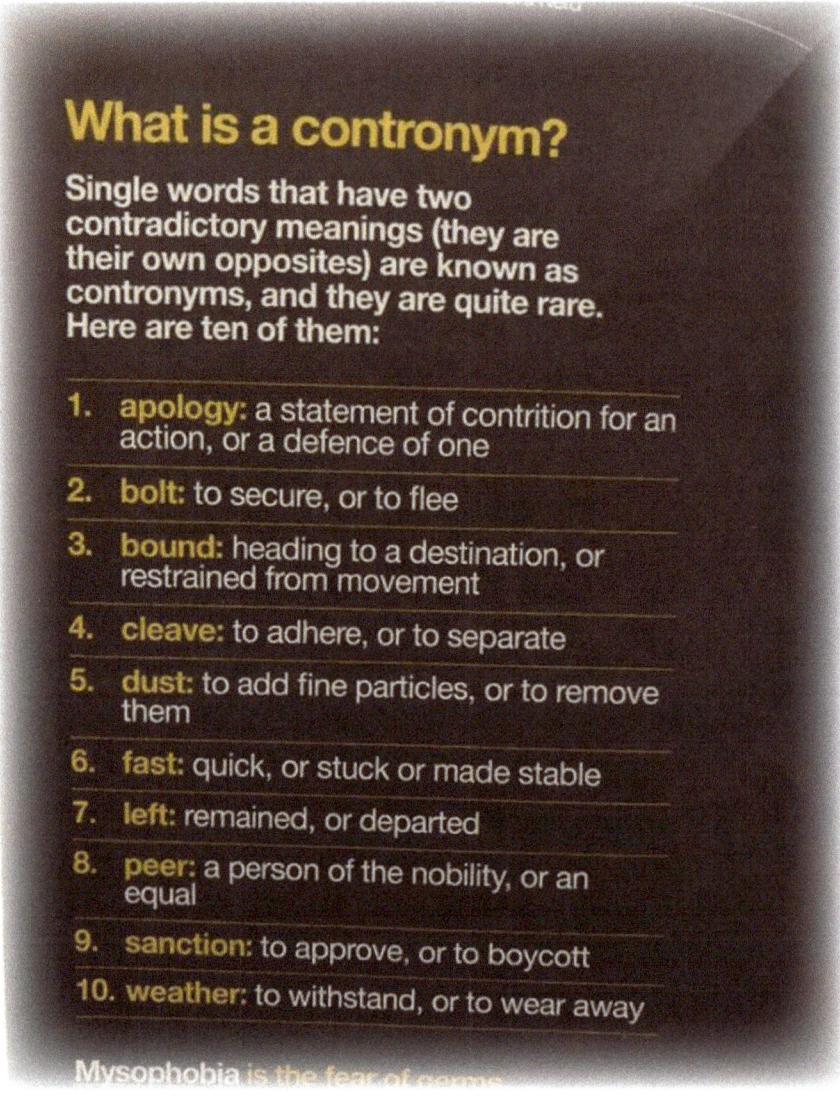

~ ~ ~

**Perspective**

**Thursday 12/3/2020** – Mass cooperation. Isn't that a marvelous thought? We need a whole lot more of that in this country. On this planet. Not just in combatting the COVID virus, but in a lot of other ways as well.

Back in 1999 I read a book by Sara Stein. I know it was 1999 because when I buy a book, I write the month and year on the first page. The subtitle for *Noah's Garden* is "Restoring the Ecology of Our Own Back Yards."

She tells about the time when she and her husband bought a piece of property and mowed it. The first indication that something was wrong, she said, was the disappearance of pheasants that used to abound on the property.

How many pheasants have you seen in your neighborhood lately?

But she had a solution. If everybody in a subdivision would maintain woods along the back of their property, tree lines along the sides, then wildlife would have a safe place. I'm attaching a photo I took of page 50 that explains it. If you want to know more about this, look for a copy of *Noah's Garden*.

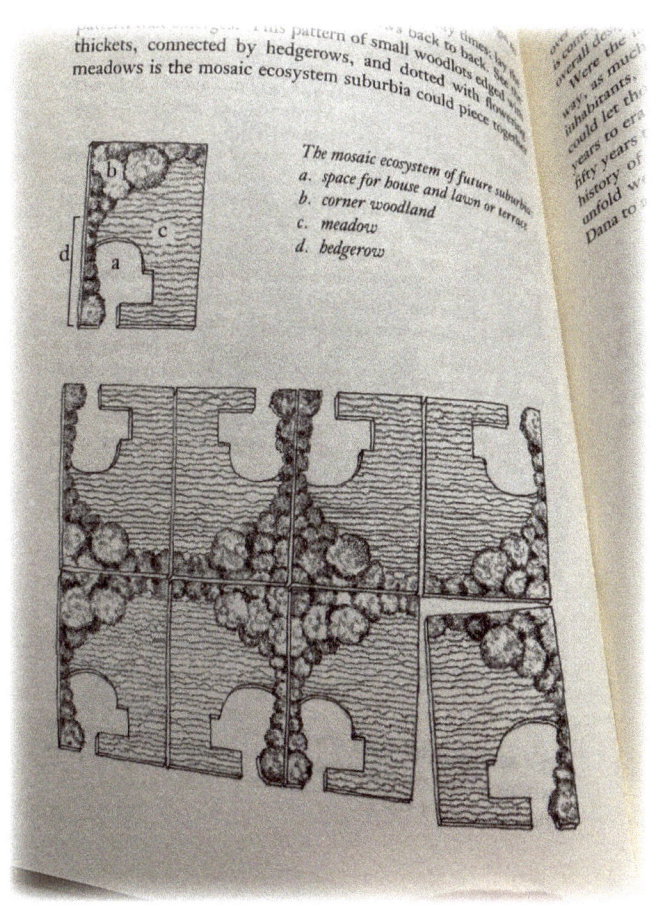

~ ~ ~

**For Music Lovers**

**Friday 12/4/2020** – Did you ever think much about different languages? I lived overseas for four years when I was a kid (Air Force family) and was constantly in awe of the people who spoke two, three, even four languages. I always wanted to be able to do that, but my parents were not linguistically adventuresome, and I didn't know how to go about learning another language while I lived in the isolated community that was our Air Force base.

There are other kinds of languages, though, besides the spoken ones. Think of music's do, re, mi, fa, sol, la, ti, do. When I learned that language, it was like a whole new world opening up to me.

Then there are these other languages we learn to interpret at an early age:

1. Reading facial expressions (not always easy now that we're wearing—or should be wearing—masks);

2. Listening—really listening—to a conversation so we can pick up the nuances of the tone of voice, the periodic silences, the way someone may grope for a difficult word;
3. Watching weather patterns as they swirl around us and interpreting what Mother Earth says to us every day.

How many languages are you conversant in?

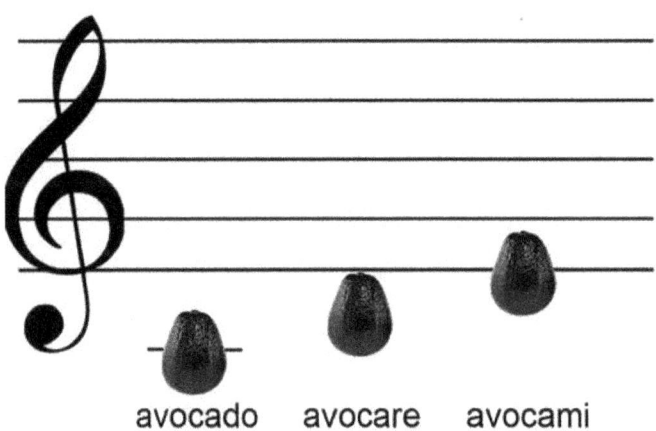

~ ~ ~

**Air & Space 7/1/20**

**Saturday 12/5/2020** – So many years ago that I can't even recall when it was—nor do I remember where I was—I saw a monument to (I think) the Canadian Air Force. Or maybe it was in London and the monument celebrated the RAF. At any rate, I walked from some sort of air and space museum into a curved pathway that led to one of the most peaceful interior spaces I've ever seen.

The centerpiece of the exhibit, the monument, was a plaque (was it on the wall or on the floor? The floor, I think) that said *Ad Astra Per Aspera.* I had to dig through my almost forgotten high school Latin lessons to come up with something closely akin to "We strive to reach the stars." Not an exact translation, certainly, but it struck a note that reverberated in my heart at the time.

And I decided to reset my course to find my own personal star, to add more meaning to my life. I was vitally aware of the people who were being honored by that memorial, but I also knew that their motto could speak to me on a more personal level. At least, that was what I heard that day.

This silly photo may be celebrating "air and space," but that unknown monument is what will always come to my mind when I hear those three words.

Crystal Clear

~ ~ ~

**3 - 6 - 9**

**Sunday 12/6/2020** – I love this chart. I'm going to let you figure it out for yourself. It's so darn logical (after all, it's math!) that it's truly beautiful. Elegance, I think, is the word that mathematicians use.

While we were talking about languages a couple of days ago, I didn't think to mention the language of mathematics—certainly a language that can be spoken universally. Give me a blackboard and a piece of chalk, and I can "talk" to anyone else who loves math.

Darn it. As far as I know, they don't even make blackboards anymore. Oh well, the idea is still valid.

| 111 | 222 | 333 |
|---|---|---|
| 3 | 6 | 9 |
| | | |
| 444 | 555 | 666 |
| 12 | 15 | 18 |
| 3 | 6 | 9 |
| | | |
| 777 | 888 | 999 |
| 21 | 24 | 27 |
| 3 | 6 | 9 |

# Fran Stewart

~ ~ ~

**Women**

**Monday 12/7/2020** – *Question:* What do fire escapes and windshield wipers have in common?

*Answer*: They were both invented by women.

These were answers to a need that a woman saw. And then she did something about it. This reminds of the time many, many years ago when I (and every other female I knew) hated the horrible belts we had to wear each month to hold our sanitary napkins in place. That was a problem, and my solution was to take strips of Scotch tape, fold them over into an inside-out ring, and use them to stick the pad to my underpants.

I was a teenager who knew nothing about patents, but if I had known I might have pursued the idea and come up with something simpler and more commercially viable than rings of Scotch tape. Several years later, Kotex started putting out napkins with adhesive strips. <<sigh>> My idea, but somebody else invented what I had only tinkered with.

What sort of need do you see? Have you considered tinkering around to find a solution? Remember to patent it.

~ ~ ~

**Replacing Sorry**

**Tuesday 12/8/2020** – Several months ago I had a conversation that evolved into one of those close, spoken connections women are so beautifully capable of. At one point, we both were on the verge of tears. She wiped her eyes. "I'm sorry I'm so emotional."

I couldn't reach out and touch her arm, but I reached into the eight-foot space between us. "Please," I begged her, "don't ever apologize for showing emotion. Our emotions are what connect us. Our emotions are what make us human."

I wish I'd had this meme available at the time to show her. But I can start living it as an example—not just to her, but to everyone I know. They'll get to "receive my gratitude instead of my negativity." I like that.

Will you join me?

> lately i've been replacing my "i'm sorry"s with "thank you"s, like instead of "sorry i'm late" i'll say "thanks for waiting for me", or instead of "sorry for being such a mess" i'll say "thank you for loving me and caring about me unconditionally" and it's not only shifted the way i think and feel about myself but also improved my relationships with others who now get to receive my gratitude instead of my negativity

~ ~ ~

**Without Pi**

**Wednesday 12/9/2020** – As I've been compiling all these FB posts of mine to include in the three-volume public memoirs I'm publishing, I realized how often I refer to 3.1416. Pi is such a useful concept. A lot of mathematics would fall apart without it.

But I never, ever thought of it in the way this meme shows it.

The world needs people who see things from a quirky new angle. Sometimes it brings us a laugh. Sometimes it opens up a whole new dimension.

What's quirky about your thought processes today?

p.s. Those three volumes I mentioned? They're called *Clear as Mud*, *Clearly Me*, and (coming soon) *Crystal Clear*. It's my CLEAR series—and I'm darn proud of this accomplishment.

~ ~ ~

### Both Sides

**Thursday 12/10/2020** – Yesterday we were talking about quirkiness. Today let's talk about power.

There were a whole lot of years of my life when I was afraid to step into my power. Heck, I was afraid even to acknowledge that I could possibly have any. As a result, I finally reached a point where I ran away—the only way I knew to deal with a difficult situation.

Was my action a mistake? Yes and no. *Yes*, when I look back and see how things could have been a lot less traumatic for all concerned if I had had the skills to step up and express myself. *No*, when I look at how everything eventually worked out, when I look at the lessons I learned, when I see how I was forced to grow through the whole process.

What about you? Do you acknowledge your power and at the same time, do you appreciate your vulnerability? Is your core rock solid, but your heart gentle? Can you spring from a calm center to defend yourself or those you love?

I didn't back then. It wasn't, back then. I didn't know how, back then.

Now, I do; it is; and I can.

> You can be vulnerable and still be powerful. You can have a gentle heart, but still be rock solid at your core. You can be as calm as a breeze, but as fierce as a tiger. The best people embody both sides.

~ ~ ~

**Not Flat Enough**

**Friday 12/11/2020** – Ever felt like this? I used to lie down and let people walk over me. "We need somebody to chair this project." Okay. "We need to raise more money." Okay. "We need somebody to do all the bookkeeping." Okay. "We need …" And so on down the line.

One day I woke up to the fact that I wasn't enjoying any of these projects I'd taken on just because somebody said, "We need…"

That was the day I began backing out of all these jobs, finding people to replace me—and if I couldn't—simply resigning. Guess what? All the jobs got filled one way or another. Now if I take on a project or agree to a task, it's because I'm fully committed to it. It's something I believe in. It's something I care about.

If I don't feel that way, then my answer is a simple no. After all, if *you're* committed to it, if you believe in it, if you care about it, then you might want to do it yourself.

I'd hate to take that option from you.

> "You can lie down for people to walk on you and they will still complain that you're not flat enough."
>
> Live your life.
>
> — Mature Gambino

# Fran Stewart

~ ~ ~

## I Kid You Not

**Saturday 12/12/2020** – I kid you not. This is the actual transcript of part of an online chat I had with one of those techies who are supposed to help people. He shot off these three chat-notes to me after having not been able to address my problem:

> I understand I already forward this to our technical team regarding about it
>
> But I cannot guarantee about it but when will they apply the changes on our platform. Since there's a lot of costumers having new ideas or changes for the platform
>
> But thanks for bring this one up Noted!

I'm glad to know a lot of *"costumers"* are having new ideas, but what about the rest of us who don't know how to sew very well?

~ ~ ~

## How to Attend a Concert

**Sunday 12/13/2020** – This is a really good list, but I'd like to point out one particular item on it: the third one from the bottom of the right-hand column: how to attend a concert or a performance.

I know this will date me, but I've never been to a rock concert. I didn't go to Woodstock way back when (I didn't even know it was happening until well after it was over). I never saw the Beatles in person (and didn't care to).

The concerts I've attended over the years were community bands, orchestras, choral groups. One of the most moving parts of a live performance, if it's been a memorable one, is that moment of mystical silence at the end, before the applause erupts. It's one of the greatest compliments an audience can give a performer, but it's something no rock group or rapper or country singer will ever experience, because audiences at concerts today don't seem to understand the force of silence.

Think about it—if the music has moved you almost to tears, or to a sense of exaltation, why would you want to break that magical connection that exists between you and the person/people on stage? When your applause does break free, it's liable to be raucous indeed. But the real gift to the performer was that moment of silence.

Maybe we should add "How to be quiet" to the list.

## 40 OLD-FASHIONED SKILLS THAT KIDS NEED TO KNOW TODAY!

- How to write a letter
- How to make a phone call
- How to take a message
- How to get to know an older person
- How to play with a baby
- How to sew on a button
- How to make a genuine apology
- How to read slowly
- How to hammer a nail
- How to shake hands
- How to introduce yourself
- How to take notice of needs around you
- How to make scrambled eggs
- How to balance a checkbook
- How to see a job through to completion
- How to write a thank-you note
- How to do laundry
- How to take care of a garden
- How to fix something instead of replace it
- How to plan a healthy meal
- How to hang a picture
- How to wash dishes
- How to make a budget
- How to wait and save for something
- How to check tire pressure
- How to ask questions to get to know someone better
- How to read a map
- How to find a book in the library
- How to seek counsel from someone more experienced
- How to care for a pet
- How to select a gift that the receiver will appreciate
- How to admit a mistake
- How to set the table
- How to iron a shirt
- How to give someone the benefit of the doubt
- How to weigh out the pro's and con's of a decision
- How to have good table manners
- How to read a recipe
- How to attend a concert or performance
- How to do something well, even if no one is watching
- How to be KIND!

~ ~ ~

**Two Kinds of Wrinkles**

**Monday 12/14/2020** – Wrinkles don't bother me. Some of the best role models in my life have been wrinkly old women. And now I have to recognize that I've become a wrinkly old woman myself. Not that 73 is all that old. (If you're younger than 30, please don't guffaw. You'll—hopefully—be in this same place someday.)

Mother Ebbesen taught me that the mind was more powerful than any physical disability. Her wrinkles came from pain, but also from laughter. Miss Johnson introduced me to Shakespeare and thereby changed my life. Her wrinkles had nothing to do with her impact. Mrs. Van Aken taught me that mystery writers could have a lot worth saying, and thereby helped lead me into a satisfying life of writing mysteries that featured a bipolar character. Her wrinkles never could mask her generous heart. Shirley Murray showed me how journaling could help put life into perspective. Her wrinkles softened her face when I looked at her across the desk where we worked together.

These were all women with soul. I owe them a very great debt.

~ ~ ~

**Survivorship Bias**

**Tuesday 12/15/2020** – *Survivorship Bias*. Had you ever heard that term before? I know I hadn't, until I saw this explanation. It's worth reading.

It reminded me of a chapter in *"Depression Visible: the Ragged Edge"* by Diana Alishouse. She talks about the number of famous people who have or are assumed to have had bipolar disorder. There's even a list of them on page 20. Composers, astronauts, writers, actors, poets, presidents, TV news anchors, artists. These were the ones who made it, the ones who didn't succumb to despair (or at least they didn't until after they became famous). These are the ones who kept going doggedly despite the overwhelming challenge of depression. These are the planes that made it home.

This is a picture tracking bullet holes on Allied planes that encountered Nazi anti-aircraft fire in WW2.

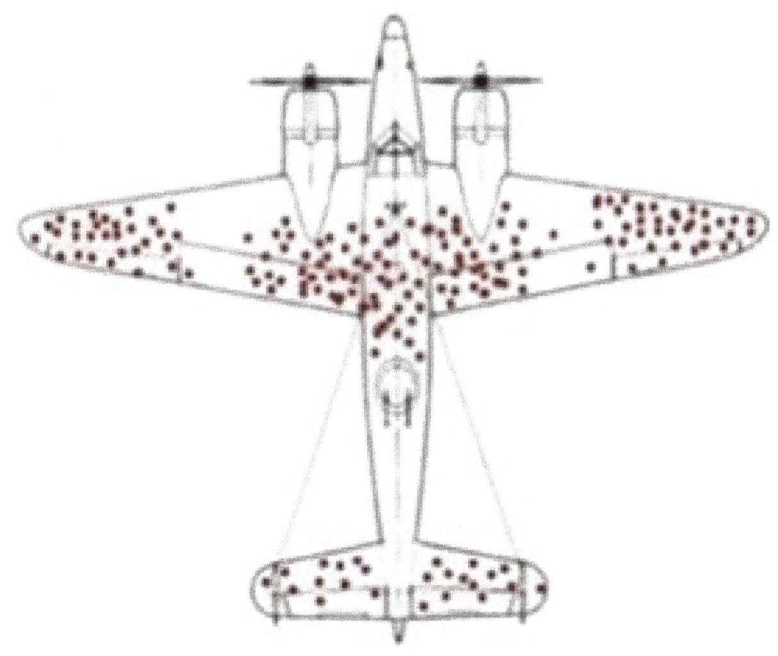

At first, the military wanted to reinforce those areas, because obviously that's where the ground crews observed the most damage on returning planes. Until Hungarian-born Jewish mathematician Abraham Wald pointed out that this was the damage on the planes that *made it home*, and the Allies should armor the areas where there are no dots at all, because those are the places where the planes won't survive when hit. This phenomenon is called survivorship bias, a logic error where you focus on things that survived when you should really be looking at things that didn't.

> We have higher rates of mental illness now?
> Maybe that's because we've stopped killing
> people for being "possessed" or "witches."
> Higher rate of allergies? Anaphylaxis kills,
> and does so *really fast* if you don't know
> what's happening. Higher claims of rape?
> Maybe victims are less afraid of coming
> forward. These problems were all happening
> before, but now we've reinforced the medical
> and social structures needed to help these
> people survive. And we still have a long way
> to go.
>
> Source: marzipanandminutiae

~ ~ ~

### Word Puzzles

**Wednesday 12/16/2020** – Just between you and me (see number 24), let's have some brain-growth today. For years people believed that brain cells, once destroyed, could never be regenerated. Turns out that that's true, sort of. But what CAN happen is that the brain cells which are left can figure out new neural pathways in order to make up for the missing cells.

Obviously this is a vast oversimplification, but I rather like the idea that each time I work a puzzle (particularly a fun one), I'm exercising those existing brain cells and maybe making it a little easier for them to do their job—especially if they'll have to fill in somewhere at a later date.

In re-reading my grandfather's diaries which he kept from 1910 to the day before he died in 1967, I was struck by one entry where he said, "Today I am 65 years old and I feel that old too. Am very tired tonight."

I'm almost a decade older than he was at that time, and my heart goes out to the people such as my grandparents who lived through hard times that aged them in ways I can hardly imagine.

I told my daughter that if I ever get to the point where I can't brush my own teeth or wipe my own bottom, then she's welcome to pull the plug.

Meanwhile, I'm gonna take those morning walks and work those puzzles and read and knit and play with Fuzzy Britches and listen to music. Keep those brain cells on their toes!

# Crystal Clear

## INTERPRET THE FOLLOWING:

| | | | |
|---|---|---|---|
| 1. SAND (boxed) | 2. MAN / BOARD | 3. STAND / I | 4. R\|E\|A\|D\|I\|N\|G |
| 5. WEAR / LONG | 6. R-ROADS-A-D-S | 7. ↓ T O W N | 8. CYCLE CYCLE CYCLE |
| 9. LE VEL (offset) | 10. O M.D. PH.D. B.S. | 11. KNEE LIGHTS | 12. III I / OO |
| 13. CHAIR | 14. DICE DICE | 15. T O U C H ↓ | 16. GROUND / FEET FEET FEET FEET FEET |
| 17. MIND / MATTER | 18. HE'S / HIMSELF | 19. ECNALG | 20. DEATH / LIFE |
| 21. G.I. / CCC CCC C | 22. ___ PROGRAM | 23. (BLOUSE vertical in C) | 24. YOU JUST ME |

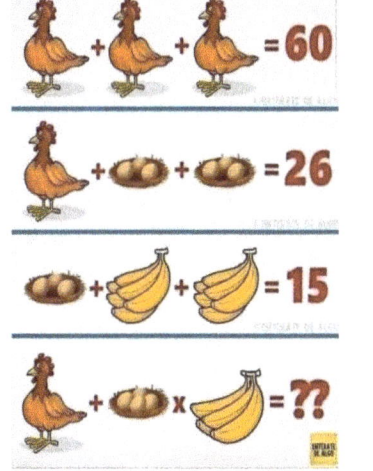

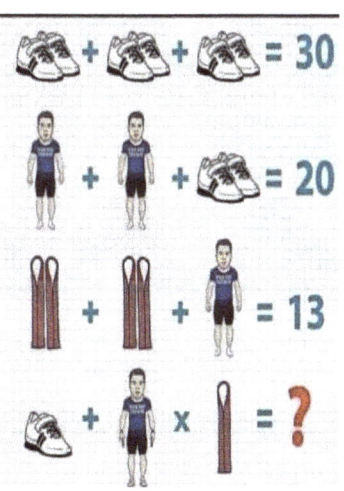

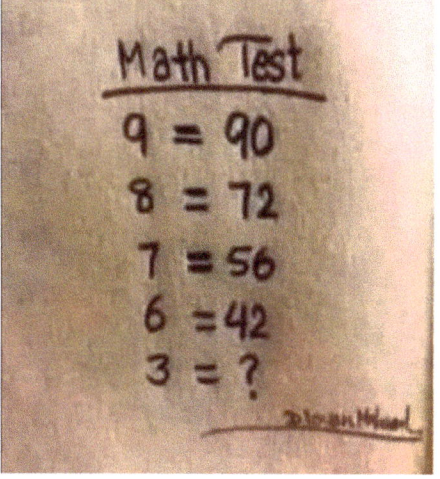

Math Test
9 = 90
8 = 72
7 = 56
6 = 42
3 = ?

## One More Thing

**Thursday 12/17/2020** – If you're grieving a loss this holiday season, I'd like to wrap my (virtual) arms around you and simply cry with you. There are well more than a quarter of a million families who will be without someone this year—someone who might have survived if we had taken the COVID-19 threat more seriously right from the start.

Please—do your part to protect others around you. Wear a mask. Wash your hands. Send virtual hugs. It's not too much to ask.

~ ~ ~

### Fewer Selfies 1/16/20

**Friday 12/18/2020** – Throughout this past year, I've posted an awful lot of selfies. It seemed like a good idea at the time. But after seeing this, I'm thinking I may have been a bit skewed in my thinking.

Fortunately, this year is almost over, and I won't be posting any more selfies on Facebook. Now, if I only had some fresh-picked ANYTHING to show you . . .

Oh wait! I do have some! The potatoes came from the bucket with the vine the deer ate several times earlier this summer. I finally moved it onto my back deck, and there was only about a month of growing time, so I was delighted to get one potato to eat, and one to think about. It's so tiny compared to the tip of my pinkie finger. Not even an eighth of a bite …

~ ~ ~

**Typo**

**Saturday 12/19/2020** – And now, for Saturday's laugh:

# Crystal Clear

~ ~ ~

**Hyperbole (11/3/2020)**

**Sunday 12/20/2020** – Last month, when I was listening to the elections reporting on WABE, my local Public Radio station, I heard someone ask about the "hyperbole" that had been floating around. The only trouble was, the reporter pronounced it as *three* syllables with the accent on the first syllable: HY-per-bole (with a long ō).

What????? On national public radio????? The word is *four* syllables long, with the accent on the second syllable: hy-PER-bo-le (with a long ē sound in the last syllable).

What does this have to do with anything? And why am I still wondering about it more than a month and a half after it happened? This is what I'm feeling like:

I know the English languages changes. It's vital; it's alive; it's dynamic. But, really, folks, there are a few shifts that aren't dynamism—they're just plain mispronunciations. Let's stop that so I can get back to important stuff—like rabbit typos. Or trying to stand on my head.

And in the picture on the next page, I had no idea about #2.

If you do a search for *mispronounced words*, you be sure to find a good list (or two or three or four…)

~ ~ ~

**Watch Compass**

**Monday 12/21/2020** – Did you know this? I certainly didn't. All these years I've depended on my handy pocket compass, and I didn't really need it as long as I have the watch I've worn ever since the day in 2002 when my father died and I took it off his wrist.

Now, during this time when so much healing is necessary, if only we could find a moral compass that was as simple to use, as simple to follow.

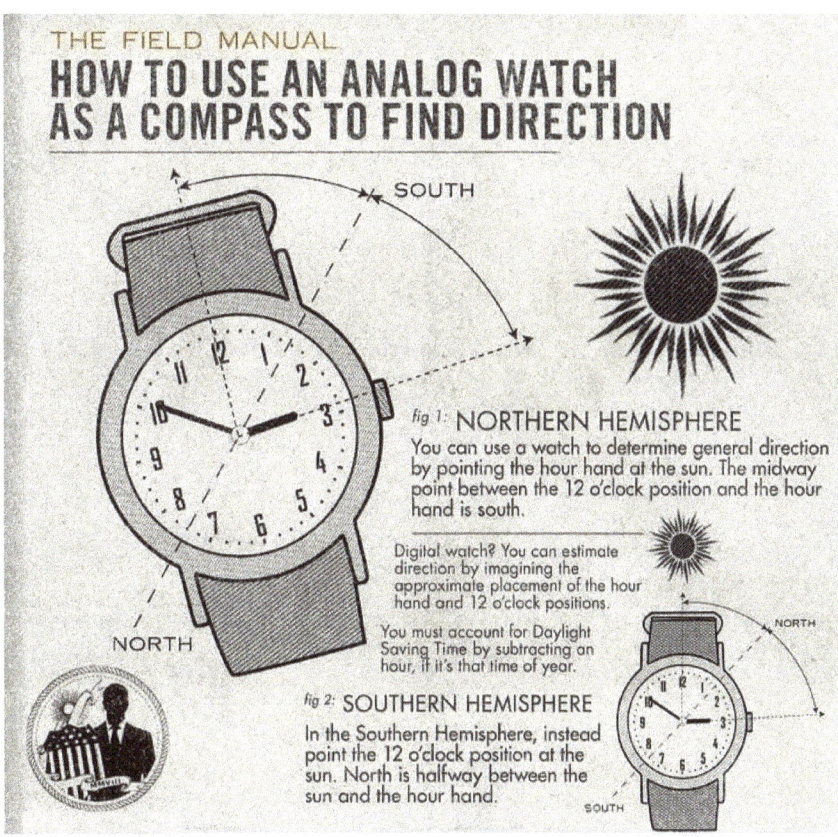

~ ~ ~

**Definitely a Radical**

**Tuesday 12/22/2020** – I wasn't very old when I began to question the pictures I saw in a lot of books and a lot of churches. You know the ones—the fair-skinned, clean-haired fellow surrounded by a bunch of guys who look as preppie as he does. Or the golden-haired little angel perched on his mother's knee—his blue-robed, fair-haired mommy—surrounded by blonde angelic figures.

# Fran Stewart

It sort of reminds me of all the memes I see on FB nowadays—the white guys conquering mountains with stunning vistas stretched out before them; the (invariably white) women doing yoga poses or blowing dandelion seeds into the wind or contemplating a cup of (herbal) tea.

After this last election, the county I live in now has a Board of Commissioners on which everyone is a person of color. Everyone. And I say hurray. It's about time.

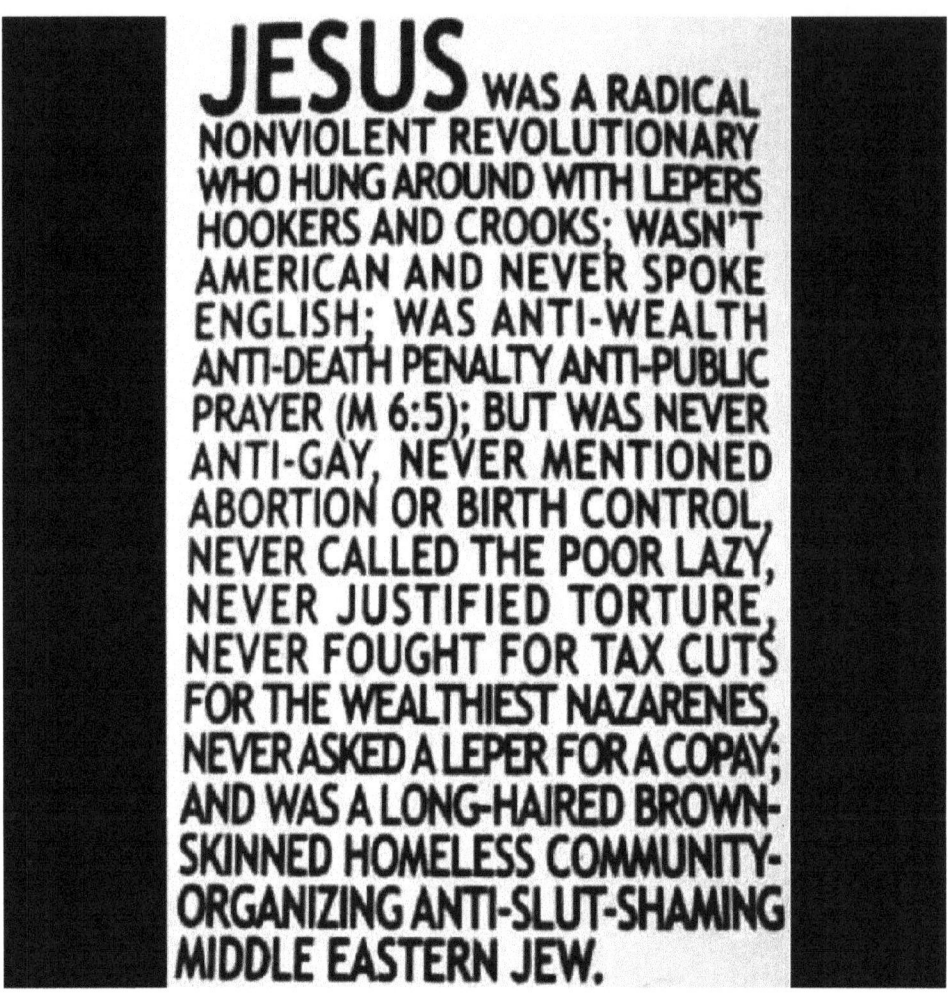

~ ~ ~

**Pete**

**Wednesday 12/23/2020** – I love this story. We can all make a difference, a big difference, by being true to ourselves and refusing to bow to what is most certainly wrong. Here's what happened:

In the 1970s, Francisco Franco's fascist government was still in power in Spain, but a growing pro-freedom movement invited Pete Seeger to give a concert in Barcelona. The stadium where he was to appear was packed with a hundred thousand people.

As Pete prepared to go on, government officials handed him a list of songs he was not allowed to sing. Pete looked at the list and said, "But that's pretty much everything I'd planned on singing."

"No," they insisted. "You must not sing any of these songs."

He took the list and strolled onto the stage. Holding it high he grinned. "I've been instructed not to sing any of these songs, but I reckon I can play the chords and let YOU do the singing."

Everyone knew the words, of course. They'd sung them for years in secret. Now they sang aloud, defying those who wanted to shut out the sound of freedom.

It's a good lesson to remember.

~ ~ ~

**Reading to Babies**

**Thursday 12/24/2020** – If you're giving gifts this Christmas, I hope you're giving books. Even more, though, I hope you're giving the lap to sit on while the reading is happening.

Whatever you choose to give at this time of year, and whatever you receive, I hope you'll remember that I appreciate you. You've enriched my life, your comments, your willingness to share.

This old mama loves you.

> man the crazy thing about babies is that like, some people would think that reading a baby a book about farm animals is teaching them about farm animals, but really it's teaching them about the concept of a book and how there's new information on each page of a single object, but *really,* beyond that, it's teaching them how language works, and beyond *that* it's *really* actually teaching them about human interaction, and *really really* it's them learning about existing in a three-dimensional space and how they can navigate that space, but *actually, above all* it is teaching them that mama loves them.

### Reasons for Rejoicing

**Friday 12/25/2020** – There are always lots of reasons to rejoice. Family, friends, health, cats (or dogs or hamsters or bunnies), books, our senses (sight, hearing, taste, touch, smell), sunsets and sunrises, the constellations, the green of spring, the glory of autumn. The freedom we have in this country to believe as we choose to believe.

No matter what your reasons to rejoice, please remember them—not just this day, but every day.

*Photo Credit © Eli Reiman*

~ ~ ~

### Happy Boxing Day

**Saturday 12/26/2020** – Happy Boxing Day.

Traditionally, in the UK and countries tied to England, boxing day is the day to give gifts to people who have served you during the year. It's something maybe we should pay more attention to.

Think of the mail carriers who are out there in all sorts of weather sometimes until well after dark. Think of the people who deliver your newspaper, the people who stand for hours at a time checking out groceries, the ones who work in the library where you waltz in so blithely and take a book from the shelf. Think of the teachers and the medical personnel who've made your life richer and safer.

There are so many out there to whom we owe an incredible debt of gratitude. So why not give a few gifts AFTER the season? Just to say thank you.

~ ~ ~

**Pando**

**Sunday 12/27/2020** – When I think of the magnificence of this earth, I'm truly humbled. I lived in Colorado for five years when I was a kid, and the aspen trees were always my favorites. At the time I had no idea how connected trees were to each other, but now that I know, I find it hard to understand how anyone can look at a tree and not be inspired.

Wouldn't it be lovely if people felt connected to each other the same way trees do?

This is Pando, but it isn't a forest– it's all one tree. Each trunk of the Quaking Aspen is genetically identical and connected by a single root system that's at least 80,000 years old, which means it's one of the biggest and oldest living things on Earth.

~ ~ ~

**Feathery Beak**

**Monday 12/28/2020** – Hobbits have fuzzy feet. Ravens (like this one at the Tower of London) have feathery beaks. Dinosaurs, it turns out, had lots of fluff and feathers. Now, as I sit here on a cold morning, having just come in from a cold walk, I wish I had feathers or fur or hair on my ankles.

Luckily, several years ago I knitted some leg warmers—long tubes of soft yarn that I can pull on whenever I need them.

Trouble is—I can't find them!  <<<sigh>>>  I need a smaller house.

Crystal Clear

~ ~ ~

**Stewardship**

**Tuesday 12/29/2020** – Back in 2019 I sent out a newsletter announcing that I had started my own publishing company in order to protect my royalties and my copyrights for my children and grandchildren after my death. I received this reply from Candace, a woman who is a colleague of mine in an organization we both belong to:

# Fran Stewart

> "You used great wisdom in stewarding well both your intellectual properties and your income stream. Maybe you should consider a name change: *Fran Steward*!"

It reminded me of something that happened back when I was a senior in high school. Our English teacher assigned us the task of doing a research project of some sort that related to the English language. And then we'd have to present an oral report about our findings. I can't recall what I chose to write about, but I distinctly recall what one of the boys in the class reported on. I don't remember his name, but I certainly remember his topic.

He chose to look into the origins of last names—specifically the last names of all of us students in the class. One girl's name connected her to French royalty; several of the names were reflections of who started the family: Johnson (John's son), Robertson (Robert's son); another one's name came from the trades—in fact, there were a number of those names, such as Barber, Smith (blacksmith, most likely), Wright (wheelwright). He saved what he considered to be the best—i.e. the punch line—for last. "Then there's Stewart." He smirked openly at me. "It means the one who kept the pigs."

The class (everyone, that is, except Frances Stewart) roared.

You know how fragile we are at that age. I took that to heart (especially the sneer and the laughter) for years until one day I happened to mention it to my sister.

She turned up her lip. "What did he know? The stewards were the ones who were responsible for maintaining the wealth of the lords they served—lords who were so busy fighting they couldn't be bothered with practical matters. Those upper-class people would have starved without their stewards overseeing the care of their livestock and their crops."

Wish somebody had told me that way back when.

## Penultimate Day

**Wednesday 12/30/2020** – Today is the penultimate day, not only this year but also of these FB posts of mine. I've enjoyed the journey in so many ways, not only the challenge of posting every day, but the chance to share my memories with you.

One of those memories is the way I first heard the word *penultimate* on NPR. I discovered National Public Radio at least forty years ago when I lived in Vermont. I'd stopped in to visit a friend and heard the loveliest music. "What record is that?" to which they replied, "It's not a record, it's public radio." Those few words changed my life.

When public radio was founded, back in 1969, the chair of the FCC, Newton Minow, called commercial television "a vast wasteland" and called for programing in the public interest. I'd like to think that when I began writing my Biscuit McKee Mysteries almost 20 years ago, that I was seeing a need for a different kind of mystery—one that would step into what I saw as a wasteland of either flippant or gory stories and be a shining example of how mystery writers could educate their readers about social concerns such as bipolar disorder and suicide prevention. I saw my books as being in the public interest.

I wish now that I'd known more about marketing so my message could have reached more people sooner.

Still, those books and these mini-memoirs of mine are—I hope you'll see it this way—in the public interest. They've also been lots of fun for me to write. They've stretched my mind and exercised my intellect; they've helped me look for humor and let me recognize the places where I could be of service to others; they've connected me to *you* through your comments, your messages, and your emails.

I'd say, all in all, it's been a productive journey. I hope you agree.

p.s. I know I used this same picture almost two years ago, but I had something altogether different to say about it at the time. Just think about it—any life event you look at today will appear different than it did when it first happened. (Just a little lesson from my memoirs classes.)

# Fran Stewart

~ ~ ~

## The Last Chapter

**Thursday 12/31/2020** –I've warned you about this several times over the past two months. Today is the last day I'll post anything to Facebook. There are several reasons:

1. I decided after watching the Netflix documentary *The Social Dilemma* to deactivate my personal Facebook page. After all, I almost never look at it. Each morning I sit down and open the bookmarks I have programmed into my laptop so I can check out the FB pages of my children, grandchildren, and a couple of dear friends. Other than that, I see no reason to wade through volumes of posts that show up on my page even though I've tried to fix my settings so that won't happen.
2. When I deactivate my personal Facebook page, that will eliminate this author page, since the two are inextricably linked together.
3. When I deactivate the FB page(s), I'm not sure whether everything that I've posted so far on this page since 2012 will disappear or whether there just won't be any more posts. I imagine all the virtual connections that cyberspace has created over the years will also disappear, which means you won't be following me anymore.

My understanding is that I will no longer be able to post comments to those pages I mentioned above in reason #1—since my FB identity will be nonexistent. I should (I think) still be able to use Messenger.

Tomorrow morning, check out what I'll write on my new daily website journal: franstewart.com/fransjournal. And feel free to leave a comment. See? We can keep in touch after all.

In the meantime, I wish you the very best always and all ways. Remember that old song?
> *The breeze and I*
> *Are whispering goodbye ..."*

*Photo credit: Yellowideas Photography © 2004*

~ ~ ~

Thus ends Crystal Clear, the third book of my CLEAR series. I haven't stopped writing my daily thoughts, although I'm no longer going to post any of the public ones here on Facebook. My private musings go into the hand-written journal I sit down and write each night before I go to bed. Someday—a long time from now, I hope—my granddaughter will inherit those.

The musings that are okay for public consumption? As I've told you, I'll continue to write them each day on my website journal, and—who knows?—maybe in another year I'll publish them as the 4th book in this series.

In the meantime, thank you. Thank you for traveling this journey with me. It's been fun, hasn't it?

With ((virtual)) hugs,

    --Fran/Mom/Grannie/Auntie/Sis/Tree and so on

www.ingramcontent.com/pod-product-compliance
Lightning Source LLC
Chambersburg PA
CBHW051353110526
44592CB00024B/2969